Airborne Dreams

AIRBORNE DREAMS

"Nisei" Stewardesses and Pan American World Airways

CHRISTINE YANO

DUKE UNIVERSITY PRESS *Durham & London 2011*

© 2011 Duke University Press
All rights reserved.

Printed in the United States of America
on acid-free paper ∞
Designed by Jennifer Hill
Typeset in Scala
by Tseng Information Systems, Inc.

Library of Congress Cataloging-
in-Publication Data appear on the last
printed page of this book.

Contents

CONDUCTING RESEARCH
THE "PAN AM WAY"

I FEEL COMPELLED to say something about the processes of this research project, primarily because in many ways my experiences speak directly to the image and practices of Pan Am. This project has lived under a lucky star since its inception in April 2005, when I read a small announcement in a Honolulu newspaper about a fiftieth-anniversary luncheon being held by former Pan Am "Nisei" stewardesses. I knew nothing about this group of women. However, Pan Am was an entirely familiar name: the glamour airline of world travelers; the carrier that promised a ticket to the moon; the company whose name still graced a skyscraper in Honolulu; the airline whose bag we mocked as a symbol of nerds; and the corporation whose precipitous fall from grace marked the passing of an era. Pan Am for me was both the stuff of dreams and the mark of the Jet Age.

I missed the luncheon, but a couple of the organizers agreed to meet me at a neighborhood Starbucks. That meeting was the true beginning of this project, as the two former Pan Am stewardesses, now in their sixties, spoke with me at length and with great enthusiasm. In their stories I found tantalizing elements: romance (and less sex than one might imagine), race, tears, melodrama, money, glamour, and the swinging 1960s. The combination was irresistible. The two put me in contact with other women like them who met me at coffee shops and libraries and invited me into their homes, and the corpus of interviews grew. The women posted news of my research in the newsletter of the local branch of World Wings International, the organization of retired Pan Am flight attendants, and soon e-mails and faxes arrived, from former "Nisei" stewardesses in Hawai'i and from those living elsewhere. I was overwhelmed by their numbers and their enthusiasm. Never had research subjects come knocking at my door, asking to be let in. I quickly applied for university summer research money, and the person in charge of grants turned out to be a long-time Pan Am buff who embraced my project with personal relish. It seems that wherever I turned, Pan Am—that is, the loyalty of employees and customers alike that keeps the company alive—was there, enabling the project. Clearly Pan Am lives between the thoughts, actions, and sheer will of its former employees and fans.

Only seven months after my research began, I gave a public talk on the topic. The room was packed and the response enthusiastic, generating another web of contacts. These included a former steward at Pan Am, as well as a graduate student working on a related topic. He lent me his Pan Am books; she gave me the name of a contact at the National Air and Space Museum (NASM) of the Smithsonian. Serendipity prevailed. I was on my way to attend a meeting in Washington and arranged to visit NASM and meet with researchers there. Again the project met with enthusiasm, and I applied and later received a grant as the Smithsonian's Verville Fellow to conduct research for a year. By the time I left for Washington in August 2006 I had taped thirty interviews and received e-mailed or faxed responses to my questions from several more. All told I had over five hundred pages of transcribed interviews to work with, accumulated in a short amount of time primarily through the networking of former employees and enthusiasts of a company defunct for fifteen years. I was stunned.

At the same time, I felt that this was a story that needed to reach a broader audience than an academic book ordinarily would. To that end I arranged for an exhibit entitled "Airborne Dreams: Japanese American Flight Attendants and the Development of Global Tourism in the Pacific" at the Japanese Cultural Center of Hawai'i (JCCH) from November to December 2006. I worked with a committee of former stewardesses and employees who rummaged in their closets and collections to come up with uniforms, bags, mementoes, scrapbooks, and even a complete china set. I asked myself and them, Could this have happened with any other airline? Who would have kept such things? Their answer to me was "no!" They explained the specialness of the airline, their deep attachment to it and the attachment of others. And it was true. Pan Am buffs, family, and friends came out of the woodwork for the opening of the exhibit, recalling the good old days when flying Pan Am meant dressing in hat and gloves and toasting champagne over the Pacific. Each one had a special story about Pan Am to tell. I attempted to capture some of the stories through a nine-minute video of interviews shown continuously at the exhibit. I also held a panel discussion on the opening night of the exhibit, featuring two of the original stewardesses hired in 1955. To my surprise one of them wore the uniform from the period, complete with gloves, hat, nylons, and heels. A person attending commented, "It was like seeing a vision from the past!" The enthusiasm was put to work: "Nisei" stewardesses acted as docents on Saturdays throughout the run of the exhibit. I wanted to create a space within the exhibit for the public's voice, and thus designated a blank wall dedicated to "Pan Am memories." Over the course of the exhibit it filled with people's handwritten 3" by 5" cards, several of which I quote throughout this book. As a bonus coda, the Smithsonian curator Tom Crouch arranged for a portion of the JCCH exhibit to be displayed at the National Air and Space Museum Steven F. Udvar-Hazy Center, near Dulles Airport in Virginia, where it remained on a two-year loan through May 2009.

In the same way that Pan Am's "Nisei" stewardesses became media darlings while they flew, so too did the exhibit about them garner media attention (see e.g. "Airborne Dreams" 2006). A newspaper article and photo spread proved providential, as former stewardesses sent electronic versions of the clipping to each other. One of these landed in the hands of a World Wings member in Miami, who contacted me just as I was about to leave for a trip there to conduct research at the University of Miami, which houses the Pan Am archives. As luck would have it, the weekend of my arrival coincided with three Pan Am social events: the Christmas party of World Wings International, Miami chapter; the annual party of the Pan Am pilots' association; and the annual gathering of former Pan Am employees, which included the sale of memorabilia. At each of these events I met former Pan Am employees who told me their stories, and got acquainted with the infamous partying, Pan-Am style. I saw firsthand what many of the women I interviewed could only describe, and what these Pan Am devotees in Miami recreate yearly—boisterous conviviality, some of it alcohol-infused, much of it tastefully executed. This was the "cocktail generation" come to life (cf. Adinolfi 2008).

The timing of the three events in one weekend was no accident: all the participants relished the opportunity to commemorate the date of Pan Am's last flight out of Miami, its home base. Employees even now remember bidding a tearful farewell to the airline as they watched that last plane take off. Although many of them continued jobs in other airlines—the Pacific routes taken over by United Airlines in 1986, the Atlantic routes by Delta Airlines in 1991—they all say that the Pan Am experience was supreme and unique. Further, they all say that to this day their loyalty rests with Pan Am, and they prove it by their continuing participation in these events yearly, through membership in Pan Am employee organizations, and some as members of the Pan Am Historical Foundation. Clearly this kind of ethnohistory lives.

A last episode: in October 2006 I received an e-mail message from a woman helping to record the memoirs of Eugene Dunning, a longtime Pan Am steward and trainer. Dunning had been based in Honolulu at the inception of the "Nisei" project in 1955 and was a big champion of what he considered the "special qualities" of the stewardesses' service. Dunning had heard of my research through the Pan Am grapevine and wanted me to interview him. This request was not without its difficulties, especially since Dunning lived in northern California, had suffered a stroke some years ago, and moved only with the help of a walker. But in what former employees call Pan Am can-do spirit, we arranged the interview, including my stay at the home of his memoir recordist. The upshot was pure Pan Am: after our three-hour interview and a tour of his memorabilia, Dunning was energized. His eyes shone as he handed me three books on Pan Am that he had written, described his plans to write two more on his experiences, and began making arrangements to visit the exhibit in Honolulu and reunite with the "Nisei" stewardesses. Indeed, a few months later he returned to Honolulu for a Pan Am visit.

This description of the processes of my research is far more self-indulgent than it needs to be, but I include it with a specific purpose. In only a short time I have been able to gather a considerable amount of data and meet countless people through the goodwill and sheer force of a living and enthusiastic network known as Pan Am. The very same aura that the company conveyed in the years covered by this book, 1955–72, continues into the twenty-first century and propels my research. Pan Am engendered such loyalty and enthusiasm among its employees that nearly twenty years after its demise, these same employees are eager to spread the word, to confide their love of what one stewardess called her "first boyfriend." It is the Pan Am network—formally through organizations such as World Wings International, and informally through e-mail, faxes, and phone calls darting around the globe—that has taken my research into places I could not have imagined.

The closeness of this research to the Pan Am network has been both boon and bane. I have taken full advantage of the network, but recognize that the research is based primarily on those with utmost goodwill toward Pan Am. Thus I have not had access to many who had negative experiences with the company or who have been highly critical of it, although this was not for want of trying. Admittedly, therefore, this work veers toward the celebratory. I have tried to counterbalance this to a certain extent with my own critical distance and comparative perspective, but the weighting of my sample is undeniable.

I have referred briefly to "the Pan Am Way" and the "Pan Am can-do spirit," both invoked frequently by the people I have been researching. What they mean by this is in large part the subject of this book: how a large, prestigious corporation such as Pan American World Airways could encompass the very subjectivity of its employees. This includes the "Nisei" stewardesses, whose racialized position with the airline enabled Pan Am to better perform its claim to global supremacy of commercial aviation in the 1950s and 1960s. These women who enabled the airline's imaging found that their work experiences stimulated their own development as people, and specifically as "Pan Am people." Theirs is a story that is echoed by many other women who worked for Pan Am, including those I met at the World Wings luncheon at Tavern on the Green in New York and Christmas parties in Miami. However, I argue that the "Nisei" stewardesses' stories run with a twist of race behind them that colors their experiences in highly particular ways. That twist is the fundamental subject of this book.

Throughout this book, parenthetical references of the form "(PAA 1970–72)" indicate that the source of a quotation is a stewardess who worked for Pan American World Airways during the years given.

Acknowledgments

MY FIRST DEBT goes to the former employees of Pan American World Airways. This book is entirely dependent upon the goodwill and enthusiasm of the women and men I interviewed, and especially those who helped with the exhibit and videotape. I would like to thank especially (in alphabetical order) Marilyn Boock, Hiromi Grantham, Jacqui Higa, Eva Kama, Charlotte Yamashiro, Jane Noe, Aileen Sodetani, Mae Takahashi, Cynthia Tsujiuchi, May Tsukiyama, Aggie Von Brimer, and Minnie Yoshimori. This is indeed their story, and I feel privileged to be able to tell and interpret it. They are a class act. Special thanks to Eugene Dunning and Sue Miller in California and Alicia Smith in Miami for their hospitality and enthusiasm.

A big thank-you to the staff and volunteers at the Japanese Cultural Center of Hawai`i: Brian Niiya and Brian Suzuki. Special recognition and thanks to the gallery director Christy Takamune, who designed the exhibit in Honolulu and bore the brunt of the stress in my absence. These three filled in at a crucial time when I left for Washington with only the promise of an exhibit. *Mahalo* to those involved in the video production: Chris Conybeare (producer), Cliff Watson (camera), and Joy Chong-Stannard (editor). The resulting video bears the mark of their fine professionalism.

My time spent in Washington at the Smithsonian's National Air and Space Museum truly molded this work in ways I could not have foreseen, especially as I was inspired by people such as Dom Pisano and Ron Davies for whom aviation studies are a lifelong pursuit. This work has been greatly strengthened and broadened because of them. A special thanks to Tom Crouch, who dreamed easily and generously of bringing "Airborne Dreams" to Washington, then continually paid the high price of his dreams in efforts that went beyond his initial imagining. I am particularly grateful to Jenifer Van Vleck, Yale Ph.D. history student, who shared the year at NASM and time at the University of Miami with me as a Smithsonian fellow writing a dissertation on the role of commercial aviation in United States foreign policy. I found Jen's seriousness of pursuit and high intellectualism inspiring and know that a rich career awaits her. My thanks also to the staff at the University of Miami Otto G. Richter Library, Pan American World Airways Archives, for their gracious helpfulness.

I thank especially my colleagues and friends at the University of Hawai`i: Mari Yoshihara, Ric Trimillos, Ben Finney, Hal McArthur, Nancy Cooper, and Linda Crowder. Thanks too to the research assistants Rachel Spitler, Paul Christensen, Shawn Smith, Yoko Kurokawa, Hirofumi Katsuno, Noriko Sanefuji, Sebastian Fite, and Takashi Miura for their help in transcribing, gathering, translating resources, and helping to pull everything together.

A special, fond mahalo to Corky White, who read first drafts of all chapters, commented critically and enthusiastically, and remains a cheerleader of this project. Writing a book is a daunting and lonely task that would have been far more difficult without her as my muse.

I have benefited greatly from being able to present my work at meetings of the American Studies Association, the American Anthropological Association, the Japan Anthropology Workshop, and the Association for Asian American Studies. I have also presented portions of this work at the Reischauer Institute for Japanese Studies, Harvard University, and at the University of Hawai`i. Colleagues at these meetings and elsewhere have helped me consider my subject more thoroughly; they include Laura Miller, Jan Bardsley, Carolyn Stevens, Ellis Krauss, Michael Bourdaghs, Kevin Doak, Christopher Gerteis, and Ted Bestor. I am also grateful to the two anonymous reviewers at Duke University Press for their insight and suggestions, as well as to Ken Wissoker. This is a better work for my reconsideration of the material based on their comments.

I am deeply grateful to institutional sources of funding: the University of Hawai`i Research Relations Fund which provided seed money for the project, and especially the Smithsonian National Air and Space Museum

(Verville Fellowship). While in Washington I also benefited from a Visiting Researcher position at Georgetown University, enabled by Kevin Doak.

Above all, thanks go to my family—Scott, Eli, and Marika, and my parents. Scott did double duty, reading the final draft and commenting. They are and have always been my emotional mainstay. I am indebted to them because they allowed me to bring these airborne dreams to fruition.

THE PAN AM SKIES AS FRONTIER
OF JET-AGE MOBILITY

17 MAY 2007. Tavern-on-the-Green restaurant, Central Park, New York. Annual luncheon of the Manhattan chapter of World Wings International, the organization of retired flight attendants of Pan American World Airways. The day exults in the glories of spring: brisk air, clear skies, brilliant azaleas. Even as I exit the subway at 72nd Street on the Upper West Side, I notice a couple of women who I guess may be headed to the same event. It is something about their age, dress, and purposefulness that provides clues. We diverge at the park, but sure enough, when I enter the restaurant there they are, just ahead of me, still engaged deeply within the buzzing excitement of their own company. I am here as an observer of the luncheon and as a researcher of a small group of women among the 240 in attendance. The majority of women in attendance are white: Americans and Europeans based in New York who flew for Pan Am until its demise in 1991. There are also a handful of women who stand out because of their African ancestry, part of Pan Am's program in Africa in the 1970s, as well as another handful of Spanish-speaking women hired from South America in the 1960s and 1970s. The women I am researching are of Asian ancestry: they flew in an even earlier racialized program of Pan Am's, from 1955 on. They were called "Nisei" (second-generation Japanese American) stewardesses, even if not all of them were second-generation or Japanese American. By calling these women generically "Nisei," Pan Am built into the group the cultural capital of Japanese American war veterans whose heroism during the Second World War made the name synonymous with patriotic Americans of Japa-

nese ancestry.[1] From 1955 to 1972 they shared a base in Honolulu as part of Pan Am's Asian-language personnel.

The noise level in the room reaches a fever pitch as the women call out to each other, hug and kiss, pass around drinks, take photos, and regale each other with stories of the high adventures of their careers flying around the world. A husband of a Pan Am flight attendant once laughingly characterized these women to me as a bunch of raging extroverts. Walking into a room such as this, it is hard not to agree. Of course many reunions share a high level of excitement and nostalgia. But this one strikes me differently. These stories are more exotic because of their locales—Beirut, Karachi, Tokyo, Paris. Many of those in attendance were involved in historic events, such as the Vietnam baby airlift of 1975 just before Saigon's fall. Many met and served kings, queens, presidents, and movie stars. These women weave bonds over the heady adventures that marked their careers, as well as to the company that traded on glamour in the air. Fifteen years later, theirs is a high-energy, continuing sorority of Pan Am.

Within the boisterous group in New York, the stewardesses on whom I focus present a slightly different picture. The five women of Japanese ancestry share the laughter and excitement of the day. But for the most part they are a little more reserved and a little less boisterous than the others in the room. Their voices are toned down a notch. Some were born in Japan, others in Hawai`i, still others in California. They interact readily with the other women present, yet they retain a distinctive place racially and culturally.

This book focuses on their stories within this group, in a high-profile corporation and occupation, situated in a particular era. It explores the complex intertwining of three distinct strands: Pan American World Airways, "Nisei" stewardesses (and their Japanese American context), and the Jet Age during which this story begins. I argue that the "Nisei" stewardess' presence as the Asian (American) woman aloft helped to solidify Pan Am's position as "the world's most experienced airline," demonstrating the company's knowledge and mastery of the globe exactly when technology claimed to shrink distances. At the same time, Asian and Asian American women gained a foothold in cosmopolitanism and globalism, breaking out of their family's expectations and mastering their own worlds within the context of postwar America. Let me begin their stories here in 1955.

On 13 October 1955 Pan American World Airways stunned the commercial aviation industry by ordering the largest fleet of commercial jet aircraft in the world—twenty Boeing 707s and twenty-five Douglas DC-8s—and officially ushering in the age of jet travel and global mass tourism. In that same year the company hired the New York architect Edward Barnes to design what was to become a familiar logo worldwide: a stylized globe in a trademark azure, emblazoned with five uppercase letters in a crisp, serifed font: PAN AM. The logo, which seemed a fitting match to the company's slogan, "World's Most Experienced Airline,"[2] would come to symbolize not only an airline but also an empire and the dominance of postwar America in the world.

Yet another Pan Am milestone event of 1955: the airline embarked on a new personnel program, creating a "Japanese-language position" (eventually extended to other Asian languages, including Mandarin, Korean, Thai, Vietnamese, and Tagalog) for stewardesses on each of its Tokyo-bound and eventually round-the-world flights, and recruiting women of Japanese ancestry to fill them. United States immigration laws forbade hiring Japanese nationals for the job; instead the airline turned to Japanese Americans.[3] These "Nisei" stewardesses were among the first nonwhite stewardesses in Pan Am and other airlines' employ. However, this breaking of the racial barrier was not a matter of civil rights but a carefully drawn corporate practice to compete with a newly emerging Japan Air Lines, which began domestic operations in 1951 and expanded to international travel in 1954. This book links these events of 1955—jets, logos, and Asian (American) women—as part of a well-crafted strategy to assert global domination by an American corporation. Here is the story of Pan American World Airways at its peak in a new industry of Jet Age mobility and global tourism.

How was Pan Am's world constituted by these women, for what purposes, under what circumstances, and with what kinds of far-reaching implications? The globalism of these airborne dreams embody what I call Pan Am's frontier ideology—an aggressively competitive, masculinist business culture that constantly emphasized its primacy in the creation of empire. By focusing on one airline from 1955 to 1972, during which Honolulu was Pan Am's "closed" Asian language base (all flight attendants based in Honolulu were required to speak an Asian language; in effect, this meant racialized hiring in that all were of Asian ancestry), this book examines more generally the politics and practices of postwar America during the Jet Age.

Understanding the story of Pan Am's "Nisei" stewardess story means disentangling three strands: Pan American World Airways, Japanese American history and the Japanese American postwar experience, and the Jet Age.

By 1955 the Pan Am brand was already known throughout many parts of the world. For many people in countries throughout the Pacific, Asia, and Africa, Pan Am possessed a unique presence as the premier symbol of air travel, modernity, and the United States. Significantly, Pan Am was the carrier that first brought air mail service to many of these places. The arrival of a Pan Am airplane meant the arrival of these regions in a larger world of communication, foreign goods, and technology.[4] Pan Am had the routes, the technical prowess, and the prestige, like no other airline. As the commercial aviation historian Ronald Davies emphatically states, "Pan American was the only mega-carrier in airline history. No airline will ever dominate the industry like Pan Am. It set the standard to which all other carriers had to aspire" (personal communication, 14 May 2007). I examine this domination within the context of 1955, a time when the events analyzed here were not isolated practices: they helped to define the Jet Age and shape commercial aviation. These were airborne dreams: for Pan Am, extending an empire of global travel; for the women, propelling themselves into that world as newly forged cosmopolitans. These airborne dreams emerged as part of the techno-fantasy of the Jet Age, encompassing an emergent sense of globalism in postwar America.

It matters less that other airlines may have done similar things at the same time or even earlier. For example, British Overseas Airways Corporation (BOAC) flew jets in 1952,[5] as well as hiring women from Hong Kong, India, and Pakistan as "assistant stewardesses" and ground staff in 1949.[6] Likewise, by 1955 Thai Airways, Northwest Orient Airlines, Air India International, KLM Royal Dutch Airlines, and Air France all employed Japanese women as flight attendants (*Nippon Times*, 20 September 1955, 6). However, most of these other programs and practices were relatively short-lived. More important, none of these practices set an industry standard as did Pan Am's actions did. As Davies asserts, while the airline was in its ascendancy, "whatever Pan Am did, all other airlines had to sit up and take notice" (personal communication, 14 May 2007). In short, defining the commercial aviation "frontier" required more than establishing practices and policies: achieving that sort of impact depended on having power and prestige.

From a business standpoint, the case of JAL and Pan Am demonstrates the complex entanglements of American companies and foreign start-up airlines during the postwar period. After the end of the Second World War, Japan had been barred from the manufacture and possession of aircraft by the Potsdam Declaration in 1945. In 1951 Japan was granted one domestic airline, with flight operation entrusted to a foreign airline. That provision brought about the formation of Japan Air Lines Company Ltd., which entered into an operational agreement with Northwest Airlines.[7] With the signing of the San Francisco Peace Treaty in 1952, JAL was allowed international routes. These started in 1954 with flights between Tokyo and San Francisco by way of Wake Island and Honolulu. Pan Am's primary concern was always to maintain and expand its ridership; whenever a new airline entered the market—such as JAL—it immediately tracked any new competition. The question is, who was flying and how did this affect marketing? Pan Am's memoranda on JAL make it clear that the airline's concern was as much with Japanese passengers as with American travelers flying to Japan (Milley 1955a; Milley 1955b; Milley 1955c).[8] Pan American's plan to hire "Nisei" stewardesses may have taken the Japanese language into consideration, but many of the passengers to benefit from their hiring were in fact American.

It also matters little that the Pan Am empire eventually failed in 1991, when the airline industry had changed and the company had difficulty adjusting its formula to altered conditions. In fact, the airline's embeddedness in a particular period was part of its downfall. What matters is that Pan Am's position as a global leader during the postwar period, and the company's vision of itself as defining an Americanist vision of progress, growth, and empire, was an integral and infectious part of the times.

One of the themes running through this book is that of the frontier. In this I take my cue from the promotional rhetoric of the airline, as well as from the women, who in their interviews with me may not have used the word so much as spoken of its elements. The frontier is also a theme of technology, commerce, and mobility in Jet Age America, the period spanning the 1950s to the early 1970s. Thus I have found the concept to be a useful structuring principle in analyzing both macro and micro phenomena. The frontier works as an *emic*—that is, a historicized, contextualized—concept of Pan American World Airways, "Nisei" stewardesses, and the Jet Age. But a few comments are in order if we are also to make it an *etic*—that is, heuristic, external—concept of analysis.[9]

Frontier, as a conceptual site, underwent revisions from wilderness to battlefield and more recently to the space of encounter (Kaplan 1993, 16). Stemming from the work of Frederick Jackson Turner (1861–1932), the frontier thesis is a century-old cornerstone of American history. Turner's thesis states that the very character of the nation has been shaped by the concept and presence of a frontier, framed as a geographic space of freedom, conquest, and individualism (Turner 1992 [1920], 38). The thesis quickly gained enthusiastic adherents but also prompted its share of critics, including "new western historians" who equated "frontier" with outdated Anglocentric, sexist, exceptionalist, and triumphalist versions of American history (Limerick 1994). The concept of the frontier thus obscures the underlying power struggles that made it possible. A recent edited volume by Bradley Parker and Lars Rodseth, *Untaming the Frontier in Anthropology, Archaeology, and History* (2005), revisits the concept and finds continued usefulness if its meaning is extended to include a "shifting zone of innovation and recombination" "lying on the margins or in the interstices of cultural networks," a "[contact] zone of interaction between peoples" (Rodseth and Parker eds. 2005, 4, 9, 10). Once the dynamics of power relations are brought within its purview, this sense of the frontier as a contact zone of peoples, images, and assumptions plays a central role in my research.

Frontier readily calls up highly gendered and racialized images from the past: white, masculine explorers conquering colored, feminized "virgin" territory. Thus frontier ideology rests in implicitly gendered and racialized metaphors extended to technology, mobility, government, business, and social control. The white masculinity of the frontier ideology includes assumptions of character building incorporated within the concept of leaving home. The romanticism of "Go West, Young Man" lay not only in the "West," where young white men were supposed to go, but to the uncharted interior of personal development. That this territory of personal development remained the purview of white men tied the imperative of leaving home to gender and race. Pan Am's program of "Nisei" stewardesses subverted this stereotypical construction doubly by providing the means by which Asian and Asian American women left their homes far behind and built careers in the frontier of the air. "Go West, Young Man" could be reconfigured as "Go

East (and everywhere else), Young Woman." In this updated frontier story, the "Nisei" stewardess displaced the Turnerian white settler.

That displacement was only partial. In the global airline business, race played an important role in promoting a white corporate image, selling nonwhite tourist destinations, securing mainly white passengers, and displaying some of the industry's well-trained nonwhite hires. Pan Am was expert in this. The "Nisei" stewardess—as a member of a safely feminized, former enemy race—could now take care of people and expertly attend to customers. Hers was the ultimate professional assimilation, by which she gained access to a cosmopolitan world. The mobility of "Nisei" stewardesses, the possibility of "going everywhere," lay within the requirements set forth by Pan Am and the expectations of the Jet Age. The irony that this occurred within the parallel, non-intersecting context of highly contentious black-white race relations in the United States, discussed in chapter 1, sets the stage for this book.

Through racial images, frontier also calls forth empire. Indeed, Pan Am's "empire of the air"—at least during the period examined in this book—rested upon a promotional foundation of frontier. In the hands of Pan Am's president Juan Trippe, no port of call was too small, no destination too remote, no foreign government too intractable to deter expanding the empire. Pan Am's appetite for empire seemed insatiable, but of course it was not the only airline lusting for empire. The American entrepreneur Howard Hughes and his Trans-World Airways (TWA) were Juan Trippe and Pan Am's chief rivals. In spite of certain victories by Hughes, Trippe's airline remained the one to beat. His triumph continues today in a legacy of nostalgia to which no other airline comes close, as I discuss in chapters 2 and 6.

The frontier has been explicitly labeled American, reinscribing boundaries—as well as the boundlessness—of the nation. In this Pan Am's frontier project of Jet Age empire may be seen as particularly American, characterized by a bold can-do spirit, a limitlessness, and aggressive strategies of capitalist enterprise (cf. Courtwright 2005). This characterization is well suited to Juan Trippe as a personality and business leader, as well as to Pan Am (see chapter 2). Pan Am's frontier to conquer was postwar America's, sharing with it the contentions of gender, race, and empire.

In these various ways Pan Am used frontier language and ideas to promote itself as a public servant, a pathbreaker for America, and the leader of a new era called the Jet Age. The frontier of Pan Am included international routes as well as "international" peoples. Thus, the "Nisei" stewardess program could be seen as fitting neatly into the airline's ambitions. Pan Am's frontier created a contact zone of mobility and interaction that became part of the airline's fame (cf. Pratt 1992). This sense of pioneering previously uncharted waters of race, language, and culture helped substantiate Pan Am's—and postwar America's–claim to empire, the central subject of this book.

STRAND TWO: JAPANESE AMERICAN HISTORY
AND POSTWAR EXPERIENCE

This story begins only ten years after the end of the Second World War, during which persons of Japanese ancestry living in the United States suffered a highly racialized policy of barbed-wire containment and publicly enforced assimilation, established by President Franklin Roosevelt through Executive Order 9066.[10] Internment defined persons of Japanese ancestry as racialized enemies against the United States and its allies. The majority of Japanese Americans in Hawai`i were spared, in part because they made up over 37 percent of the population and were needed for labor (Nordyke 1989 and table 3-1); however, they did not escape the public distrust and overt racism of the war, and they were asked to rid themselves of all material vestiges and practices of Japanese culture. Indeed, the racialized atmosphere of wartime inevitably colored the lives of all persons of Japanese ancestry living in the United States. Even before the war anti-Japanese sentiment shaped the experiences of immigrants from Japan and their descendants in the United States in the form of employment policy, housing practices, and exclusion laws, of which wartime policy was but a culmination.

With contract immigrants having arrived from Japan since 1885, by 1955 the historical depth of Japanese Americans in the United States had extended to three or four generations. With characteristically low rates of outmarriage, at least until the postwar years, Japanese Americans tended toward social and commercial ethnic enclaves. Understandably, each succeeding generation held weaker ties to Japan and less familiarity with Japanese language and customs. Wartime greatly accelerated and enforced these processes of assimilation, in the continental United States through

short, it was exactly the promise of occupying a frontier niche in a glamorous occupation—at least for a period of their young adult lives—that fueled many of these women's dreams.

The Jet Age is the crucial stage setting for those dreams, including the intertwined personal and corporate elements of this story. The synonymity of the airplane, and the jet in particular, with modernity (or "supermodernity," according to Auge), links travel in the Jet Age with the class- and race-specific figures of the premier travelers, the "jet setters" (Auge 1995). Enthusiasm for a Jet Age peopled by jet setters captivated the Euro-American public as the epitome of modernity awash in techno-utopic fantasies. However, these fantasies were shared unevenly by groups, depending on their social class, urban or rural status, proximity to centers of power, and race or ethnicity. Even within one social class, the genders participated differently: women continued to perform window dressing for the age, while men could dream of piloting the new aircraft. The shrinking of the globe by jet travel meant that foreign (or foreign-looking) women could embody exoticized Jet Age glamour. The "Nisei" stewardesses were part of this. Pan Am was not the only airline that flew jets or hired foreign and foreign-looking women. But it was the airline whose name and prestige rang as a symbol of the aircraft and the lifestyle associated with it.

In addition to the seductions and promises of newfound globalism, the Jet Age encompasses a highly contentious era marked by the civil rights movement from the 1950s on (as I discuss in chapter 1) and the rise of feminism in the 1960s and 1970s. It occurs within the context of newly established institutions of globalization: the United Nations (1945), a symbol of international authority housed in the United States; global economic organizations such as the World Bank (1944), the International Monetary Fund (IMF, 1944), and the General Agreement on Tariffs and Trade (GATT, 1947–94; replaced by the World Trade Organization); and collective security organizations such as the North Atlantic Treaty Organization (NATO, 1949). Thus the shrinking of the world by jets was not only the purview of business and leisure but also a critical part of America's postwar history of international engagement.

Throughout the book I use the word "cosmopolitanism" to suggest the physical and conceptual crossings of geopolitical borders—that is, worldliness within a particular historic conceptualization of the "world." However, this is worldliness and mobility with cautionary tales built into its usage. Stuart Hall describes an optimistic cosmopolitanism of choice that draws on a wide range of meanings and "cultural repertoires" (2002, 26). In this view cosmopolitanism opens up a range of choices that mononational or monocultural practices do not. It is within this fairly benign and historicized view of cosmopolitanism—as orientation, competence, and choice built upon mobility—that Pan Am's "Nisei" stewardesses may be discussed in accord with their own times.[14]

This is not to deny the highly problematic political contexts within which these orientations, competencies, choices, and mobilities exist. As Ackbar Abbas points out, elective cosmopolitan mobility takes place only in particular privileged settings: "metropolitan centers where movement and travel are undertaken with ease and where the encounter with other cultures is a matter of free choice, negotiated on favourable terms" (2000, 771). This brand of cosmopolitan mobility, in other words, ignores conditions of movements and displacements that occur in less than ideal conditions. Disadvantaged cosmopolitans include refugees, diasporic subjects, migrants, and exiles.

The contemporary debates on cosmopolitanism—and the attendant sense of inhabiting a position as a "citizen of the world"—center around issues of power and mobility. Craig Calhoun asks: "What does it mean to be a 'citizen of the world'? Through what institutions is this 'citizenship' effectively expressed? . . . How does this citizenship contend with global capitalism and with non-cosmopolitan dimensions of globalization?" (2002, 89). The key to answering these questions lies in expanding the concept to include a range of conditions and effects; thus, not "cosmopolitanism" but "cosmopolitanisms." As the editors of a key volume on the subject contend, "Cosmopolitanism must give way to the plurality of modes and histories . . . that comprise cosmopolitan practice and history. We propose therefore that cosmopolitanism be considered in the plural, as *cosmopolitanisms*" (Pollock, Bhabha, Breckenridge, and Chakrabarty 2000, 584). In this pluralistic, decentered view, the idea of cosmopolitanisms opens up the possibility of multiple modes and loci of power, multiple practices and histories, and multiple assertions, definitions, and mobilities, each to be examined in its own context.

This book examines these three strands—Pan Am, "Nisei" stewardesses, and the Jet Age—as intertwined aspects of one story. At the macro, industrial level, I look at the role of "Nisei" stewardesses in Pan Am's postwar frontier ideology and the practices of empire of the Jet Age; at the micro level, I analyze the role of Pan Am's company practices and on-the-job experiences during the Jet Age in shaping the lives of "Nisei" stewardesses. This is therefore as much a story of an airline and a group of women as it is the story of an era. It is a story that juxtaposes the intimacy of racialized bodies with corporate and national aspirations of empire. This book recognizes the premise of two recent edited volumes, *Haunted by Empire: Geographies of Intimacy in North American History*, edited by Ann Stoler (2006), and *Moving Subjects: Gender, Mobility, and Intimacy in an Age of Global Empire*, edited by Tony Ballantyne and Antoinette Burton (2009): that the realm of the intimate (bodies, emotions, dreams) is crucial to consolidating the power of empires, even as relations of empires may help structure the realm of the intimate (Stoler ed. 2006, 4). What this book shares with those other volumes is a focus on the closeness of the encounter as it shapes mobile subjects—"bodies on the move"—here, sites of affect and labor on which corporate empire depends (Ballantyne and Burton eds. 2009, 8).

The braiding of the story includes contradictions. Although the women were officially hired for their Japanese language skills, only a few spoke Japanese fluently. Perhaps more important than language, what Japanese American (and later other Asian and Asian American) stewardesses gave Pan Am was the "look" of exotic cosmopolitanism, especially in their Asia-bound and round-the-world service. Thus under the banner of language, Pan Am spotlighted race as a marketing strategy to prove its prestige, extend its command of international airspace, and display its mobile cosmopolitanism. These elements—prestige, airspace, and mobile cosmopolitanism—all constituted primary pillars of Pan Am's postwar frontier.

The braiding also includes different levels of cachet. Pan Am was not the only one to benefit from its program. "Nisei" stewardesses gained tremendous exposure to a larger world far beyond their local upbringing. Working for Pan Am as a flight attendant became an education for these women in cosmopolitanism and gendered service. For many it also became a touchstone in the formation of their identities. This holds true for women whose very subjectivity continues to be wrapped up with Pan Am decades later, as well as for women whose Pan Am employ was only a brief interlude. Once a Pan Am stewardess, always a Pan Am stewardess—this is what many of the women I interviewed say. Although they represent those who hold that status particularly dear, they are not alone in this assessment. Thus for many members of an older, general public, knowing or finding out that a woman had previously flown for Pan Am gives her a certain cultural cachet that tends to follow her for years after her flying days have ended. This book examines that cachet as a product of corporate, personal, and historical interventions.

The contradictions and the cachet belie the double-sided nature of mobility itself. As Tim Cresswell puts it: "Mobility as progress, as freedom, as opportunity, and as modernity, sit side by side with mobility as shiftlessness, as deviance, and as resistance" (2006, 1–2). That is, the enhanced mobility afforded by the Jet Age did not come without brakes placed upon the social changes that it wrought. The same speed that enabled people to circle the globe also prompted second thoughts about where the new mobility might lead, as well as the unequal resources that allowed some to move with greater ease than others. "Nisei" stewardesses of the Jet Age shared some of these ambivalences: while some families toasted their daughters' newfound place in a prestigiously mobile, white world, others cringed at the thought that their daughters were now on so public a moving stage, serving drinks at high speeds and altitudes. In both cases, public mobility became the source of prestige and shame. Inhabitants of the social and technological frontier of the Jet Age, "Nisei" stewardesses occupied the limelight of mobility marked by ambivalence.

That ambivalence contributes to what John Urry calls a "mobility system"—an infrastructure of technology, information, social relations, and business practices that makes movement possible, predictable, and commercially feasible (2007, 12–14). The Jet Age created its own mobility system whose hallmark was its very frontier-like quality. As I discuss in chapter 1, enabling the Jet Age required building jets and reducing air time and costs, but more importantly educating the public as to the safety and reliability of this new form of travel. The shrinking distances and quickened pace of jet-fueled mobility did not necessarily come easily or evenly.

Weaving together the three strands of the story brings to the fore key questions. What did it mean to be cosmopolitan during the Jet Age? What kinds of cosmopolitanisms were produced by postwar globalization, techno-utopias, and rising challenges to existing racial and gender structures? Put succinctly, how are frontier and cosmopolitanism intertwined? If frontier expresses, among other things, the cultural impact of the Jet Age, and cosmopolitanism is part of the discourse surrounding the assimilation of ethnic minorities in the United States, then the "Nisei" stewardess sits at the nexus of frontier and cosmopolitanism. She inhabits the frontier of Pan Am's empire exactly because of her assimilation, performing corporate Jet Age multiculturalism. One might consider this a form of postcolonial cosmopolitanism—the orientations and competencies of global consciousness founded in power-infused practices of race, class, and gender. Indeed, this is a story of corporate subject making in its production and performance of cosmopolitan selves as part of the Jet Age.

This observation holds particular force for Asian Americans, a diverse group whose histories have been interlaced with the displacement of migration shaped by governmental prohibitions, restrictions upon citizenship, and, eventually, hollow praise as model minorities.[15] An invitation to take part in the white cosmopolitanism of the time can be viewed as an achievement within the framework of the assimilationist politics that have galvanized the group. The invitation did not come without a struggle; not everyone agreed on the terms of assimilation, and the disagreements sometimes surfaced in the form of labor disputes and student strikes.[16] These disagreements demonstrate that many Asian Americans engaged in more critical engagements with cosmopolitanisms that were not complicit with mainstream power. By contrast, "Nisei" stewardesses generally toed the line. They combined a kind of political conservatism with personal liberalism—they were risk-taking conservatives—a combination that may hearken back to the continuing tie of the airline industry with the military (cf. Courtwright 2005). They took their place within the desires and competencies of global consciousness that defined Pan Am's cosmopolitanism. How they negotiated the terrain of that global consciousness is the stuff of this book.

This, then, is a story of intertwined dreams—frontiers, mobilities, postcolonial cosmopolitanisms—that link the corporate and the personal. That this story takes place in the air—that its dreams are *airborne* dreams—carries its own significance. I argue that the mobility enabled by flying itself, especially during the Jet Age, plays a part in both corporate and personal aspirations, shaping the horizon of expectations, weeding out the faint of heart, propelling the heady limitlessness of those aspirations, all within the context of particular class-based possibilities. This book tells the tale of an uneven global romance with and in the air at a time when flying was not yet commonplace or degraded.

In this romancing of the air, key issues prevail to structure the intertwining of the personal and the corporate. Race overlaps with gender overlaps with class, in an overdetermined sense of postwar mobility and postcolonial cosmopolitanism. These issues mark the particularities of time and place, making the story of Pan Am and its "Nisei" stewardesses a case study in the larger history of postwar America during the Jet Age and its own negotiations of race, gender, and class. In no small way, these airborne dreams inscribe both the possibilisms and problematics of a dreaming nation within them.

LAST TURNS OF PHRASE

Finally, a few words of explanation about terminology. Throughout the book I place "Nisei" in quotation marks to emphasize that this was a convenient label rather than a sociological fact. By the program's end in 1972, very few of the women involved were actually second-generation Japanese Americans. Some were third-generation, others were Japanese nationals, still others were of different Asian ancestry. However, this was a label that stuck and to which the women themselves answer. I also use the somewhat awkward construction "Japanese (American)" to emphasize the popular conflation of Japanese and Japanese American women by the American public.

I also use the term "stewardess" when referring to female flight attendants of the 1950s and 1960s. I was instructed on this by a member of the Miami chapter of World Wings International, who made the differentiation clear. She and others emphatically told me, "We were stewardesses, not flight attendants," pointing out that during the years of their employ, the label signified a glamorous female position. It was not until the 1970s that the gender-neutral term "flight attendant" became an official label, marking the influx of men to the profession and women's growing feminist consciousness (Barry 2007, 206, 266 n. 61). Thus "stewardess" it is, with its implications of a particular period in constructions of gender, race, class, globalism, and commerce.

One

1955

Postwar America, Things Japanese, and
"One-World" Tourism

There are no distant places any longer: the world is small and the world is one.

WENDELL WILLKIE, *One World* (1943)

LET US SET THE STAGE for the "Nisei" stewardess by examining 1955 as the year of a particular confluence of events for Pan Am (jets, logos, and Asian women) and the United States. Within the events of 1955 I focus on everyday popular culture and middle-class consumption, Cold War tensions, and key events in race relations. This was the cusp of the Jet Age, when African American struggles were juxtaposed with a taste for exotic women from the Asian American "model minority." Asian American stereotypes found their way into the marketing of mass tourism and girl-next-door stewardesses, exotic and otherwise. In this "Nisei" stewardesses played their role, shaping postwar America's conceptualization of itself and its role in the new internationalist "one-world" order.

In the view of Wendell Willkie, Republican nominee for president in 1940 and author of the words quoted above, overseas travel would teach ordinary citizens and leaders alike the utopian lessons of "one world." Willkie and others saw overseas travel as fostering global peace and understanding by effacing national boundaries in favor of one-world citizenship. Anthony Sampson argues that airlines are "among the most national of industries, inextricably bound up with their home country's ambitions and security" (1984, 19).[1] Thus wherever Pan Am flew, it carried the American banner. America's exceptionalism was Pan Am's exceptionalism. Pan Am's "frontier ideology" as represented by its practices in 1955 thus constitutes a critical dimension of globalism in postwar America. Willkie's one-world utopianism of air travel—contextualized within the events of the year 1955 and images of Asian women—remains firmly tethered to nationalist configurations.

THE YEAR 1955: MOVING IN AND MOVING OUT

That both the Jet Age and Pan Am's "Nisei" program began in 1955 is no accident. The year was pivotal for various "frontiers" in the United States, as culture went global, the Cold War reaffirmed Asia as an international hot spot, and the civil rights movement was born. A sense of newness—that this was the start of an era—engulfed the American public. Pan Am presented itself as one of that era's pioneers, with "Nisei" stewardesses playing an important part on its corporate stage.

The turn to the new took place within what has been characterized as a culture of containment; this refers primarily to controlling the perceived threat of communism during the Cold War, but also to the social control centered around female domesticity, heteronormativity, and the nuclear household. Elaine Tyler May's seminal work *Homeward Bound* (1988) paints a picture of middle-class life and the American dream that has become an iconic symbol of the 1950s.[2] This was a dream not equally shared or practiced across the country, however. In *The Way We Never Were* (2000) Stephanie Coontz criticizes the dream as a historical fluke and a media-based image rather than a reality. In a provocative rejoinder to May's work, Joanne Meyerowitz juxtaposes counterhistories of women of color and different sexual orientations, class positions, and regional backgrounds in an edited volume boldly titled *Not June Cleaver* (1994) (referring to the mother figure in the postwar television situation comedy *Leave It to Beaver*). As Meyerowitz argues, "The sustained focus on a white middle-class domestic ideal and on suburban middle-class housewives sometimes renders other ideals and other women invisible" (4).

One purpose of this book is to interrogate how essential parts of the June Cleaver ideal superimposed themselves upon other women such as "Nisei" stewardesses through industrial practices that were racialized, gendered, and commodified. The "Nisei" stewardesses became hostesses, à la

June Cleaver, in the air, while setting themselves apart in other ways. Instead of being confined to the home, they built careers flying to the farthest reaches of commercial aviation. That they did so through the refraction of race colors their stories with the exotic appeal of the incipient Jet Age.

In 1955 Ray Kroc opened his first McDonald's restaurant in Des Plaines, Illinois,[3] Disneyland opened in Anaheim, California, Elvis Presley struck a deal with "Colonel" Tom Parker to manage his career, and James Dean died in a one-car crash near Cholame, California. It was against this background that Pan Am embarked on its effort to hire "Nisei" stewardesses, symbolizing the beginning of postwar American domination of popular culture globally. Nothing captured middle-class life more than consumption, what Lizabeth Cohen calls a "consumers' republic"—"an economy, culture, and politics built around the promises of mass consumption, both in terms of material life and the more idealistic goals of greater freedom, democracy, and equality" (2003, 7). In postwar America to buy was to be a good citizen, helping the economy to recover after depression and war. Consumption— and especially international air travel on a carrier such as Pan Am—thus became a political virtue.

One of the major effects of the Cold War was the turn to Asia by the United States, as it waged the Korean War from 1950 to 1953, maintained major military bases in Japan, South Korea, and the Philippines, and became embroiled in conflicts in Vietnam. This turn to Asia had direct repercussions for Asian Americans: the Cold War spotlight tied Asian Americans more closely to their ancestral homeland, causing some to question once again their American identity (Lim 2006, 124). More importantly, the act of placing Japanese American women aboard a prestigious airline such as Pan Am took on added symbolic significance. When all eyes were turning to Asia, they could be displayed as a triumph of assimilation and mastery of the world. Pan American's hiring of Japanese (American) women in service roles performed the global politics of postwar America.

The year 1955 also saw the birth of the civil rights movement, which was sparked by two events: the murder of a fourteen-year-old African American, Emmett Till, in Money, Mississippi, for purportedly whistling at a white woman, and the arrest of an African American woman, Rosa Parks, for refusing to give up her bus seat to a white man in Montgomery, Alabama. The resultant protests and intense focus on African American injustices deflected attention from other nonwhite minorities, including Hispanics and Asian Americans. There were no demonstrations by Japanese Americans, no boycotts or protest marches in the 1950s or 1960s. But this only meant that Japanese Americans had a different, more circumspect public face—that of a "model minority"—quiet, hard-working, and highly assimilable. It is for this reason that Pan Am hired "Nisei" stewardesses, or at least the Japanese Americans who constituted the early and definitive groups of stewardesses. Frank Chin calls the model minority image "racist love," "expressed in the form of praise" (1976, 556–57). Heaped with praise, Japanese American stewardesses provided Pan Am with an exoticized presence (and Asian language), without the encumbrances of more contentious minority populations.[4] "Nisei" stewardesses were racialized as acceptably, even desirably, women "of color."

In her study of multicultural marketing, Arlene Davila paints a somber picture of ethnic relations: "The fact that multicultural marketing ends up pitting one ethnic group against another in terms of who is advertising-worthy and who is not . . . means the gains of one group (in terms of public exposure or advertising revenues) amount to a loss for another" (2001, 237). Thus the elevation of the "Nisei" stewardess must be seen in relation to the relative absence of other women of color in the air. Although Pan Am hired Hispanic stewardesses as far back as 1950, these women, based in Miami (an "open" Spanish-language base that included non-Spanish speakers), flew primarily the Latin American routes. By contrast, "Nisei" stewardesses, based in Honolulu (a "closed" language base, housing only those who spoke an Asian language), flew not only to Asia but also on Pan Am's round-the-world flights. All of Pan Am's westbound Flights 001 (originating in San Francisco and traveling around the world with stops in Honolulu, Tokyo, Hong Kong, Bangkok, Calcutta, Delhi, Beirut, Istanbul, Frankfurt, London, and New York) and eastbound Flights 002 uniquely maintained a "Japanese-language position" (eventually extended to other Asian languages), to be filled singly by a "Nisei" stewardess. Thus Hispanics and Asian (American) stewardesses received different treatment in terms of their language-base identity, as well as their routes.

Pan Am's establishment on its round-the-world flights of positions reserved for speakers of Japanese and other Asian languages reflected not only a customer base that may have included Japanese (or other Asians) but also an eagerness to employ model-minority "Nisei" stewardesses as part of a racial, cultural, and linguistic display when circumnavigating the globe. Furthermore, "Nisei" stewardesses predated any African American hire by Pan Am by ten years: the airline took that step only in 1965, under pressure from the National Association for the Advancement of Colored People (NAACP). (The airline's argument that it hired on the basis of language rather than race—therefore denying any special place for African Americans—proved ultimately unconvincing.)

In these ways, the complexities of race in America in 1955 found corporate expression in Pan Am's differential hires of the 1950s and 1960s. Within the hierarchy of minorities in the United States, Asian Americans sometimes occupied a top rung as "honorary whites" or "near-whites"; at other times they were viewed as "just like blacks," even as "forever foreigners" (Okihiro 1994, 33; Tuan 2003; Davila 2001, 231; cf. Lowe 1996).[5] The tension between these variable positions was exactly the dilemma of the "Nisei" stewardess—domesticated enough to wear the Pan Am uniform, even while framed as racially exotic. She inhabited the racialized interstices that combined orientalism, model-minority assimilation, and marketability in ways denied to other women of color. Notably, the Japanese- Asian-language position on Pan Am's round-the-world flights was hers and hers alone.

Race relations in the United States may be viewed against the backdrop of a photo exhibit, "The Family of Man," at the Museum of Modern Art in 1955 for which the photographer Edward Steichen was the curator.[6] The exhibit opened in January to great acclaim and public interest; 503 amateur and professional works by 273 photographers, covering 68 countries, sent a powerful message to the American audience.[7] The exhibit used race as a spectacle of difference, even as it set aside the volatility of actual race relations in the United States. Looking past domestic inequities so well dramatized in 1955, the exhibit displayed a romanticized, humanistic view of world harmony, utilizing a visual "rhetoric of unity" (Sandeen 1995, 2). Some of the same assumptions of racial display and visuality undergirded Pan Am's hiring of "Nisei" stewardesses, balancing unity and assimilation with difference. Although Pan Am's was a business strategy, not an artistic or "humanitarian" one, the American public was already inured to some of the same principles expressed in Steichen's exhibit and book. Pan Am banked upon the allure of particular forms of racialized difference, made acceptable within model-minority femininity and reconfigured to corporate specifications.

What, then, constituted this model-minority femininity? I turn now to various postwar images of Japanese (American) women in order to frame more closely Pan Am's "Nisei" stewardess program. These images formed part of the reason why Pan Am wanted "Nisei" stewardesses in 1955, as well as creating a bank of stereotypes against which the women worked and that they manipulated and sometimes resisted. In examining these images I do not mean to imply that there is either a single gaze or a unidirectional one. Rather, part of the project of this book is to embrace multiple vectors of subjectivity by interweaving corporate and individual gazes. I also acknowledge that the images of Japanese (American) and other Asian (American) women were both overlapping and distinctive. The overlap in images lies in processes of racialization; the distinctiveness is due in part to wartime imaging that drew careful boundaries between Japan and other Asian nations and peoples, as well as the experiences of American soldiers in occupied Japan. Renee Tajima points out two seemingly contradictory aspects of Asian female media images pertinent to our discussion—their invisibility and their marked quality (1989, 314). In other words, Asian women typically appear in supporting ("invisible") roles of a drama, rather than as the main character; they are also rarely portrayed as "ordinary" people. The question that arises is what practices these images enable or promote. As David Palumbo-Liu is careful to point out: "Sometimes racial others are read as synonymous with the general exotica of modern forms; at other times, they are markers of a 'racial frontier' that cannot be crossed without cost" (1999, 83).[8] Pan Am crossed that racial frontier specifically by drawing upon exoticized images of Japanese American women, carefully assimilated within the professionalism of the company's Tunis blue uniform.

The Euro-American image of the geisha—a highly sexualized figure whose existence centers around serving men—dominated the postwar view of Japanese (American) women.[9] In fact, the geisha image can be seen as the exemplar of a host-guest relationship that points directly to the flight attendant profession. This shared concept lends itself to a shared fetishization. Najeeb Halaby, head of Pan Am from 1969 to 1972, was known to have referred to flight attendants as "geisha," suggesting that his stewardesses "should be more like Japanese geisha girls, prepared to flatter and entertain the male passengers" (Kane with Chandler 1974, 52). Hiring "Nisei" stewardesses drew Pan Am that much closer to the "geisha girls" whom Halaby and others lauded.

Whether the image of geisha in postwar America was historically accurate is less revealing than how the image served particular purposes in the American fantasy. Thus it does not matter that originally geisha (i.e. performers of art) included men, but it does matter that the image of geisha was sexualized as serving (and servicing) men. As Kelly Foreman argues, "The strength and continuity of the 'geisha-girl' image [in the United States] stems from its usefulness in defining American gender roles, that 'geisha-girls' serve as a vibrant source of female 'other'" (2005, 37). Through the geisha image the guest-host relationship readily elides into an idealized service culture that elevates guest-males by means of attentive, solicitous host-female pampering. This kind of gendered pampering rests at the crux of the geisha image—as well as Halaby's directive.

The geisha-laden stereotype finds expression in books, plays, operas, and films, the most notable being *Madame Butterfly* (1904), Puccini's opera based on the novel *Madame Chrysantheme* (1887) by Pierre Loti.[10] *Madame Butterfly* adds qualities of loyalty, suffering, and sacrifice to the geisha image, acting as a primer on interracial, international liaisons. It enacts a prototype of a young woman (not coincidentally, a geisha) who sacrifices everything for heterosexual love. That this love is interracial and international portends the tragedy of the encounter. In postwar America that prototype distilled the allure and danger of the exotic—and became part of the assumptions under which Pan Am's "Nisei" stewardesses worked.

The Second World War provided the American public with a host of images of Japanese women, from alluring geisha to the highly demonized Tokyo Rose (the taunting female American voice broadcast to American soldiers in Japan), and later the "Hiroshima Maidens," a group of young Japanese women disfigured by the atomic bomb and brought to the United States in 1955 for plastic surgery (aboard a Pan American flight). For people in various American communities, those images became part of a lived reality when six to seven thousand war brides from Japan were resettled as a result of the War Brides Relocation Act of 1945.[11]

Japanese war brides prompted a flurry of big-name Hollywood films about Japanese-American interracial romance.[12] Within the fictive framework, the American public could negotiate some of the ambivalences and complexities of this wartime byproduct. One notable film is *Sayonara* (1957), originally a novel by James Michener (1953). In the novel and film, Lloyd Gruver (Marlon Brando in the film version), an American military officer who has fallen in love with a Japanese star actress announces, "I concluded that no man could comprehend women until he had known the women of Japan with their unbelievable combination of unremitting work, endless suffering and boundless warmth" (Michener 1953, 128; quoted in Yamamoto 1999, 41). It was this combination of work, perseverance, and warmth that created the model-minority reputation of "Nisei" stewardesses. Interracial romance such as this throws the gauntlet at western women's feet, validating the "unbelievable combination" possessed by Japanese women. The lesson of the Japanese woman made her an ideal to be read against the independent postwar American woman as part of the project to refeminize American middle-class women.

This gauntlet—the Japanese or Asian (American) woman as exemplar of the nostalgized femininity that white women have lost—brings us full circle to the geisha image with which our discussion began.[13] The image reinforces western elements of heteronormative desirability in its sexual and racial dimorphism: short, delicate Asian females contrast with taller white males. Furthermore, bodies echo personal gendered traits: submissive, passive Asian females contrast with dominant, aggressive white males. These kinds of gendered, racial stereotypes of Japanese and Asian (American) women work precisely because they reinforce a Euro-American sexual ideology. They may be "exotic," but their difference works within an existing Euro-American system rather than challenging it in any way.

The image implicitly critiques those left outside its bounds—white women and Asian men—while celebrating the figure whose subjectivity seems to steer the course: the white male. Where does this leave Asian (American) women? As objects of desire, are they allowed by this image also to become subjects of their own choosing? As Traise Yamamoto points out, "For all their visibility as sexually exotic objects, Asian American women remain invisible as subjects, within both dominant discourse and much feminist discourse" (1999, 67). My discussion here is built on images and therefore leaves little room for women to "talk back." I analyze the images merely to establish the setting in which we may better examine both Pan Am's policies and the women who filled the company's ranks. Yet in the chapters that follow I show how the "Nisei" women did indeed talk back, whether in words or actions. In contrast to Pinkerton's Madame Butterfly, who remained at home waiting for her lover, these women took to the air, gaining a command of foreign ports of call far surpassing those (men and others) left at home. They effectively turned the geisha stereotype on its head, even while maintaining a foothold within it.

Gina Marchetti's analysis of Hollywood depictions of "yellow peril" romance is instructive: "Functioning as spectacle, race, ethnicity, and gender exist as ahistorical, set, preordained, and unchangeable. Spectacle provides those exaggerated moments in which the social boundaries are most clearly demarcated" (1993, 215). The images I have been discussing lie exactly in those "exaggerated moments"; but it is their very overdetermined nature and the women's surpassing of their boundaries that make this examination critical for understanding Pan Am's "Nisei" stewardess program. As Yamamoto points out, "Despite fluctuating levels of benignity and hostility between Japan and the West in the twentieth century, the construction of the Japanese woman as the site and sign of access has remained relatively constant" (1999, 24).[14] That Pan Am positioned "Nisei" stewardesses as "sites and signs of access" speaks to the stereotypes and images of Asian women as well as to the equally devastating stereotyping of other women of color (Hispanics, African Americans) considered less amenable to that "access" role. In the airline's eye the "Nisei" stewardesses may have been women of color, but they were not "colored." Within the structures of this contradiction—of color, but not colored—"Nisei" stewardesses inhabited their corporate role. The power to cross the frontier of Japan in postwar America's business culture lay in the hands of Japanese (American) women, whose images positioned them within a highly desirable path enhancing Pan Am's global power.[15] That these women were able to incorporate that position within their own subjectivity for their own purposes is part of the realization of these airborne dreams.

In contrast with the many images of Japanese (American) women indelibly inscribed in the public imagination in postwar America, another group of Japanese American women received little or no media exposure—those who joined the Women's Army Corps (WAC) and Army Medical Corps during the Second World War. Brenda Moore's insightful study of this group provides a valuable point of comparison with "Nisei" stewardesses (2003). Although initially barred from service, Japanese American women began volunteering for the WAC from November 1943. Like their male Nisei counterparts eager to prove their American patriotism, some enlisted directly from internment camps. The U.S. War Department initially expressed interest in the women for the same reason that Pan Am reputedly did—for their Japanese-language skills. Some received additional language training specifically for their military assignments as members of the Military Intelligence Service and eventually did translation work. Many more, however, held clerical positions in integrated units alongside white women. Moore analyzes the experiences of Nisei WACs through the framework of "subjective turning points"—"dramatic changes in life histories . . . that separate the past from the future; people refer to themselves in terms of who they were before and after the event" (Elder, Gimbel, and Ivie 1991, quoted in Moore 2003, 149). Indeed Nisei WACs view their military experience as defining "turning points" enhanced by travel, education, independence, and marriage (2003, 165). In this way they preview some of the ways "Nisei" stewardesses say their lives were changed by their Pan Am years. In spite of different circumstances and reasons for employment, both groups of women found that their racialized hire and work experiences defined them.

THE POWER OF THE GIRL-NEXT-DOOR IMAGE

Let us turn briefly to the girl-next-door image—white, middle-class, and unmarried—as a structuring principle of the stewardess profession, and ask what its implications are, particularly as refracted through the lens of the "Nisei" stewardess.[16] First of all, she is a "girl." Unmarried, she brings youth and, by implication, her "virginal" freshness and sexual availability to the cabin. The job does not require much experience, which suggests that attending to the safety needs of passengers is not foremost among the job's responsibilities. To the contrary, youth is a fundamental part of the image, and the supply of "girls" is ever renewable, which points to the importance of the presentational, sexualized aspects of the job.

Second, the image suggests familiarity and accessibility. The girl next door is the girl within reach. She is democracy incarnate: not a distant figure on a pedestal but a down-to-earth female found everywhere. She is empathetic because of her gendered "instincts" and because she has a similar background. We know her, but more important, she knows us. Thus class and race are essential components of the empathetic intimacy that enhances the stewardess position. Here is where Pan American's "girl" differed: with a passenger.list that included people from different countries, with a crew that likewise included not only Americans but Europeans and now women of Asian ancestry, the "neighborhood" of the cabin constituted a zone of encounter, sometimes more than familiarity.

Third, the girl next door helps define and characterize the "neighborhood." She symbolizes the unity of the neighborhood and unifies those who look upon her. The model for her neighborhood rests not in the big city, but more specifically in the American idealization of the small town, a tightly-knit, face-to-face community where everyone knows each other. The reputation of the small-town girl characterizes the stewardess as friendly, humble, and unsophisticated—qualities that "Nisei" stewardesses claim of themselves. She is purportedly also highly trainable: the same reputation that paints "country boys" as good soldiers makes small-town girls next door into good "wives" in the airplane cabin. Both reputations rest on the assumption of old-fashioned values that emphasize loyalty and humility.

Fourth, the girl-next-door image is embedded in white, middle-class virtues—"wholesomeness"—that define public morality. The suspicion shrouding "public women" in the past could be ameliorated in part through espousing the private virtues of "respectability." That respectability included knowing the ways of housewifery. Thus stewardesses were encouraged to perform the role of hostess, with the cabin as their living room. By emphasizing wholesomeness and respectability (in part by hiring nurses in the early years), airlines defended their display of women. The work of moral rectitude landed in the lap of the girl next door.

Fifth, the girl next door was an ideal for more than just the American stewardess. As Barry notes, "The celebrated sky girls of the United States grew in international prestige, representing American womanhood abroad and setting the benchmark for airline hostesses around the world" (2007, 53). That womanhood may have been raced, classed, and characterized to American specifications, but those specifications became synonymous with the prestige and modernity of air travel. Thus American aviation, which set the standard in its technology, also set a standard through a kind of service that emphasized a feminized cabin, with polished air hostesses at its helm.

What is perhaps more important than analyzing the girl next door as an ideal is considering what that ideal excludes. Or, in the context of "Nisei" stewardesses, what the inclusion of females from other racial and ethnic groups suggests about the image. Whose neighbor is she, and what does her inclusion say about the neighborhood? Does she extend the neighborhood as part of a new racial frontier? Or is she upheld as a model of the taming of that frontier? Turning "Nisei" women into girls next door may be considered nothing less than Pan Am's achievement of ultimate assimilation through professionalism. The "Nisei" stewardess—rather than others such as African Americans or Hispanics—was the model-minority success story in the air.

COLD WAR TOURISM: FRAGILE CONTACT ZONES IN THE JET AGE

Although the 1950s and 1960s have been characterized as decades of containment, they may also be seen as a period of globalism and expansion, during which the United States promoted ideals of international integration. Statistics on international tourist arrivals paint a clear picture, charting the rapid increase between 1950 and 1975 (quoted from World Tourism Organization; Sharpley 2002, 16):

1950	25,282
1960	69,320
1965	112,863
1970	165,787
1975	222,290

The decades 1950–60 and 1960–70 saw the number of international tourist arrivals increase by over 100 percent, and the decade 1965–75 nearly did as well. Caught up in "one world" idealism (expressed in the epigraph that begins this chapter), Americans reached beyond their shores both by bringing the world in and by moving themselves out in the form of people-to-people diplomacy, academic exchange programs, and international tourism. In a sophisticated analysis of the period, Christopher Endy writes of overseas tourism as a postwar "consumer diploma": "Travel promotion . . . reflected an expansive American nationalism and optimism in the power of American consumers" (2004, 34). Helped by rising incomes, expanded consumer credit, increased routes, more and faster planes (jets), lower fares (tourist class in 1952; even lower economy class in 1958), governmental support and promotion of tourism, and attention from the mass media (travel sections in newspapers; Hollywood films), Americans traveled overseas as never before. But where were they going? Europe still garnered the lion's share of overseas travel, with trans-Atlantic tourism doubling between

1953 and 1959, and doubling again to 1.4 million passengers by 1965 (Endy 2004, 128–30). Travel to Asia and the Pacific increased as well during this period, but remained a small fraction of the overall total: in 1950 the Asia-Pacific accounted for 0.8 percent of all international travel, increasing to 1.0 percent in 1960 and 3.0 percent in 1970 (Warn 1999, 27 and figure 3.3).

"One world" included Asia, in particular because the United States maintained a military presence through wars, occupation forces, and permanent military bases. The Cold War provided the political reason for America's Asian presence; as mass tourism grew, leisure provided the economic and cultural interface. Exoticism—with a particular focus on Asia—became one source of Jet Age entertainment, as well as prestige. As Johanna Omelia and Michael Waldock recount: "More and more exotic decor, elaborate meals, and extensive in-flight service were used to entice passengers and differentiate the airlines. Most airlines featured lounges sporting interesting themes to spark the imagination of travelers. . . . In 1955, Northwest introduced its Fujiyama room, a lounge in the lower level of Stratocruiser decked out in Asian splendor 'symbolizing the other lands we serve beyond the Pacific. When you step down the stairway from the main deck of the Northwest Airlines Stratocruiser into the Fujiyama Room, you enter another world, tasting the charm of the Orient'" (2003, 58; photo of Fujiyama room, 2003, 69). Just as Northwest Airlines boasted of its Fujiyama lounge, Pan Am boasted of its women through its "Nisei" stewardess program. Here was the girl next door as professional as the next, but with specific racialized difference that added exotica to the experience aloft. "Tasting the charm of the Orient" on Northwest was mere simulacrum; on Pan Am a passenger could be served by a woman of "Oriental ancestry." What the airlines shared was the exoticism of imagination. Northwest's Fujiyama lounge was not necessarily the sort of lounge that was found in Japan, but what was imaged as "exotic Japan." Meanwhile, Pan Am's "Nisei" stewardesses provided the advantage of looking "exotic," while speaking perfect English and knowing American culture. In this they embodied the humanist ideals of Edward Steichen's *Family of Man*: Pan Am represented the world as one big, happy family.[17]

The American tourist in the postwar period was "the modern mobile subject" (Von Moltke 2005, 123). Mobility became a symbol of the modern, enabled through technology, prosperity, and a budding appetite for travel. Kristin Ross's study of private motorization in postwar France explains the new euphoria of "pure speed," of a hurtling through space that created new subjectivities and an expanded sense of the nation (1996, 21–22). What Ross explains of cars is all the more true of airplanes, especially jets. The middle-class citizen could participate in "pure speed," participating in the expansionist "one world" through tourism. And the travel experience could begin even before one's plane lifted off, in a cabin inhabited by the faces and voices of the (would-be) "foreign"; this was part of the effect of having "Nisei" stewardesses on board. The irony of the "Nisei" stewardesses is that they gave the airline the look of foreign, even if most were born and bred in the United States.

Travel—whether real or "armchair"—allowed millions of ordinary Americans to participate in the drama of United States expansion (Klein 2003, 107). During the postwar era traveling abroad was a patriotic imperative, even if only a few Americans could afford to do so. To this end Wendell Willkie's statement is prophetic for its visionary idealism.

It is also prophetic as the basis upon which the "contact zone" of mass air travel captured the ideology of international relations. As formulated by Mary Louise Pratt (and later taken up by James Clifford), contact zones are "social spaces where disparate cultures meet, clash, and grapple with each other often in highly asymmetrical relations of domination and subordination" (Pratt 1992, 4; Clifford 1997). The fragility of the contact zone of tourism lies in negotiating the terms of "meetings, clashes, and grapplings," here specifically in terms of race and nation. The anthropologist Edward Bruner calls the touristic encounter a "borderzone," "an empty stage waiting for performance time, for the audience of tourists and for the native performers" (1999, 158). Inevitably the stewardess is a native performer who is an intermediary between the tourist and the destination. The refracted experience of the "Nisei" stewardess, however, made her exotic presence on the stage of the cabin part of the destination itself.

That stage is not quite as empty as Bruner makes it out to be. The touristic borderzone is always filled with existing stereotypes (such as those I analyze for Japanese American women), historical conditions (such as the events of 1955), and corporate strategies (such as the "Nisei" stewardess program). These constitute a "power-geometry" of social relations (Massey 1994). The zone of encounter advances what Aihwa Ong calls "flexible citizenship": "the cultural logics of capitalist accumulation, travel, and displacement that induce subjects to respond fluidly and opportunistically to changing political-economic conditions" (1999, 6). It is the fluidity and opportunism that characterize the interaction, shaping the subjectivity of those involved in the touristic encounter, from travelers to "natives" to racialized flight crew.

Within the context of this research, the airplane may be considered a contact zone with distinctive features. As a transoceanic medium, the airplane is a temporary contact zone, whose duration generates certain kinds of interactions and relationships. Crew and passengers share a pact, bonded by the act of air travel, from its dangers to its liminality. Arthur Hailey, author of *Airport* and a pilot, writes: "Among those who fly actively and professionally, there is a camaraderie which has no parallel in any other occupation. . . . This camaraderie, this sense of unison and unity, are most evident during time spent in the air. . . . There is an awareness of having left behind the smallness and trivia of the everyday world" (quoted in Courtwright 2005, 18).

Hailey's view may be overly romanticized, yet it coincides with the notion of the airplane in flight as liminal in time and space. The airplane is simultaneously a specific physical space—i.e., "somewhere"—as well as a site that "disappears" upon landing—i.e., "nowhere." The Pan Am cabin, like other spaces through which one simply passes rather than inhabits, such as airports, highways, and supermarkets, may be considered what Marc Auge labels a "non-place"—a blank space that "can not be defined as relational, or historical, or concerned with identity" (1995, 77–78). However, Pan Am's cabin was anything but blank: it was highly in-filled with carefully chosen icons that defined the airline, from dinnerware to champagne to uniforms (and the women and men who wore them). Hiring "Nisei" stewardesses was part of the exotic "emplacing" of that cabin as part of the Pan Am brand, part of the in-flight experience.

The symbolism of the airplane as synonymous with modernity, and in particular the jet as the supreme icon of a particular point in time, centers around travel in the Jet Age with the class- and race-specific figures of its premier occupants, the "jet setters." By 1955 more Americans flew overseas than sailed in ships (Endy 2004, 128), and by the end of the decade what they flew were jets. Jets successfully bridged the frontier of overseas travel amid practices based in race, gender, and class assumptions. Pan

Am's hiring of "Nisei" stewardesses built upon and extended those assumptions, showcasing the cabin as a global space of encounter. Willkie's "one-world" pronouncement did not blunt the sense of frontier in the postwar era; rather, his words celebrated a new utopian borderlessness. Pan Am's model-minority "Nisei" stewardess symbolized that "one-world" utopia.

Two

"THE WORLD'S MOST EXPERIENCED AIRLINE"

Pan Am as Global, National, and Personal Icon

> Mass travel by air may prove to be more significant to world destiny than the atom bomb. For there can be no atom bomb potentially more powerful than the air tourist, charged with curiosity, enthusiasm and good will, who can roam the four corners of the world, meeting in friendship and understanding the people of other nations and races.
>
> JUAN TRIPPE in a speech to the annual meeting of the International Air Transport Association (IATA), 1955

THE SENSE OF POSTWAR UTOPIA found its corporate expression in the self-proclaimed "airline to the world" — Pan American World Airways. Brimming with the excitement of a new age, boasting its part in shaping that very age, pushing its political connections to the point of breaking, Pan Am bullied its way to an unrivaled position in commercial aviation. Here is the corporate strand of this book's story, told as Pan Am would have it: a frontier tale that draws upon the spirit of adventure, exploration, and conquest, even as it espouses humanitarian ideals. This is a strand of empire.

Pan American World Airways provides an excellent case study of not only empire but empire building. This was a corporation intertwined with the personality of its charismatic founder and head from 1927 to 1968, Juan Trippe (1899–1981), who for many people was Pan Am, as much as Pan Am was Juan Trippe. The stamp of his excesses was visible everywhere in the company's image and corporate practices, especially as he invoked the "frontier" in speeches and publications. The words of Juan Trippe quoted above say far more about Pan Am and its founder than they do about mass air travel, world destiny, or atomic bombs. Embedded in this declaration are the personality of its speaker and the ethos of his company: self-confident, manipulative, and autocratic. Trippe and Pan Am embodied the global- ism of 1955—burgeoning popular culture, middle-class consumerism, and *Family of Man* images, amid Cold War concerns that set America's sights upon Asia.

The story that I tell here focuses on the ambitions of Trippe to develop and exploit the frontiers of commercial air travel through a corporate cul- ture that can be described and analyzed much as one would conduct a vil- lage ethnography. Pan Am proclaimed a frontier ethos of extremes, pro- moting itself as the first, the best, and the most. Employees adopted that company ethos as the "Pan Am Way": can-do spirit, pride, pluck, luxury, prestige, technological innovation, hierarchy, loyalty, and a constant con- cern for performing and promoting the company's larger-than-life image. Image was important in everything that Pan Am did—from influencing business and governmental transactions, to convincing people around the world to fly Pan Am, to fostering identity, pride, and loyalty among em- ployees. Central to that image was Pan Am's role in defining America and the Jet Age, beginning with ordering the largest fleet of jets in 1955 and continuing by hiring women as its own international "exotics" ("Nisei"). If American exceptionalism rested on an ideology of freedom and liberty, then Pan Am's exceptionalism followed suit, proclaiming that it was em- phatically not like any other airline (cf. Palumbo-Liu 1999, 223). Pan Am's domination of overseas air travel was nothing less than postwar America's economic imperialism in practice. The American "soft power" inroads of McDonald's and Disney, born in 1955 and traveling later overseas, only re- capitulated Pan Am's domination in the air.

That domination continues to live in the twenty-first century through public nostalgia and private celebrations, as I discuss in chapter 6. Many "Pan Am people"—stewardesses, pilots, and other employees—remain strongly connected to the airline, a testament to company loyalty. Their loyalty runs parallel with a more general, commercialized public nostal- gia for Pan Am as the airline that represents the Jet Age, a glorified past of global travel. Of course not all employees remain connected to the com- pany, and not all members of the public express such nostalgia for Pan Am and the Jet Age. And yet for those who do, Pan Am lives in the preserve and consumerist practices of collective memory. As the demise of the airline in 1991 recedes, that memory is fast becoming part of a historicized moment and generational identity that embodies the spectacle of "Nisei" and other cosmopolitan stewardesses circling the globe.

JUAN TRIPPE'S WORLD: DEFINING AND
INHABITING THE FRONTIER

The story of Juan Trippe and Pan Am has been told in numerous biographies and company histories (e.g. Josephson 1972 [1943]; Daley 1980; Bender and Altschul 1982; Davies 1987; Conrad 1999; Gandt 1999; Homan and Reilly 2000; Banning 2001; Bilstein 2001).[1] In familiar phrases these personal and corporate histories draw a close link between the company and the man: the story of Trippe and Pan Am was an "American Saga" (Daley 1980); Pan Am was America's informal "chosen instrument" (Bender and Altschul 1982); Juan Trippe struggled to secure his "empire of the air" (Josephson 1972 [1943]). The phrases tellingly connect the man, the company, the nation, and empire. Trippe famously used an old idea ("frontier") to boldly proclaim a new age: in his words, the skies were "America's frontiers pushed back to infinity" (Trippe 1939). This airborne frontier represented social utopianism as well as physical expansion and conquest. Gracing the cover of *Time* on 28 March 1949, Trippe proclaimed, "Now the world is every man's oyster" (*Time* 1949, cover). By that he referred to his plan to offer economy fares to passengers, thus paving the way for middle-class tourism. The "oyster" may not have truly been available to all, but this did not prevent the pronouncement from making headlines. The Appendix provides a timeline of Pan Am events from its beginnings in 1927 to its demise in 1991, culled from printed sources and the website of the Pan Am Historical Foundation (http://www.panam.org). Here I only briefly retell parts of the story in terms of personalities and what I consider a social frontier, highlighting the place of the "Nisei" stewardesses in corporate strategy.

The story of Trippe (and Pan Am) is one of elitism, prestige, charisma, and ambition. A twenty-eight-year-old Yale graduate infatuated with flying, Trippe exploited his school ties to the fullest in gathering the financial and personnel resources to establish his fledgling company. He enlisted the financial backing of William A. Rockefeller and Cornelius Vanderbilt

Whitney in establishing the Aviation Corporation of the Americas, which eventually merged with two other companies, including one named Pan American Airways. In the merger Trippe became the operational head of Pan Am. Relying on family and school connections was not unusual, but Trippe made these ties a particular badge of identity. Pan American became known as the "Yale airline" because of the many school connections that Trippe exploited (Bender and Altschul 1982, 13). The ties between elite school (Yale) and corporation (Pan Am) remained strong throughout Trippe's tenure, marking the airline as one that flaunted success gained through wealth, prestige, and personal connections.

The links between government and Pan Am—a contract to provide postal service, the securing of international landing rights, and wartime cooperation—became part of the company's prestige and were a source of contention during Trippe's tenure. The Second World War brought Pan Am ever closer to the national political scene. First, the relationship between Pan Am and government began at home, with Trippe's marriage to Betty Stettinius. Trippe's brother-in-law Edward Stettinius Jr. eventually served as undersecretary of state to President Franklin D. Roosevelt in 1943. Second, as America's only exclusive international carrier, Pan Am stood in a unique position to assist the government through its global network. Third, Pan Am directly assisted the military by training its pilots and lending airplanes. Pan Am had the airplanes that the government needed; thus during the war the United States military officially took over Pan Am's fleet, crews, and operations. Fourth, Pan Am conducted covert infrastructural operations for the United States government, constructing bases in the Pacific, building airstrips in Central and South America and Africa, and airlifting planes, supplies, and ammunition to North Africa (Burns; http://www .panam.org). Pan Am also conducted secret missions, transporting exiled heads of state, military advisors, diplomats, and spies (Bender and Altschul 1982, 14). In January 1943 Roosevelt became the first United States president to fly overseas, boarding a Pan Am flying boat to Casablanca, where he and Winston Churchill negotiated the unconditional surrender terms for the Axis.[2]

The close ties between Pan American and the government contributed to the public impression that the airline was the nation's "chosen instrument," favored in the awarding of routes, landing rights, and other privileges. The airline received exclusive and generous mail subsidies, without which Pan Am and Trippe could not have constructed their worldwide route network. Pan Am used these and other privileges as publicity, calling itself "the second line of defense" and "virtually an adjunct of the United States armed forces" (Endy 2004, 42). Trippe would have liked nothing better than to establish Pan Am as the sole national carrier on international routes. However, in the years after the Second World War, to his great disappointment, the government continually denied him and his airline that status. Although Trippe had enjoyed previous cordial relations with Roosevelt, by 1943 he had antagonized Washington with his aggressive attempts to secure a monopoly of international air traffic. Trippe argued that other countries supported a national carrier and that the United States should do likewise. Government officials objected to the monopoly that Pan Am enjoyed, and wished to establish an open skies policy that would allow competitors into the field of international air travel.

The postwar debates centered upon open versus closed skies, freedom of the air versus "chosen instrument" sovereignty of American skies. Freedom of the air won out, and Trippe aggressively attempted to make up for that defeat. By 1955 fifteen airlines based in the United States were flying internationally, including the "Big Four" domestic airlines Trans World Airways (TWA), Eastern Airlines, American Airlines, and United Air Lines (Barry 2007, 231 n. 5). Part of Trippe's revenge for losing chosen instrument status was competing with other airlines on the basis of image—to which the "Nisei" stewardess contributed.

Image was always important to Trippe. From the beginning he showed a flair for showmanship, not for himself so much as for his company. His airline would stand out for its look and standards of discipline and professionalism, borrowed in part from the military. With flying boats made to look like yachts and uniforms inspired by naval designs for pilots and crew members, Pan Am cultivated the style of official, public service (Sampson 1984, 46). Maintaining a dignified, nautical theme, he called his airplanes "clippers," a name that distinguished his airliners from others.

In his speeches Trippe directly invoked the notion of frontier. In one speech, entitled "America in the Air Age" that he delivered in 1944 at UCLA and Berkeley, Trippe began thus: "A hundred years ago, the West Coast was the frontier which inspired adventurous Americans with dreams of nation-building. Here, a daring, forceful and intelligent people set up a new watch-tower from which American eyes might scan the vast reaches of the world" (1944, 1). In Trippe's words America held stewardship over the rest of the world, keeping watch, maintaining peace from a vantage point that one must assume focused on Asia. Trippe compared westward exploration of the United States in the 1800s to the new frontier of overseas travel pioneered by Pan Am. Continuing his comparison, he asserted: "In blazing a trail across both oceans and to all five continents, our thousands of [Pan Am] employees, here and abroad, have had some of the same vision and pioneering spirit that marked the settlement and development of this great State [California]. Their outlook, from the very nature of their work, has been a world outlook, not limited to any one seacoast or section" (Trippe 1944, 2). Here as elsewhere Trippe invoked the frontier to convey the newness of the age, its widespread effects, and Pan Am's helmsmanship of the endeavor as "an instrument for expanding horizons" (Trippe 1944, 9).

The sense of frontier is nowhere better inscribed than in Pan Am's stake to history through its self-proclaimed "firsts." Its list of company firsts in promotional literature of the late 1970s included the following:

First American airline to use radio communications (1928)
First airline to develop and use instrument flying techniques (1929)
First airline to operate scheduled trans-pacific service (1935)
First airline to provide transatlantic passenger and mail service (1939)
First airline to operate a scheduled commercial round-the-world service (1947)
First airline to provide tourist-class service outside the continental limits of the U.S. (1948)
First airline to order U.S. commercial jet transports (1955)
First airline to establish a global electronic reservations system—Panamac (1962)
(News release; NASM F1P-167000-70)

What matters here is not the veracity of the claims so much as the existence of the list itself and how the notion of the company as a pioneer shaped attitudes toward Pan American. These "firsts" contributed to Pan Am's public image, as well as the crucial private image of the company for its employees.

Flight attendants and other employees took pride in considering themselves members of a company that could boast such "firsts." If Pan Am could claim a place in history, then so too could the company's workers.

One stewardess who flew with Pan Am in the 1970s recalls, "The experience was like getting a master's degree in the world. I just can't put a price on what I learned from the people I flew with and the places I went. Occasionally, we participated in history, like evacuating the refugees during the Fall of Saigon." This critical notion of being an important part of the national scene, especially as it extended to other parts of the world, bestowed upon employees a share in the company's place in history.

The list of firsts broached various frontiers: Pan American's firsts extended into the social realm by opening markets and air mobility to the middle classes. Trippe proclaimed his goals to democratize air travel upon the christening of *Jet Clipper America* on 16 October 1958: "The new jet aircraft is going to move people, mail and cargo—more of them, more swiftly, more safely, more economically, than any plane ever built anywhere in the world before. This is a development true to our most essential purpose and policy: to serve not an elite of the fortunate—but all the people—as fully and efficiently as all our skill and striving can make possible" (Trippe 1958). In this speech and others Trippe invoked frontier idioms in emphasizing the airline's pioneering efforts in both technological and social engineering.

Reconfiguring the public face of his airline from an elite carrier to one ferrying the masses became a neat feat of persuasion, echoing democratic and humanitarian ideals in line with the times. As set forth in Trippe's speech from 1955 quoted at the beginning of this chapter, mass tourism—enabled by programs such as the hiring of "Nisei" stewardesses—promoted nothing less than mass "friendship" and "understanding." That these humanitarian ideals coincided with corporate profit making was an assumption left unspoken.

ETHNOGRAPHY OF AN AIRLINE: THE ETHOS AND
PRACTICES OF THE "PAN AM WAY"

In the twenty-first century talk of branding—a configuration of distinctive traits that sets one product apart from another—has become a commonplace fixture of our consumer lives. But even in an age of branding the degree to which former Pan Am employees I spoke with claim the distinctiveness of the company's identity is notable. I refer to the ethos and practices of the company as the "Pan Am way," taking my cue from the many references made by marketing, but more important, by former employees. Juan Trippe's quote at the beginning of this chapter encapsulates the Pan Am way by its brash performativity, placing itself at the center of the world that it would create through the Jet Age. The frontier sense of the Pan Am way marked vision, innovation, empire, and most of all, prestige.

The prestige system in which Pan Am operated derived from its unique position as the premier international carrier of the United States. Even after other American carriers began to fly internationally, Pan Am had set the pace and standard, so that it still retained a distinct position. That position began with the legitimacy of the airline as the United States government's mail carrier and extended to the commercial realm. In flying exclusively overseas, the airline's image rested at the forefront of the engineering needed to travel long distances.

As an overseas carrier, Pan Am had to compete on a larger international stage. It emphasized the cosmopolitanism of its service, offering what it advertised as the best of the best. In its heyday the company boasted that it served the food of Maxim's of Paris to its first-class passengers. Indeed, within the nascent international tourism trade, Americans looked to Pan Am as the expert on foreign countries, because the company traveled regularly there. One "Nisei" stewardess from the 1960s (PAA 1966–86) explains: "Because Pan Am had all the routes, I think they commanded a lot of respect. No one else could touch their route structure. And I think there was a little mystique about Pan Am at that time. Pan Am had a lot more savvy internationally. They were more sensitive to the different cultures, because they had been in different cultures and worked with these people for years." With the most extensive network of any airline in the world, Pan Am could become the expert of the world to the world, publishing its own travel guides and educating the novice traveler.[3]

Through long-distance travel Pan Am's employees themselves earned bragging rights to cosmopolitanism. This cosmopolitanism worked in two ways: they knew the world, and perhaps even more significantly, the world knew them. A slogan from a company jingle sums up the Pan Am brand of ownership: "You call it the world, we call it home." The rights to call "the world" "home" gives particular significance to the countless photographs of Pan Am stewardesses in far-flung locations in several countries. If one is to believe the company jingle, they were not traveling the world; they were merely inhabiting their "home." According to the women I interviewed, everywhere they went they were recognized and generally admired as Pan Am stewardesses. The mystique of Pan Am extended easily from routes to stewardesses in uniform. But even out of uniform, a group of American women of approximately the same age, sharing a particular kind of grooming and physical attributes, staying at Intercontinental hotels, dining at particular restaurants, and shopping at particular stores were often assumed to be Pan Am stewardesses. This includes "Nisei" stewardesses alongside their white co-workers.

The Pan Am stewardess—like other stewardesses—often acted as the public representative of the company and sometimes the nation. In effect the airline well understood that it put its best public relations foot forward through the figure of the female flight attendant. A photograph from 1947 depicts a white Pan Am stewardess in uniform being presented with a gift basket by a Filipino man, while other white men look on. The caption reads: "From the *Manila Times*, February 27, 1947: 'First US Flight Stewardess Due to Arrive Today. . . . vivacious Yvonne Olivier, the first stewardess to travel on a Pan American Clipper from the United States to the Philippines.' After being greeted by the press, Philippine General Romulo presented her a beautiful basket of native fruit at the 'swank' Manila Hotel. Then she was shown the sights of the city and given an official welcome at Malacanan Palace, official residence of the President of the Philippines. In the evening she danced the night away at a special reception" (*World Wings International 2007 Calendar* 2006). This Pan Am stewardess and others acted in their capacity as informal diplomats for the United States. For the airline, attracting favorable media attention was always the point, and stewardesses in uniform drew cameras by offering a photo-op that few could resist. In no small way the Pan Am stewardess provided a corporate and national spectacle, particularly in third world countries.

Part of the spectacle lay in the uniform, invoking military prestige and American corporate power. Part of the spectacle lay in the woman's body, invoking the cosmopolitan female whose personal knowledge of the world surpassed that of most people she met. Hers was a body with the transgressive potential of one who traveled the world, symbolically contained in a Pan Am uniform of professionalism.[4] She was the girl next door with a difference: her global travels transformed her into a worldly sophisticate.

Besides the ethos of the company, derived from its long-distance, international carrier status, another interconnected part of the Pan Am way was luxury and prestige. In spite of its pioneering economy-class fares, the prestige of the airline rested in the way it promoted itself as an exclusive club. A "Nisei" stewardess who flew in the 1960s and 1970s recalls: "It was like a country club mystique with the Pan Am execs. They were very good at spending money. I mean, they catered to people. I remember this Mr. X; he used to go L.A. to London regularly. He had his own tin of caviar. His personal tin. He was an alcoholic, and they would let him bring his own label of white wine to drink. On the way back from London, they would mix him his own little concoction and bring it on in these Johnny Walker Black Label bottles. And he always sat in the same seat with his own tin of caviar. I thought it was just mind-boggling." Pan Am's "country club mystique" lay in members understanding country-club ways—knowing how to extend personalized, first-name-basis, elite service, especially to regular first-class customers. What was critical was the notion that Pan Am understood upper-class ways, because it was part of them. The company not only served caviar but knew the taste of it as well as its passengers did. This is the elitist legacy of Juan Trippe and his cohorts. As one passenger from the period succinctly recalls, "No one did it as well as Pan Am did" (Miller, card).

The service that Pan American offered was designed to be suitably upper class: respectful and even formal, rather than familiar. Thus Pan Am's girl next door stood slightly apart (and above) others. One flight attendant who flew with Pan Am in 1966 and subsequently for United Airlines from 1986 on contrasts the two airlines: "United's [Air Lines] thing is 'Friendly Skies.' Well Pan Am was totally different. It was very formal, very respectful. You didn't get down and dirty with the passengers. I mean, you really didn't. It was very formal. The way we were expected to act on the airplane was more like you were a hostess. Not the kind that would get touchy-feely stuff. That was never part of the job. We really couldn't do that. It was more formal." According to this stewardess, the formality of Pan Am service was more easily managed than the friendliness of United Airlines in terms of emotional labor. She continues, recalling Hochschild's work on the stresses laid upon those whose job depends upon emotion management (1983): "I hate that 'Friendly Skies' thing. I want to shoot the person [who made it up]— it's very hard to live up to that, you know. I mean not everyday you want to be friendly. But that was a difference in the mind set, because United was basically a domestic carrier. Americans are more friendly and outgoing. You can't do that when you have all multicultural people, because a lot of Middle Easterners, Asians, they're very formal. And you do not approach them in an informal way. And that was very important at Pan Am, being able to distinguish how you would be able to react" (PAA 1966–86). Thus the respectful formality of Pan Am service was a matter of multicultural management as well as social class. The "Nisei" stewardess contributed to this by her own addition to a multicultural cabin crew.

If part of Pan Am's ethos rested in multiculturalism, it was due to a sense of empire, and nothing epitomized that empire better than its signature buildings. In 1963 Pan Am opened the largest commercial office building constructed at that time, on prime real estate on Park Avenue in New York.[5] With the words "PAN AM" emblazoned at the top of the building and a heliport on the building's sixtieth floor, the Pan Am building quickly became an icon of the cityscape. In typical Pan Am style, it was bigger (seventh-tallest in the world), bolder, and more commanding than any other building around. Trippe wanted the words "PAN AM" at the top of the building to be as large as possible and illuminated as a bright, recognizable beacon.[6] At the grand opening Trippe proclaimed: "The building we dedicate today . . . will be a monument to our civilization and to our free-enterprise system. Its size is impressive. It is the largest office building in the world" (Trippe 1963). Size here mattered as part of the immodest claims befitting the man and his sense of empire.

Tall skyscrapers were not the only edifices to promote the company. Women's bodies played their part as well. Displaying women's bodies decoratively and sometimes provocatively may not have been unusual for the 1950s and 1960s, and stewardesses' duties included promotional work and advertising. Photographs of women gratuitously filled employee newsletters: of stewardesses at a promotional event, of a movie star aboard a Pan Am flight, of a fashion show held in the air, or of Miss Universe and Miss U.S.A. being used in a promotional flight ("Miss Universe and Miss U.S.A. to Serve as Co-hostesses" 1977). Clearly women's bodies—like airplanes and skyscrapers—contributed to what we would now call Pan Am's visual "branding." In the postwar era this branding included the novelty of the "Nisei" stewardess.

The Pan Am way also included educational and humanitarian activities, especially during the 1940s through the 1960s. In this Pan Am was not unique. Reconfiguring capitalist intentions as public service makes good business sense and is thus a corporate strategy shared broadly. What is important for our story is how Pan Am's practices of "doing good" meshed with larger national visions and goals, thus configuring the airline as a public servant to the general American public (or even to the "world").

Education was one vector of civic activities. Pan Am, along with other airlines, used educational publications distributed to schools to promote "airmindedness."[7] What made Pan Am's publications distinctive, however, was that the "airmindedness" it promoted had a larger scope, encouraging international travel. Newsletters such as *Pan American World Airways Teacher*, published four to six times a year in the 1940s and 1950s, and *Classroom Clipper*, published monthly in the 1960s, provided teachers and students with geography lessons, aviation news, and company promotionals.[8] Here is the introduction to one issue from 1951: "Student and teacher exchanges are regarded by the Government as a major factor in the 'Campaign of Truth' through which the peoples of other lands are learning more about the American way of life. From this point of view, plans for educational travel during the 1951 vacation season are more significant than ever before" ("Educational Air Travel" 1951, 1).[9] In the Eisenhower era of people-to-people programs, foreign travel made ambassadors of ordinary citizens. Thus flying Pan Am—the premier international carrier—became more than a pleasurable activity: it was also an educational and patriotic one. Pan Am's adoption of public responsibility in supporting education in the United States contributed to its image as a civic institution rather than as a capitalist corporation. Pan Am may not have been alone in this, but the platform of its efforts was larger than most, shuttling students between countries, promoting civilian air travel, realizing Willkie's "one-world" dream.

The company's humanitarian efforts—albeit many with political ties—contributed to the airline's public image as well. In January 1980 the company compiled a document entitled "Chronology: Pan Am's Assistance during Times of Crisis," listing twenty-three events from 1929 to 1979 ("Chronology" 1980). The "times of crisis" included hurricanes, earthquakes, volcanic eruptions, floods, conflagration, war, and revolution in Latin and South America, Europe, Middle East, Asia, the Pacific, and Africa, as well as the "rescue" of the disfigured "Hiroshima maidens" in 1955. Whether supplying food and medicine or airlifting orphans, Pan Am worked closely with the United States government in efforts that blended political positioning with humanitarianism.

All these efforts worked. In 1960 Trippe won the International Achievement Award for World Peace, a humanitarian award given by the Chicago Association of Commerce and Industry. Pan Am's educational and humanitarian activities—worthwhile and laudable in their own right—became supreme public relations opportunities. Company newsletters highlighted these humanitarian efforts, in effect performing the company's civic worthiness before an audience of its own employees, thereby fostering corporate identification and pride. Pan Am's "good deeds" became the "good deeds" of its employees and vice versa.

Besides education and worldwide humanitarian efforts, Pan Am made it a point to be a good citizen of local and international communities. It sponsored sporting events, such as the FIFA World Cup in 1970, the Olympic Games (until 1988), and the International Special Olympics in the 1980s. In Japan, Pan Am was a major sponsor of sumo wrestling from 1961 to 1991, even after its exit from the Pacific market in 1986. The company's regional director presented the enormous Pan American Trophy to the top wrestler of each major tournament. In Miami, Pan Am annually contributed a float to the Orange Bowl Parade, often parading waving stewardesses. Pan Am played a part in beauty contests as well. From its beginnings in 1952 the Miss Universe contest in Long Beach, California, found co-sponsorship in Pan Am,[10] which flew contestants aboard its "Miss Universe Special Clipper." A photo from the inaugural event shows the beauty contest stage decorated with a huge backdrop of a Pan Am Stratoclipper ("The Most Beautiful Girls in the World" 1952, 7). In Honolulu, Pan Am was a major sponsor of the Japanese American beauty contest known as the Cherry Blossom Festival Queen Pageant, and from the second year of the contest's existence in 1954, Pan Am donated the queen's crown, thereafter known as the "PAA Crown" (Yano 2006b, 66).[11]

James Frank, longtime Pan Am employee, comments on Pan Am's community service efforts. I quote his interview at length because of his careful explanation of Pan Am's corporate and individual approaches to humanitarian endeavors: "Our main and continuing objective is to produce revenue. . . . Possibly there might not be a positive return [in profits from Pan Am's charitable ventures] in the short run, . . . However, such an effort is seen as a marketing program, a strategy, so to speak. The idea is to create a ripple effect, to provide a public service which will create goodwill and repeat passengers in the future. . . . There *is* another factor, however, which underlies everything that Pan Am has ever done, and which is a major motivating force in policy and direction. Pan Am cares! . . . Of course everybody says that they 'care about people.' But with Pan Am it is just plain true. From the top down, and from the bottom up, Pan Am cares" (Reida 1983, 2–3). Beginning with the "ripple effect" of goodwill that community service imparts, Frank explains these as indirectly linked to profits. However, soon enough he intones the catchphrase of the company, "Pan Am cares!," to suggest that this was part of company policy. Frank's talk turns from policy to legacy as he explains the history of Pan Am's "caring":

> In the 20's and 30's Pan Am was first into so many places, and this meant that there was of necessity a warm and personal type of relationship that developed with the new cities and peoples to whom we offered services. Also, we were pioneers of a sort, and had the camaraderie of pioneers. After establishing services to new areas, Pan Am often remained for long periods the only air service, and we developed a feeling of responsibility for it. The leadership of the airline felt this responsibility, and communicated it downward. . . . My point is that Pan Am personnel are unique in that they know that the carrier has the history that it does, they have unusual opportunities to involve themselves in special care situations because of our far-flung route system, and possibly most important, because they know that management expects them to offer a special service when it is possible. . . . Although it is not quantifiable, it is simple. Pan Am cares! (Reida 1983, 4, 7)

According to Frank, the "Pan Am spirit" begins historically with far-flung routes—echoing Trippe's frontier—and the paternalism of being the primary or sole carrier along these routes. (This kind of relationship is echoed by stories told to me of Pan Am in the Pacific, Africa, and parts of Asia, where Pan Am generated an American-based cargo-cult worship as the only airline connecting the populace to other parts of the world.) Embedding itself into local communities through schools, sports, and beauty pageants served the airline well. Pan Am became the American corporate fixture that linked whole communities, nations, and regions to networks of modernity and prestige. It mattered less that the airline stood to profit by that link; what concerned many people was their own membership in the network.

This is not to say that the airline—and its head, Juan Trippe—did not face criticism globally. Trippe's ruthlessly monopolistic business practices came under careful scrutiny, in particular from the same government who had utilized his networks earlier to build military bases and an operating fleet during the Second World War. What began as a close, symbiotic relationship between Pan Am and the government fell apart as Trippe applied pressure after the war to designate his airline as the "chosen instrument"— that is, the sole American international carrier. Trippe's appetite for empire knew no bounds. The denial of his request and the opening of international routes to Trans World Airways (TWA), American Export, Northwest Orient Airline, and Braniff in 1946 proved a slap in the face to Trippe and Pan Am. The role that Pan Am played in education and humanitarian and community service must be understood against the backdrop of such controversy. In these postwar years Pan Am undoubtedly reigned supreme. But it did so with its competitors—both American and foreign, such as Japan Air Lines—breathing down its neck. Thus the portrait of postwar Pan Am is as complex as that of Trippe himself—enigmatic, ruthless, arrogant, grandiose, visionary. The largesse of public service for the man and the airline came with a sharpened point, always tinged with the hunger for empire and profits.

SHAPING THE JET AGE: COMMODITY SCIENTISM,
JETSETTERS, AND THE PAN AM BAG

That sense of empire found no better expression than in Pan Am's record-breaking order of jets in 1955. Enthusiasm for the Jet Age peopled by "jet-setters" captivated the Euro-American public as the epitome of modernity awash in techno-utopian fantasies. These fantasies were shared unevenly, depending on social class, region, urban or rural status, proximity to centers of power, race, and ethnicity. Even within one social class the genders participated differently: women continued to perform window dressing for the age, while men could dream of piloting the new aircraft. The shrinking of the globe by jet travel meant that foreign (or foreign-looking) women could embody exoticized, Jet Age glamour. The "Nisei" stewardesses were part of this. Pan Am was not the only airline that flew jets or hired foreign and foreign-looking women. But it was the airline whose name and prestige rang as a symbol of the aircraft and the lifestyle associated with it.

The public did not accept jet travel or the Jet Age without a degree of skepticism. At its most basic level the public still needed to be persuaded to fly. Jets represented the latest technological wizardry involved in what Robert Smith has called "commodity scientism"—the commodification of science and technology: "When science itself is commodified, the products of a market-aimed technology are mistaken for the scientific process, and those products, like science, become invested with the inexorable, magical qualities of an unseen social force" (Smith 1983, 179). This recontextualiza-tion of technology is exactly the message of Trippe's speech quoted at the beginning of the chapter, inflating the importance of jets, assigning to them a humanistic importance in their ability to transform the world.

Pan Am issued pamphlets on the new Jet Age to travel agents and pas-sengers, heralding the company's technological and social accomplish-ment. One of these, "Jet Clippers Are Here; One of America's Proudest Moments; A Bright New Day for You," boasts of corporate achievement and exudes unabashed patriotic pride in its promise of a techno-utopic Jet Age: "Come with us to meet a new miracle. . . . A great and powerful sky giant— a new kind of air transport that can make all your most wonderful worldly dreams, and many you never thought of, all come true. It's the magnificent new Pan American Jet Clipper—the Boeing 707" ("Jet Clippers Are Here" 1958, 2, 4).

The pamphlet announces the new frontier of jet travel as a source of patriotic excitement. As it describes the physical sensation of riding a jet, it purrs with sensualized astonishment that any machine could be both that quiet and that powerful. "In the air, you hear a low hum—or perhaps you'd describe it as a pleasant whoosh. . . . Also contributing to this delightful feeling of hush, is the amazing lack of vibration. The drink on your table, a coin on edge, a standing pencil—choose your own test of steadiness, and be amazed. . . . Result—the most restful and relaxing air trip you've ever known" (ibid., 4). According to the pamphlet, jets will change the bodily ex-perience of travel and even change people's ideas: "Jet Clippers mean a *new concept* of the world you live in" (ibid., 2; emphasis in original). That new concept meant a spatial and temporal reorientation of a shrunken world traversed in a fraction of the time previously taken.

Pan American's consumer scientism rested partly on its claim to Jet-Age utopianism. Pan Am referred to itself as an "aerial ambassador of American industry," with Trippe espousing "the firm belief that his airline was bringing a benevolent form of capitalism to less-fortunate nations" (Gordon 2004, 39). Trippe expressed this utopianism repeatedly: "In this Jet Age, we Americans have available a new "magic carpet" to make new friends abroad and new business partners as well. Yes, if we elect to . . . we Americans can . . . assure ourselves the best chance for world peace. (Trippe 1960). In Trippe's vision jets were indeed "magic" as a vital part of his— and America's—frontier. Jets would provide the miracle elixir to pave the way toward world peace, winning the Cold War battle, connecting people in face-to-face diplomacy, and spreading economic prosperity, American style.

The Jet Age connected some ports more than others. Those frequented by the new media darlings, the "jetsetters"—wealthy cosmopolitans and celebrities—seemed like one small neighborhood of nightclubs in Paris, Rome, London, and New York. Jetsetters, whose main claim to fame was not talent but money, and the paparazzi who trailed them,[12] predated the more recent millennial extreme cult of celebrity. But even then, during this nascent period of media frenzy, these trendsetters were made, not born. An essential component of the lifestyle was the jet that took the jetsetters where they wanted to go, and among these Pan Am was iconic.

Pan Am, transporter of celebrities in the 1960s and 1970s, shared the paparazzi limelight with them. Media coverage of the Beatles' arrival in the United States in 1964 showed them disembarking from a Pan Am airplane. A nostalgia-filled Pan Am calendar of 2002 compiled photos of celebrities aboard Pan Am flights: Joe DiMaggio and Marilyn Monroe, Cary Grant, John Travolta, Lionel Richie, Marlon Brando, Robert Redford, Sean Connery, James Garner, Anthony Quinn, Chubby Checker, Chuck Berry, and Rudolph Nureyev (*World Wings International 2002 Calendar* 2001). The airline's name became synonymous with a fast-paced, glamorous lifestyle, glorified in media representations. Boeing 707 jets were featured in the James Bond films *Dr. No* (1962), *From Russia With Love* (1963), *Live and Let Die* (1973), and *Licence to Kill* (1989). Bond, the fictional secret service agent known for his gadgetry and beautiful women, including Asians, could do no better than to fly the jet-set, glamour airline, Pan American.[13] Stanley Kubrick's film *2001: A Space Odyssey* (1968) featured a fictional Pan Am spacecraft, the Orion III, complete with space-age stewardess in gravity boots. Years later the film *Catch Me If You Can* (2002) told the tale of the notorious Frank Abagnale, who had falsely posed as a Pan Am pilot in the 1960s.[14] And even more recently, Steven Spielberg's last installment of the Indiana Jones series (*Indiana Jones and the Kingdom of the Crystal Skull,* 2008) had a Pan Am plane flying the hero to Peru.[15]

The Pan Am in-flight bag—a familiar carry-on item, typically given away by travel agents and sales representatives—became a popular, fetishized symbol of the airline and the era. Its blue-grey color, globe logo, and serif lettering proved instantly recognizable to a generation of travelers and would-be travelers,[16] becoming even more a symbol of the airline world-wide than the company's tall, showy skyscrapers. If imitation was a form of flattery, then the mark of an airline's prestige may have rested in its bag's counterfeit production. According to an article in the *Clipper* in 1958, the Pan Am flight bag was already subject to such "flattery": "In Tokyo—as else-where around the world—the Pan Am flight bag is a badge of prestige and the respected symbol of the international traveler. In fact, these bags are held in such high esteem that they are counterfeited and sold on the black market. On the back streets of Tokyo counterfeit Pan Am bags are grabbed up at two dollars each and considered rare prizes at that price" ("Pan Am Flight Bag Honored by Orient Counterfeiters" 1958, 4). Owning a Pan Am flight bag meant that you had traveled internationally. Unfortunately, it also meant that your international travel might well have taken place in a large group tour, which was popular at the time with middle-class trav-elers. Passengers on these Pan Am tours each received an in-flight bag as a way of identifying them as part of the group. The ubiquity of the bag, as well as its link with group tours, made it an easy target for parody. Known in some circles as the bag of choice for "squares" (the forerunner of today's "nerds"), the bag overstayed its welcome of "cool." No true jetsetter—elite, individual, trendsetting—would be caught dead with it.

But one true jetsetter did. The famous jazz pianist Dave Brubeck dis-played no fewer than five Pan Am in-flight bags for the cover of his record-ing *Jazz Impressions of Eurasia* (1958, Columbia Jazz Masterpieces CK48531). The cover photo shows Brubeck standing before a Pan Am airplane, en-gulfed in Pan Am bags, wearing a turban, and laughing, assisted by two nonwhite women, one in a sari and the other holding a Middle Eastern "genie" lamp. In the liner notes he explains the background of the record-ing: "In early February 1958, the Quartet and I boarded a Pan American

Clipper for London. Our tour, which began in England, took us through the countries of Northern Europe, behind the Iron Curtain into Poland, through the Middle East (Turkey, Iran and Iraq) and on into India, Pakistan, Afghanistan and Ceylon. When we returned to New York in the middle of May, we had traveled thousands of miles, had performed over eighty concerts in fourteen different countries, and had collected a traveler's treasure of curios (see cover) and impressions (hear record) of Europe and Asia." Brubeck's tour was sponsored by the U.S. State Department. He was a jet-setter whose airline was undoubtedly, unequivocally Pan Am.

Pan Am's shaping of the Jet Age dovetailed neatly with its embrace of the next newest technological wizardry, the Space Age. President John Kennedy was a champion of the space program, which he included as part of his "New Frontier" program, contributing to a cultural revival of frontier discourse in the 1960s. Pan Am had a hand in this new frontier, especially since 1953, when the Pan American Airways' Guided Missiles Range Division contracted with the U.S. Air Force to operate and maintain the missile test range that included the launching site at Cape Canaveral. Pan Am's involvement with space technology and the implementation of space launches helped the company to situate itself at the forefront of national advancement, whether in jets or in rockets.

Thus when word leaked out that Pan Am might be taking reservations on a waiting list for flights to the Moon, especially after the successful Apollo 8 mission in December 1968 and the lunar landing of Apollo 11 in July 1969, thousands of would-be space travelers deluged the company with requests.[17] In response Pan Am created a "First Moon Flights" club, issuing official-looking certificates with people's names, a number (corresponding to each person's placement on a waiting list), and the signature of the company's vice-president of Sales, James Montgomery. Applicants on the waiting list received the following letter from Montgomery, which is only partly tongue in cheek, especially in its invocation of frontier rhetoric:

Dear Moon First Flighter

Thank you for your confidence that Pan Am will pioneer commercial Space travel, as it so often has here on earth. We have every intention of living up to this confidence.

The enclosed card confirms this intent, and formally recognizes your intrepid spirit. . . . Starting date of service is not yet known. . . . We ask you to be patient while these essentials are worked out. . . . Again, thank you for coming to Pan Am first. That's exactly what we intend to be. On Earth. To the Moon. Any place else. (Montgomery n.d.)

By the time the company closed the list on 3 March 1971, it had received more than 93,000 requests from people in all fifty states, as well as from citizens in over ninety other countries, including Ghana, Nicaragua, Iceland, New Zealand, Pakistan, and Ecuador (ibid.). It was only a natural progression from the Jet Age to the Space Age, and Pan Am made headlines by accompanying this progression, spotlighting its place in the new extraterrestrial frontier.

"NISEI" STEWARDESSES WITHIN PAN AM'S SOCIAL FRONTIER

The terrestrial frontier, however, was Pan Am's everyday fare, and its claim to social engineering was no less important than its technological feats. Both helped the airline lay its stakes upon empire. A promotional video from the 1970s, *Pan Am Story*, spells out the company's claim: "The goal has always been to take people where they want to go, comfortably and safely, at fares people can afford to pay, with schedules that make it possible for the average person with a two-week vacation to go anywhere in the world."

Clearly Pan Am's target—at least according to this video—was the average working person with a two-week vacation and a new, greatly expanded market of possibilities. What goes unmentioned is the structuring of people's desires—"where they want to go," "anywhere in the world"—fixed by government and business. Corporate and governmental infrastructures created air routes that determined where people could easily go; the public relations arm of the airlines worked hard to convince people that they should take airplanes to get there. The video continues: "Through the years as Pan Am led the way to the Caribbean, and into Central and South America, across the Pacific to Asia and Australia, over the Atlantic to Europe and Africa, around the world, and finally into the Jet Age, it was doing more than opening up hundreds of new routes. It was opening millions of minds to the idea of going places far from home. This year Pan Am will carry over eight million passengers to ninety-two cities on six continents, making what was once restricted to the wealthy people available to everyone. That is what the Pan Am story is really all about." The promotional video spins altruistic impulses out of profitability. According to the triumphal narrative, Pan Am's goal was not profit but humanitarian ideals, more akin to the values expressed in the *Family of Man* exhibit than to the hamburgers of McDonald's. Here lies the social frontier of postwar air travel, defined and traversed by Pan Am as the dominant airline of the United States and the world.

The pioneer of this frontier was none other than Juan Trippe. One of the classic images of Trippe pictures him in his office with a large-scale globe. Legend has it that between 1929 and 1942 Trippe would experiment with new routes by placing pins on the globe and connecting them with string. In plotting the frontier, Trippe's appetite for airborne dreams seemed limitless. In 1961 Pan Am's routes spanned more than 72,000 miles and extended to eighty countries in all continents. The empire went beyond routes and service to include hotels: Trippe purchased the Intercontinental Hotel chain in 1962. With airplanes and hotels, Trippe's globe could encompass many of a traveler's needs and much of the traveler's experience. The *Pan Am's World* video continues: "Pan Am is . . . the airline to the world. It flies to more than 120 different places on six different continents. . . . And when you get there, Pan Am is there, with the . . . comfort of Intercontinental Hotels, and everywhere, helpful people if you need them. . . . It speaks your language, and all the other languages you may not speak. No matter where you're going, it's like going to the same place. . . . Welcome to Pan Am's world!" By linking transportation and lodging, the company could offer to the middle-class traveler, Pan Am guidebook in hand, a total package of safe, predictable "exotic" travel. The "airline to the world" was more accurately an airline to Trippe's globe—travel made marketable specifically through its domestication of difference. "Nisei" stewardesses presented a prime example of this corporate offering.

The domestication of difference may also be seen as a kind of spatial ambivalence: a scrambling of spatial categories, resulting in what David Morley calls "a progressive notion of home" (quoted in Von Moltke 2005, 216). The concept of home thus extends beyond "here" to "there," in a mobile, modern frame. Kristin Ross analyzes time similarly, arguing that the postwar discourse surrounding mobility is "built around freezing time in the form of reconciling past and future, the old ways and the new. . . . Past and future are one, *you can change without changing*" (1995, 21–22).

Pan Am manipulated these modernist spatial and temporal ambivalences to convince the traveling public that it could feel "at home" anywhere in the world—that is, in the "home away from home" of Pan Am's corporate making.

The question remains: Whose home was it? By attempting to capture markets of foreign as well as American travelers, Pan Am had to negotiate the uncharted waters of offering many versions of "home." The company did so by training its stewardesses in "cross-cultural sensitivity," in consultation with "natives" from various parts of the world. It also hired some of these "natives," including women such as "Nisei" stewardesses who looked authentically "native" (here, Japanese) enough to pass corporate muster. Just as important, the company negotiated these waters of "home" within the context of an international hegemony of Euro-American culture that served French cuisine unapologetically: more than just another kind of food, it was promoted as the best, most prestigious food in the world (cf. Schwartz 2007).[18]

Indeed, you could "journey without journeying," and thus "change without changing," through Pan Am's Intercontinental Hotels, as well as on board with American and foreign stewardesses who could collectively speak any number of languages. The postwar lure of foreign travel lay in enticements that had all the rewards of status and prestige but few discomforts of the unknown. This was part of the performance of the model-minority "Nisei" stewardess as the assimilated foreign (looking) hostess. By making the unknown knowable and even hospitable, Pan Am hoped to profit from the postwar, middle-class appetite for mobility. Pan Am's business goal was to transform foreign travel from an adventure into an exotic shopping opportunity. In effect Trippe's globe condensed distances into armchair travel made possible within idioms of familiarity: comfortable airplane cabins, attentive service from girl-next-door cosmopolitans, and well-appointed hotel rooms that assured the uneasy traveler that "no matter where you're going, it's like going to the same place." Pan Am's world represented nothing less than the *Family of Man* frontier, transformed into a marketable commodity that included the model-minority "Nisei" stewardess.

Pan Am's role in blazing a prestigious, historic frontier had particular impact for Japanese American stewardesses, who within recent decades had been marginalized as potential enemies and interned in concentration camps along the West Coast during the Second World War. The Japanese

American women who flew for Pan American may have been only children or teenagers during the war, but the lessons of the war were not entirely lost upon them. Flying with Pan Am—a symbol of America in global ports of call—contributed to their symbolic incorporation into the United States. Working for the airline thrust them from the margins of citizenship to the center stage of history. Thus Pan Am's construction of itself as a national symbol served corporate as well as personal interests. It is these personal interests—those of the "Nisei" stewardess and her community—to which I now turn.

Three

"NISEI" STEWARDESSES

Dreams of Pan American's Girl-Next-Door Frontier

I daydreamed all the time whenever I saw the planes taking off. I was intent upon traveling the world. I always dreamed, what would it be like on the other side of the horizon?
                                        "Nisei" stewardess, PAA 1966–86

All the girls wanted to fly with Pan Am, because it was such a prestigious job in those days.
                                        "Nisei" stewardess, PAA 1957–86

There were a lot of girls that used to say, "I don't speak the language, but I only look like I speak the language!"
                                        "Nisei" stewardess, PAA 1955–86

THE "NISEI" STEWARDESS, racialized as the ultimate "natural" hostess, boosted Pan American's claim to the world's stage framed in terms predictable for the era. Popular culture, consumerism, race relations, Cold War tactics, and "sentimental humanism" carved out a niche for her as the Asian woman aloft. Central to defining the stage of the Pan Am cabin was the issue of language: in hiring "Nisei" stewardesses and others, the company boasted a multilingual staff, even as it looked to race.[1] At the same time, the "Nisei" stewardesses who flew for Pan Am harbored their own dreams. Examining some of their dreams and how flying for Pan Am both shaped and fulfilled them demonstrates the aspirations of personal frontiers.

Although I take "Nisei" stewardesses as a group, there were differences among them. The first of these is historical: the conditions and experiences of the mid-1950s differ considerably from that of the late 1960s and early 1970s. I thus place each interviewee in the chapters that follow within her historical time frame, specifying her years of working for Pan Am (e.g. PAA 1963–86). Note that many of the women transferred to United Air Lines in 1986, when United took over Pan Am's Pacific routes. Second, the speakers of various languages—such as Japanese, Cantonese, and Mandarin—experienced Pan Am's program in culture-specific ways. My focus in this discussion, however, is on the Japanese-language speakers, since they form the core group, both at the program's inception and later. Third, among Japanese-speakers Japanese Americans and Japanese nationals differed in how they came to be employed by Pan Am, and in some of their experiences of employment. Although I focus on Japanese Americans, I include Japanese nationals where their experiences overlapped.

Most important, I turn here more closely to the women themselves. In her study of the autobiographical works of minority filmmakers, Kathleen McHugh discusses inverting the conventional relationship between autobiography (writing about the individual) and history (writing about the larger temporal context): "Rather than history being the overarching and tacit narrative in which autobiography takes place, autobiography serves as the overarching framework within which history is explicitly narrated, situated, and embodied" (2005, 158). Here I take the women's lives and voices as the overarching framework within which the larger history of airlines, industries, and nations may be "narrated, situated, and embodied."

ON HIRING JAPANESE-LANGUAGE SPEAKERS:
THE DOUBLE-SPEAK OF LANGUAGE AND RACE

In February 1955 an article in the Pan Am company newsletter announced the birth of the "Nisei" stewardess program:

> Clipper travel between Japan and the United States by passengers of Japanese origin has become such a sizeable part of the PAD's [Pacific-Alaska Division's] business that the Flight Service department will now hire stewardesses who speak both Japanese and English fluently. In effect, this requirement means that virtually all of the new group to be employed will be Japanese Nisei. At present it is planned that twenty girls will be hired.
>
> Only by having such girls as stewardesses can Pan American make the passen-

ger who speaks only Japanese feel at home in the gracious, uncomplicated way that is standard Clipper service. ("For Finer Service" 1955, 5)

Announcements went out in the Japanese and English newspapers in Honolulu on 11 February about Pan Am's new program. The articles listed the following requirements: (1) American citizenship; (2) the ability to speak, read, and write Japanese and English fluently; (3) a height between five feet three inches and five feet six inches; (4) age between twenty-one and twenty-seven; (5) proportionate weight to 130 pounds; (6) two years of college, nurse's training, or three years' work "contributing to poise and pleasant manner in dealing with the public"; (7) 20–30 vision or better; and (8) being single and not previously married ("Pan Am to Employ Six Isle Nisei Stewardesses" 1955).

Although Pan Am had first tried to recruit Japanese American women on the West Coast, according to a Pan Am administrator at the time, it found greater success in Hawai`i. One possible explanation for this is that those in the continental United States had experienced wartime internment, something that most Japanese Americans in Hawai`i—except for Japanese-language teachers, Buddhist priests, and others with explicit and potential ties to Japan—were spared. Given the experience of racially based imprisonment, Japanese Americans in California were more sensitized to racial issues and less likely to place themselves in such a publicly exposed position as that of a stewardess flying with a prestigious major airline. Even Japanese Americans in Hawai`i were not immune to racial prejudice, before, during, and after the war.[2] One "Nisei" stewardess from 1955 describes the prejudice in Hawai`i during the war: "We couldn't even sit in the bus shelter. They would say, 'Get out of here, you damn Japs!'" A member of Pan Am's management staff in Honolulu explains, "Some of the ["Nisei"] girls [in Hawai`i] were a little apprehensive, because the war hadn't ended that long ago in 1945, and there was still resentment in the air here [in Hawai`i], about the Japanese and such."

Nevertheless, within six weeks of the original announcement Pan Am hired its first "Nisei" stewardesses, whose photographs appeared in the 31 March issue of the *Clipper: Pacific-Alaska Division*, with the caption "Hawaii Girls Join First Nisei Stewardess Class." It thus fell to Japanese American women in Hawai`i, more than California, to take up this public position. The photograph pictures three Japanese men—all principals of

Japanese-language schools in Hawai`i—interviewing two "Nisei" women. (The irony of the photograph is that Pan Am enlisted the help of Japanese-language-school principals, the very category of persons from Hawai`i who were singled out for internment during the Second World War.)[3] Thus Pan American showed a sincere regard for the Japanese language as a requirement of its "Nisei" stewardesses. It even had professional Japanese-language teachers help with the screening of applicants for the job. However, there are a number of problems with this argument.

For one, in spite of Pan Am's stated concerns, from the mid-1950s to the early 1960s the number of Japanese passengers traveling internationally was relatively small. Except for businessmen, most Japanese could not yet afford international travel, nor were they allowed to undertake it. The Japanese government did not lift foreign travel restrictions for Japanese citizens until 1 April 1964. As one "Nisei" stewardess from 1955 recalls, "Those days there weren't that many Japanese passengers per se. So when we did the life jacket demonstrations, you had one or two [Japanese] and you'd just go up to them and go over it." Other stewardesses from that period agree: many hardly used their language skills except for in-flight announcements. Even in the 1960s, with the beginning of group tours from Japan, the numbers were low. In the words of one stewardess who began flying in 1966: "There were very few [Japanese passengers]. The only large numbers we would see would be from Tokyo to Guam, since Guam was already becoming a destination for the Japanese tourist. But on other flights that we had, you had maybe a handful at most." In addition to the few Japanese businessmen, there were also first-generation Japanese Americans (known as "Issei") who traveled to Japan. But these too did not travel in great numbers in the 1950s or 1960s.

Secondly, Pan Am found it difficult to recruit suitable Japanese American women who could speak Japanese fluently, and soon reduced its diligence in screening for language. Many "Nisei" stewardesses could speak Japanese—some fluently—but many did not. One of the stewardesses from 1955 explains, "We did speak Japanese [growing up] in the neighborhood, but during the war period, we all tried to keep it down and not speak that much Japanese" (PAA 1955–57). During the Second World War Japanese language and culture were suppressed in the United States. Thus Nisei growing up in the mid-1950s in Hawai`i faced a twofold impediment to Japanese-language acquisition: although Japanese may have been the language of the home, they lived in a highly charged political atmosphere that emphasized English; and they did not have full access to Japanese-language instruction because of the closing of language schools during the war. However, the question was far less benign and more complex than one of mere emphasis and access. There were three language options for second-generation Japanese Americans: Japanese (the language of the home), a local vernacular creole ("pidgin English," the informal language of friends and the general public), and standard English (the official language of the white establishment). With the establishment of race- and class-based "English standard schools" in Hawai'i since the 1920s, and active "Speak English" campaigns during the 1940s, language was an ongoing, contentious political issue (Yano 2006b, 42).[4] In particular during the Second World War, to speak English was to perform oneself as American.[5] Social class and gender mattered as well: in wartime women's forums run by and for Japanese Americans, speaking English was evidence of a middle-class, gendered ideal known as the "American standard of womanhood" (Kotani 1985, 98). Whereas many Japanese American males often retreated into a locally based masculinity "indexed by speaking the local vernacular . . . and not speaking standard English," more females aspired to American norms of standard English (Yano 2006b, 42). In other words, males speaking non-standard English could be interpreted simply as "one of the boys"; females speaking similarly often garnered racial and class critique. Thus for the airlines, seeking females who could speak Japanese was not a simple matter but one that ran against the grain of the decades of social and political history in Hawai'i. Furthermore, by the 1960s, even if attitudes and policies changed and Japanese language schools had reopened, the speaking of Japanese was further removed by one full generation. Although some third-generation women who were hired were fluent through the particular circumstances of their families,[6] others were not. Pan Am hired them anyway, and accommodated their linguistic deficiency with company tutors and classes.

According to one of the stewardesses I interviewed, when she was hired in 1960 the only Japanese-language screening she underwent was administered by someone who did not know Japanese: "I had to read something in Japanese. It was in *romaaji* [romanization], and it was basically the announcement that you had to make. [The interviewer] wanted to hear it, but he didn't know, because he was Caucasian. But I could read it phonetically, of course, and I was hired. . . . I think if you looked Japanese and you could speak a little, they were happy to have you." The combination—looking Japanese and (minimally) speaking a little—were the basic requirements of the racialized position. One woman who flew in the 1960s ruefully admits, "It was always a joke that most of us couldn't speak the language for which we were hired. After they hired me, they sent me to language school, which was helpful, because it focused on pronunciation. We had a Japanese radio announcer here who tutored the girls" (PAA 1963–69). The company hired for the racialized look first, and then brought the women up to an acceptable level of in-flight performance through company tutors, classes, and eventually a book of in-flight announcements in romanized Japanese.[7] The reverse order of the process demonstrated the company's priorities.

The third problem lies in issues of language—both verbal and nonverbal. Japanese language marks hierarchy in highly codified ways, especially through *keigo* (formal respect terms) consisting of separate words and phrases specific to hierarchical relationships. Nonverbal respect behavior is equally important, including details of bowing (timing, depth, initiating process), comportment, facial expression, ordering of movement, and physical placement in a room. Hierarchy encompasses gender as an assumption of social relations: simply put, women wait on men—pouring their tea, serving their food, anticipating their needs. The primary Japanese travelers flying abroad in the 1950s—businessmen engaged in international work—would thus expect the highest, most exacting level of respect behavior and language from servers. For the most part the Japanese American stewardesses were not familiar with either the verbal or nonverbal expectations of Japanese travelers. The only reason why this might have been acceptable to Japanese businessmen in the 1950s who flew Pan Am was that they knew they were flying on an international airline, not a Japanese one. Out of their home turf, their expectations may have been less demanding (although see chapter 5 for exceptions to this).

Lastly, the Japanese language that Japanese Americans did speak was not necessarily that which Pan Am wanted. Japanese immigrants to the United States came from rural areas, primarily from the southwest regions. Their dialects reflected not only those areas but the era of immigration, which was in the late nineteenth century and the early twentieth. On both counts— regional and temporal—what they spoke at home differed from the Tokyo dialect that subsequently became standard Japanese. One stewardess from

1964 recalls, "Our dialect was different. Absolutely different! But through the years, we learned to adjust and speak in their [Tokyo] dialect." To raise the issue of language is not to criticize the "Nisei" stewardesses so much as to comment upon the racialized nature of their employment. "Nisei" stewardesses offered Pan Am the look of a Japanese speaker—the Asian female—and language skills that some assumed could be gained with the assistance of company tutors.

Pan Am had long employed foreign women as stewardesses. Shortly after it began hiring women as stewardesses in 1944, Pan Am recruited women from European countries as foreign-language speakers. They brought their native tongue to cabin service (as well as an "exotic" accent to the English they spoke), but they also brought an element of glamour and cosmopolitanism to Pan Am's roster. The image of Pan Am that many held in the 1940s through 1970s was wrought in part by their image—that of tall, blonde northern Europeans. Hiring "Nisei" stewardesses as "Japanese" both racialized the women and demonstrated the common practice of using language as a smokescreen for race and ethnicity.

Processes of racialization were part of the job. One example occurred on round-the-world flights. Most members of the flight crew boarded as a group and worked only segments of the journey. The "Nisei" stewardess alone accompanied the airplane from start to finish. Rather than travel as part of a crew, she worked continuously in what became known as the "J-language," or Japanese-language, position. Many "Nisei" stewardesses comment on the loneliness of their work, as different crews boarded, worked a segment, and then disembarked together. The position subsequently became racialized as that of the "Oriental" or Asian flight attendant, rather than the Japanese- or Mandarin-speaking flight attendant. One Chinese stewardess comments ruefully: "They use you. . . . They try to have one Oriental flight attendant on the airplane. I think maybe that at that time the Asia market was just beginning to come about. And so Pan Am can say [to passengers], 'We have Oriental or Asian flight attendant on board.' It doesn't matter—Japanese, Chinese. As long as they have Oriental face" (PAA 1961–64, 1977–86). It is exactly that Oriental face that configured Pan Am's airborne dreams of the period.

As one "Nisei" stewardess recounts, "It was so impressive to get on a Pan Am plane and when they say language availability, sometimes there would be like someone who speaks Mandarin, someone who speaks German, French. You know, this was [Pan Am's] big thing—fly with us, we can speak your language" (PAA 1968–86). But was it only language that was being "spoken"? I argue that Pan Am's bragging rights went beyond language to personnel and imaging: it was the tall, blonde Swede on board, as much as the language(s) she spoke; likewise, it was the exotic Asian woman who shared that center stage with the Swede (and others) in the Jet Age. Even when it was a white American woman speaking a foreign language, her linguistic ability often indexed education, worldliness, and thus social class. Because Pan Am was an international carrier, its offering of foreign languages on board made perfect sense. Having foreign-language speakers as service personnel was a practical necessity. Foreign-language-speaking stewardesses created both a welcoming atmosphere for foreigners and an exoticized "international" atmosphere for Americans and other native speakers of English. This was emphasized by hiring foreign nationals and thus imparting international "authenticity" to the airline cabin.

Most important, the airline's language program was highly sexualized. The criterion of speaking a foreign language as a minimum hiring qualification only came about with the switch from male stewards to female stewardesses. Although Pan Am had previously hired Spanish-speaking stewards, the ability to speak a foreign language was not a minimum qualification for the men's job.[8] I interviewed one steward who flew from 1942 on with no foreign language skills, and he says that he was not alone among his fellow workers. However, by requiring a foreign language of its subsequent female hires, Pan Am was able to secure for its own front-stage deployment American women with some probable level of college education[9] and foreign women. Speaking a foreign language implied overseas origins, a higher level of education (and social class), or both. What resulted was a highly gendered image of cosmopolitanism in combination with social class that became part of the public face of the company. Foreign language provided the backdrop for displaying Pan Am's mastery of the racial and gendered frontier: parading the company's "global" women asserted and performed the airline's international reach. Indeed, Pan Am's "global" women contributed to the image expressed by one of the "Nisei" stewardesses: "Pan Am was like a flying United Nations" (PAA 1966–86). She refers to both passengers and flight crew; what she does not mention is the high-profile racial and gender politics of Pan Am's "United Nations" in the air.

The first group of "Nisei" stewardesses in 1955 attracted considerable media attention, with coverage in company newsletters and in newspapers from Hawai`i to California to Tokyo to those serving Japanese immigrant communities in South America. Photographs of the first seven — May Hayashi, Ruby Mizuno, Louise Otani, Katherine Shiroma, Masako Tagawa, Jane Toda, and Cynthia Tsujiuchi — showed them decked out in uniform in a row before a Pan Am aircraft, receiving their flight pins from the governor of Hawai`i. Except for Tagawa and Mizuno, all were from Hawai`i.

As one of the seven put it, "I think we were very proud to be pioneers." Another notes that the women were "trailblazers." Both Pan Am and the women they hired configured the "Nisei" stewardess program as a public frontier. One woman from the first group recalls their fame: "Being the very first group of Nisei stewardesses, we were celebrities, and were honored by the Territory of Hawai`i. Governor King winged us and there was a great reception at the Royal Hawaiian Hotel for us. And the newspapers, every one of them covered us. I believe the news also went to South America, worldwide, 'cause I received some letters from these young men there" (PAA 1955–57).

In Honolulu the two major English-language newspapers (*Honolulu Advertiser* and *Honolulu Star-Bulletin*) carried five articles on Pan Am's "Nisei" stewardesses in 1955; by comparison, one Japanese-published newspaper in Honolulu (*Hawaii Hochi*) carried ten articles over the same period. Clearly the local Japanese American community was paying close attention because of the newsworthiness of the event: women of Japanese ancestry were breaking into a field that had previously been a monopoly of Caucasians. Pan Am used the media attention to advertise its new service to first-generation Japanese Americans, many of whom spoke limited English. An advertisement that appeared often in Japanese-language newspapers in Honolulu throughout the mid-1950s depicts one "Nisei" stewardess, May Hayashi, smiling in uniform. It reads: "One can relax comfortably with Pan American's new Japanese-speaking Nikkei [of Japanese ancestry] stewardesses. They will provide kind and heartfelt service in Japanese. As soon as you are aboard a Pan Am flight, pretty Nikkei stewardesses will take good care of you. Throughout your flight, whenever you need it, they will be

The first group of "Nisei" stewardesses, 1955. From left: Katherine Shiroma, Ruby Mizuno, Cynthia Tsujiuchi, Masako Tagawa, May Hayashi, Jane Toda, Louise Otani.

happy to assist you and provide personable service in either Japanese or English" ("Hawaii Girls Join First Nisei Stewardess Class" 1955, 2).

Pan Am took advantage of every opportunity in appealing to the potential Japanese American traveler. The pioneering activities of the women were meant to generate business—and publicity—in Japan and the United States.

The women were not the only ones singled out as pioneers. A feature article in a Honolulu newspaper in June 1955 placed the spotlight on the airline itself: "Pan American's pioneering in [hiring "Nisei"] attracted widespread attention in Japanese-American circles on the West Coast of the United States as well as here. Not only was it considered a practical thing but a demonstration of democracy in action" ("Wings to Japan" 1955). The article's reference to "democracy in action" reflected the postwar spirit of Nisei war heroes and the rising political power of Japanese Americans in Hawai`i.

The spotlight did not shine only on the first seven. The second group of

Cynthia Tsujiuchi receiving her Pan Am pin and flower lei from
Governor Samuel Wilder King, 1955.

six, graduating three months later in 1955 (Eunice Kubota, Betty Okamoto,
Nancy Shimada, Takae Tanino, Grace Yamada, and Doreen Yamanaka), also
found their photographs in newspapers. The *Clipper: Pacific-Alaska Division*
announced, "With the graduation of this class there will be a Nisei stewardess on all flights between Tokyo and Honolulu" (Pan American World Airways 1955, 3). The publicity continued through the 1950s and 1960s, with
articles and photographs in Honolulu newspapers about the women. Once
Pan Am established its "Nisei" stewardess program, having a "Nisei" stewardess on board Asian and round-the-world flights became a positional requirement. One woman hired in 1955 remembers that although she was not
yet twenty-one and thus too young to fly because of in-flight alcohol service,
she was called on board suddenly for her first flight, from Wake Island to
Tokyo, because the scheduled "Nisei" had fallen ill:[10] "I came home and I
said, 'Oh my god!' I wasn't twenty-one, international flight, serving drinks.
You can't do that. But they couldn't hire the girls fast enough and train them
fast enough."

May Hayashi in a Pan Am advertisement, 1955.

"Nisei" stewardesses became a favorite of Pan Am photographers, singled out as a group for their novelty. Pan Am's district traffic and sales manager for Honolulu, Ernie Albrecht, notes that Pan Am added other Asian touches to its in-flight service to and from Japan, such as Japanese food for on-board meals and chrysanthemums used to decorate menus— in his words, "to go along with the girls." The "Nisei" stewardesses continued to make good visual press. The 1958 issue of the *Clipper: Pacific-Alaska Division* featured a photograph and story entitled "Nisei Stewardess Anniversary": "Pan American last month observed the third anniversary of the introduction of Nisei stewardess service. To celebrate the occasion the company gave a cocktail party in Honolulu, where the girls are based" ("Nisei Stewardess Anniversary" 1958). The twenty-six whom Pan Am listed in 1958 did not include those who had already come and gone, especially as many stewardesses during that period followed the model trajectory of quitting after approximately two years to be married.

The success of the "Nisei" stewardess program and the increase in Asian passengers prompted Pan Am to extend on-board Asian languages to include Chinese (Cantonese and later Mandarin). A 1959 issue of the *Clipper: Pacific-Alaska Division* announced that the company was seeking Cantonese-speaking stewardesses: "Advertisements have been placed in Chinese newspapers and metropolitan dailies seeking girls with that qualification. . . . The Flight Service department hopes to hire 24 girls. . . . Plans have been made to start a class for 12 Cantonese-speaking girls the first week of January [1960]. These girls will be based in Honolulu and will be scheduled on flights operating between the West Coast and Hong Kong" ("Division to Hire Chinese-Speaking Stewardesses" 1959, 15). Interestingly, the Chinese-speaking stewardesses did not receive the kind of publicity—either in Pan Am newsletters or in general media—that the Japanese-language stewardesses did. For one, they were far fewer in number. Second, the racial frontier had already been broached in 1955. The new stewardesses merely joined the "Nisei" stewardesses as part of Honolulu's Asian-language base and were even lumped together as part of the "Nisei" stewardess program, which by then had become shorthand for Pan Am's "Asian" women. Third, Chinese-speaking countries did not then have the kinds of close ties with the United States that Japan did and thus did not garner the same level of media attention.

By the 1960s Asia and Asian women played an increasingly prominent role in Pan Am's plans. Travel to and from Asia increased (although see chapter 1 for its limits), often with new destinations. At the same time Pan Am was finding it more difficult to fill its Asian-language positions. The headline of an article in a Honolulu newspaper in February 1963 reads: "Isle Girls Who Speak Japanese or Chinese Scarce, P.A.A. [Pan American Airways] Finds" (Waters 1963, 7). To overcome the difficulty Pan Am set up a language laboratory in Honolulu where stewardesses could record their in-flight announcements for grading in Tokyo or Hong Kong; if the level of speaking was unacceptable, the women would have to study at the language laboratory (ibid.). In 1964 Pan Am recruited more "Nisei" stewardesses for its San Francisco base, to serve increased traffic between Japan and Latin America ("Japanese Girls Join Ranks of Stewardesses for Pan Am" 1964). The group of four "Nisei"—Hazel Hagio, Jean Miyamasu, Frances Moriwaki, and Tule Murakami—was the first to train in Miami specifically for the Latin American Division. They catered primarily to Japanese businessmen traveling back and forth to São Paulo, where a sizable population of Japanese immigrants and their descendants lived, and where Japanese industrial giants such as Mitsubishi and Panasonic had gained a foothold. In 1965 Pan Am introduced more Asian hires: "Six Malaysian girls recently graduated from Pan Am's stewardess school in Miami, the first of 75 girls from the Malay Peninsula being recruited to cater to the whims of our passengers on Pacific air routes" ("Six Beauties from Malaysia Flying Pacific for Pan Am" 1965). And in 1966 Pan Am's in-house newsletter the *Clipper* announced the first stewardesses hired directly from Japan with the headline: "First of New Japanese Stewardesses Graduate" ("First of New Japanese Stewardesses Graduate" 1966).

The photographs accompanying these articles depicted a before-and-after transformation that became a visual trope of the airline's representation of "exotic" women: a before photograph shows the women standing in a row in indigenous costume; an after photograph shows them emerging from Pan Am training center, smiling in crisp blue-grey uniforms. The transformation was a testament to the power of Pan Am and the malleability of Asian women, newly trained to serve "the whims of our passengers."

The year 1966 marks what the Japanese commercial aviation industry defined as a crisis. Citing "fierce competition now being witnessed by airlines operating international lines [in Japan]," an article in *Air News Japan*

First of New Japanese Stewardesses Graduate

MIAMI, FLORIDA—East is meeting West—and a lot of other parts of the world—here these days.

The East is represented by seven diminutive, soft-spoken Tokyo girls who are the vanguard of the first group of Japanese to be trained as stewardesses by Pan American for its worldwide routes.

They are being especially recruited for services mainly on the U.S. airline's growingly-popular transpacific flights. However, since all the girls speak English as well as Japanese, they will be equally adept at making Clipper passengers feel at home on flights in other parts of the world where there are sizeable Japanese colonies, such as Brazil.

Some Japanese-speaking stewardesses, chiefly girls from Hawaii or Stateside girls of Japanese parentage, have been serving aboard Clippers. These are the first from Japan.

From their arrival—attired in brilliantly elegant ceremonial silk kimonas, befitting the special occasion—the Tokyo girls were the center of attention. However, they quickly settled down to the busy routine at Pan Am's international stewardess training school.

Room With Americans

During their off-duty hours, the Japanese girls share four-girl suites with American stewardess trainees, generally with two Japanese girls sharing with two American girls. In classes, however, the Japanese girls will be meeting and rubbing elbows with many of the young women of 40 different nationalities who today make up Pan Am's air hostess group.

Although they are 9,000 miles and a world away from home, the Tokyo trainees find themselves beset by the same doubts and worries that affect most of the 1,200 students who are selected for the international stewardess college each year. They are paid regular salaries while in training, but almost all fret over whether the budget they brought from hom will last until the first paycheck arrives.

For a quick and nourishing repast, and one easy on the budget, they have discovered, you can't beat hamburgers and ice cream. They dine at the company cafeteria, the coffee shop or dining room of their hotel. Rice is no problem, because American Southerners love rice, too.

Early invitations to sight-see among the fabulous attractions of the Florida Gold Coast have been declined in favor of studying the stewardess manual, polishing English and writing postcards to mail home. Later the girls who know how to drive hope to summon enough courage to chauffeur themselves and their compatriots in a rental car, since Pan Am trainees are allowed special rates.

"But everybody drives on the right side of the road here, I don't know that I will be brave enough to try," said Teruke Shinozaki.

Pan Am Prestige

Tall, pretty Susan Sinclair, a former stewardess who supervised their training until they graduated September 23, impressed on them the responsibilities of their position. Recalling that Pan American pioneered air service across the Pacific, she told them, "Pan American's prestige is being entrusted to your hands. In your job you will have more contact with the passengers than the captain who pilots the plane, or many people who have worked for the airline 30 years."

By the time the trainees have won their wings each one will represent a $3,000 investment on the part of Pan Am. A pregraduation training flight will have taken them halfway around the world, to Europe or Latin America and the port of their choice. It is impossible to estimate how many individuals will have participated in putting the polish on their international aerial education.

EXCHANGING CEREMONIAL COSTUMES for Pan Am uniforms are these seven pretty Japanese gals, the first Japanese ever to be trained at the Stewardess College. They are shown upon their arrival in Miami (top) and following graduation five weeks later. From left to right are Teruke Shinozaki, Azumi Izawa, Yukiko Watanabe, Kazue Kanda, Kumiko Sadamitsu, Seiko Nakamuto and Kazue Hara.

Announcement of the first stewardesses from Japan in the *Clipper*, 1966.

reported the following the recommendations made by Japan's Supreme Export Council: (1) expand international lines; (2) extend diplomatic negotiations; (3) strengthen Japan Airlines' competitive power through continuing governmental financial assistance; (4) increase crews on Japan Airlines' international flights; (5) promote foreign tourism to Japan through Japan Airlines; and (6) promote the use of Japan Airlines by Japanese travelers ("Government Urges Measures to Improve Aviation Accounts" 1966). The race to fill international flights was clearly heating up, and the Japanese government was doing all it could to enhance Japan Airlines' competitiveness.

In that same year, in response to the increasing number of Japanese traveling abroad, Japan Airlines' "Fly Japanese" campaign in the United States, the increasing difficulty finding Japanese Americans with adequate language skills, and a change in United States immigration laws, Pan Am began hiring Japanese nationals (Ferguson 1966). Immigration to the United States had been restricted since 1924 by national quotas that favored northern Europeans, while prohibiting Asians as an "undesirable race"; the Immigration and Nationality Act of 1965 abolished quotas and generally allowed far greater numbers of immigrants from Asia and non-European countries in general. The change came just in time. On 4 November 1966 the twenty-first United Nations General Assembly declared 1967 as the International Tourist Year with the slogan "Tourism, Passport to Peace." By October 1967 the *Japan Times* reported, "International Tourism Booming," citing both a steady increase in visitors entering Japan and Japanese tourists traveling abroad ("International Tourism Booming" 1967). Although foreign carriers had hired Japanese stewardesses before, this was the first time the hiring occurred on a large scale.[11] Pan Am announced its new stewardesses with photographs and an article on the first graduating class from Japan: Kazue Hara, Azumi Izawa, Kazue Kanda, Seiko Nakamuto, Kumiko Sadamitsu, Teruko Shinozaki, and Yukiko Watanabe. Striking exactly the same poses as the Malaysian women before them, the Japanese women were shown being transformed, wearing first native costume and then the Pan Am uniform. The article emphasized how the women had worked hard to metamorphose from "diminutive, soft-spoken Tokyo girls" to cosmopolitan Pan Am "air hostesses"—in short, from East to West:

> East is meeting West—and a lot of other parts of the world—here these days. The East is represented by seven diminutive, soft-spoken Tokyo girls who are the vanguard of the first group of Japanese to be trained as stewardesses by Pan American for the worldwide routes. From their arrival—attired in brilliantly elegant ceremonial silk kimonas [sic], befitting the special occasion—the Tokyo girls were the center of attention. However, they quickly settled down to the busy routine at Pan Am's international stewardess training school. . . . For a quick and nourishing repast, and one easy on the budget, they have discovered, you can't beat hamburgers and ice cream. . . . Early invitations to sight-see among

the fabulous attractions of the Florida Gold Coast have been declined in favor of studying the stewardess manual, polishing English and writing postcards to mail home. . . . In the school's Cordon Bleu kitchens, the girls who have never cooked much besides sukiyaki will learn to prepare and serve a seven-course gourmet dinner, five miles high in the air, with Maxim's of Paris flair. . . . When they come up to that festive Friday graduation, wearing red roses and gold wings on their high fashion uniforms, the latest crop of girls in Pan Am blue will represent the best efforts of two worlds. ("First of New Japanese Stewardesses Graduate" 1966)

The article exoticized the Japanese women as strangers to hamburgers and ice cream who knew only sukiyaki. But here, through training, Pan American's cosmopolitanism worked its magic, performing an erasure of difference. Most important, the article portrayed the women as exemplars of assimilation ("model minorities," following the Japanese American example). They did not come by their transition easily; even while they maintained close relationships with their families they were required to work diligently and make sacrifices—still, a small price to pay for the privilege of shedding their "silk kimonas" for "high fashion uniforms." By meeting East and West, this "latest crop of girls" would contribute to the prestige of Pan Am. Thus Pan Am embedded the exotica of foreign women, as well as their assimilation through training in an "American atmosphere."

Much of what the film critic Gina Marchetti writes about Chinatown can be said about Pan Am's "Nisei" stewardess: "As pure style and as spectacle, . . . [she] fulfills a commercial hunger for a domesticated otherness that can represent both the fulfillment of the American myth of the melting pot and play with the dangers of the exotic" (1993, 204) Pan Am's "Nisei" became a metonym for the exotica of Asia as well as a mark of Pan Am's achievement in domesticating "otherness." European women did not have as great a cultural distance to bridge. But Asian (American) women marked an exotic remove from Euro-American culture, and Pan Am had to go to great lengths to recast them in its own American corporate image. Pan Am could boast its retinue of domesticated, model-minority exotics. It was both their foreignness and the company's effort to overcome it—a testament to its training expertise, its command of the world, and the women themselves—that enhanced the image of the airline.

As discussed in chapter 1, Pan Am's stereotyping of Asian women as combining feminine appeal and service was in keeping with images of the

Cover feature, *Life*, Asia edition, 1966.

1950s and 1960s. A feature in *Life* magazine (Asia edition) from 1 May 1967 proclaimed, "Newest Stewardess Fad: A Japanese in Every Jet," with a photographic spread of Japanese stewardesses from eleven carriers: Pan Am, Qantas, BOAC, Scandinavian Air Service, KLM, Air France, Lufthansa, Air India, Northwest, Alitalia, and Canadian Pacific.

The article provided a litany of qualities that purportedly made Japanese women particularly suited to the job: "While the Japanese airlines have always been aware of the attributes of Japanese women, the foreign carriers only lately have discovered their unique talents. 'It is her air of serenity and gift of grace that makes the Japanese stewardess such a sought-after member of the airlines' crew,' says one Lufthansa official. An Air India representative adds admiringly: 'Their ability to stand up to strain better than others is a major asset.' . . . 'A Japanese woman knows how to serve and desires to serve,' says Ursula Tautz, Lufthansa's chief of stewardesses. Alitalia's general manager for Japan, C. A. Squarci, adds, 'Japanese men expect to be spoiled and pampered with service.'" ("Newest Stewardess Fad" 1967, 42–43). Whether it is her "air of serenity," "gift of grace," strong body, or cult of service, the article proclaimed the Japanese woman to be a special boon to international travel. What made her an even better asset, at least to the other airlines, was that she came at bargain prices: according to the article, most of the carriers paid the Japanese women less than other stewardesses ("Newest Stewardess Fad" 1967, 42). By contrast, Pan Am hired Japanese women at the regular union pay scale, and afforded them the opportunity to live in the United States (Honolulu) — making the airline a particularly attractive employer for many women in Japan.

These women added to Japan's increasingly prominent international face, as Kyu Sakamoto's song "Sukiyaki" became an international hit in the summer of 1963 and the Tokyo Olympics were held in October 1964.[12] "Sukiyaki" gave a light, upbeat face to Japan, blending familiar musical idioms of western pop music with Japanese lyrics. To this day "Sukiyaki" is the only Japanese popular song to successfully bridge the Pacific and make it to American charts. Sakamoto's performance was an "ethnic novelty act" performed by a non-threatening, "cute" Asian man (Bourdaghs 2005, 254, 255). In contrast to a novelty hit that trivialized Japan, the Tokyo Olympics were a large-scale, prestigious international event that gave Japanese people a sense of their place in the world. As the world traveled to Tokyo and an increasing number of Japanese traveled abroad, 1964 was a year when many Japanese felt that they had left their war loss behind and reemerged as world players with a global vision of themselves and their own mobility. Women who applied to become international flight attendants with Pan Am represented this vision exactly. In choosing to fly for Pan Am, they were opting out of a more predictable life close to home in favor of foreign employment that would take them away from Japan, if temporarily. Few of them thought that taking such a job meant changing their life path permanently.

The "Nisei" stewardesses were a racial hire under the banner of language. However, in the early 1970s, when Pan Am was pressured to hire nonwhites, it responded differently, recruiting on the basis of race to fill quotas. According to an article in the *Clipper* in December 1971, Pan Am had committed to adding a hundred African American and Puerto Rican flight attendants, more than fifty of whom were chosen to begin training in Miami in 1972. One of the recruiters was herself African American: Alice K. Brown, a flight attendant with Pan Am since 1970. In an article published in the *Clipper*, Brown explains some of the hurdles to racial hiring: "'Recruiting stewardesses from the black and Puerto Rican minorities is no snap. . . . Trying to get applicants from minority groups is a special problem. . . . Girls with college backgrounds are prone to go into teaching and other professions and never give airline work real consideration as a career'" ("Alice Erasing Effects of Myths" 1971). Brown's point is well taken. Women of color seeking upward class mobility would more likely take an established, stable, long-term, middle-class job such as teaching than the more tenuous, potentially short-term, ambiguously classed job of a flight attendant.

Two years later, the airline reported that it had about a hundred African American flight attendants in its employ, but was still recruiting more. Coincidentally, this was the same period that Pan American was also recruiting women in Africa to add—in the words of one stewardess from Ghana hired in 1973—a "pan-African look" to the airplane cabin (see note 1). In March 1973 *Inside Travel News* interviewed the African American flight attendant and the recruiter Sharon Taylor: "We offered jobs to 105, but only 57 made it through Pan Am's Training School in Miami. . . . We are looking for more, but they don't seem to want to come aboard. . . . Just getting people to interview is the hardest part. . . . Last year I requested ads on local Black radio stations and in newspapers, but only had about 30 responses. I guess young Black people just don't believe Pan Am is for real" (quoted in Leibowitz 1973, 12–13). Taylor's difficulties highlight some of the problems in recruiting minorities into an airline that had so clearly imaged itself as white and élite. According to Taylor, the problems begin with minorities' lack of trust in the sincerity of the airline, not believing that Pan Am is "for real." That distrust led minority women to ignore company recruitment. Even when selected for the job, the rigors and unfamiliarity of training proved to be a stumbling block, creating a self-reinforcing loop of difficulties for minority hiring.

Of course the problem lay not only with minorities but in the lap of Pan Am as well. The company's recruitment efforts could be seen as tentative forays into minority hiring, looking to fill quotas to address the concerns of specific groups (African Americans, Puerto Ricans) while ignoring others. The company did not, for example, recruit in Chicano areas of California or Texas. Thus Pan Am's effort to prove that it was "for real" was as strategic and selective as anything the company had ever done. It targeted those groups that would make the biggest visual impact, lending the look of an integrated cabin.

FINDING THE JAPANESE AMERICAN GIRL NEXT DOOR

Apparently enough Japanese American women did believe that Pan Am was for real, whether in the 1950s or the 1970s. In spite of the airline's white, élite image, many accepted the corporate dreams of getting both the Asian language and Asian-looking women on board. It was not always easy to find suitable Japanese American women who could fulfill the linguistic, aesthetic, and social requirements of the job. In several cases women were invited by informal recruiters to apply. Pan Am relied on personal scouts who went beyond the standard procedure of placing public advertisements to find suitable women. Many people—including those who were not necessarily employed by the company—were constantly scrutinizing, assessing, and recruiting for Pan Am. For these informal scouts and others, the gaze was upon the current crop of Japanese American women. One woman I interviewed was asked about possible employment as early as 1950 by her teacher, an older woman of Japanese ancestry, at a vocational school in Honolulu. At that time her teacher knew that Pan Am was looking for women who could speak Japanese. The interviewee met airline requirements and showed leadership skills in serving as president of her class, but was not interested in employment at Pan Am. Among other reasons, she perceived that her parents would never allow her to travel away from Hawai`i. What is surprising about this woman's story is the early date of the incident: it precedes by four years Japan Airlines' start-up in the international market (and thus, Pan Am's official rationale). What is not surprising is that Pan Am had its eye on Japanese (American) women as part of a marketing strategy, using the women in its employ to boast its global domination.

A recruiter for Pan Am in the early 1960s (herself a "Nisei" stewardess) summarizes the desirable physical and social qualities of job candidates at the time. She looked for a specific personality type ("bubbly") and was interested in how applicants answered questions and demonstrated poise and an ability to communicate. She looked for particular physical features besides the requisite height of five feet, one inch—lowered by this time to accommodate the "Nisei" recruits—and proportionate weight: clear skin, straight teeth, well-formed ears ("if they protrude and they're bigger, it's not gonna look good with a hat on"), and dainty hands. Several of these desirable physical features may have been class-coded (as discussed in chapter 2), including those related to skin, teeth, and especially hands. The recruiter recalls: "I used to look at their hands. Because, you know, you serve people with the trays. I used to look at their hands to see if they were nice. Not necessarily all manicured, but it's because you're gonna bring food there" (PAA 1955–86). She is not speaking here of cleanliness but of a class-coded look: white, smooth hands with slender, tapered fingers, which looked as if they were not accustomed to hard (outdoor) labor. This may have been a particularly sensitive issue given the plantation background of many Japanese American families.

Another "Nisei" stewardess-turned-recruiter in the 1970s searched overseas throughout various Asian countries, as well as Europe and the United States. Besides the physical requirements she discusses the psychosocial dimensions of the ideal: "We looked at an individual's personality—were they engaging? Were they withdrawn? We looked at work experience—if they had public contact experience? What did they do? I don't know if there's a look [for which we were recruiting], say. If I can recall, someone who was more—composed; not necessarily your friendly, homespun, Midwestern girl. I mean, because Pan Am flew international, and the type of passengers who flew international were certainly different from those who flew domestic" (PAA 1968–86). Fitting the ethos and image of Pan Am meant extending the girl-next-door ideal beyond "friendly, homespun" standards to a more nebulous cultural flexibility. At the very least, a stewardess needed to demonstrate her openness to engaging the world as her neighborhood.

One part of the interview process that several women mentioned was the requirement that they walk across the room before the watchful eyes of the interviewers. Perhaps it was because the procedures of beauty contests were public knowledge, or perhaps because there was a more generalized awareness of the spotlight upon women in everyday life as well as in the stewardess industry, but the applicants took this kind of scrutiny for granted and never thought to question its relevance. In fact, walking in public before many pairs of critical eyes was a fundamental part of the job that many women acknowledged. "I was wearing a two-piece suit, and they wanted to see what I looked like. So they asked me to pull my jacket back tight, and they had me walk across the room. [Laughs] I walked across the room, walked back, and they said, 'Okay, we'll be letting you know in about a week or so.' And then I got an invitation that I was accepted" (PAA 1968–86). Some women anticipated "the walk" with dread: "They said, 'Can you just walk around the room?' I had to walk for them. They wanted to see if I was bow-legged, and I was. And I remember I was dreading it, because I know I'm bow-legged and I had to walk straight" (PAA 1963–86). This woman's interpretation of the walk was that the company was looking for a racial "Achilles heel"—the bowed legs that the woman saw as a flaw. Even if it was not, the woman's dread suggests a racial interpretation of the selection process.

A general company flight service application and rating sheet from 1972 provides telling traces of corporate values and recruitment strategies. Although by this time Pan Am and other airlines were not allowed to discriminate on the basis of age or sex, and therefore these company documents should pertain equally to female and male applicants, the language used and judging criteria imply female candidates. Besides the data that one might expect (including height, weight, and measurements "for purposes of uniform sizing"), the application asks candidates to indicate any scars, birthmarks, or missing teeth. The language used to rate candidates provides clues as to what the company sought in its flight attendants. I list all the rating factors to give an indication of the thoroughness of the process, their subjectiveness, and the values revealed by them:

PHYSICAL APPEARANCE: from "pretty, handsome, attractive, striking" to "homely, hard, matronly, dissipated, unaesthetic"

GROOMING: from "meticulous, chic, immaculate" to "sloppy, untidy, tacky, slipshod"

VOICE: from "resonant, varied tones" to "abrasive, monotone, shrill"

SPEECH: from "fluent, excellent grammar and vocabulary, eloquent" to "poor grammar, limited vocabulary, affected, slurred, slipped, inarticulate, disorganized"

WARMTH AND LIKEABILITY: from "exceptionally personable, projects warmth" to "cold, aloof, snobbish, unfriendly, introverted, self-contained"

TOLERANCE: from "empathic, concerned, compassionate" to "hypercritical, fault-finding, dogmatic, intolerant"

ENERGY LEVEL: from "lively, energetic, vigorous, fast-paced" to "lethargic, listless, slow paced, overly deliberate"

MATURITY: from "even-tempered, self-controlled, thinks through actions" to "childlike behavior, naive, emotionally volatile, impulsive"

ALERTNESS: from "sharp, intelligent, resourceful, rapid comprehension, anticipates questions" to "slow to respond, doesn't seem to understand, dull, rarely volunteers information or takes the lead"

POISE: from "self-assured, confident, polished, graceful" to "anxious, nervous, ill-at-ease, tense, awkward, easily rattled"

ENTHUSIASM: from "extremely well motivated, strong interest in job" to "superficial interest in job, low interest in job"

COOPERATIVENESS: from "open, adaptable, gracious, obliging" to "hostile, defensive, antagonistic, evasive, resistant." (Pan Am Flight Service Interview Rating 1972)

Although there may be different interpretations of the language used in the rating sheets, a picture emerges of the ideal Pan Am flight attendant. The rating sheet clearly selects for a particular type of congenial, positive, energetic team player. The interviewers select for the performance of youth, giving negative points for being "matronly." They select for a particular type of femininity that is not "hard," "abrasive," or "shrill," but "warm" (here I purposely juxtapose adjectives used for elements such as physical appearance and voice with those relating to emotions). Interviewers select for social class and education, giving negative points for clothing that is "tacky," as well as for an "inarticulate" person with "limited vocabulary." It is a balancing act to find a candidate who is "sharp, intelligent, resourceful" but not "hypercritical, fault-finding, dogmatic." She must thus be able to control a situation—quickly, gracefully, poised—without always letting people know it. In short, she should be the perfect hostess.

According to one woman who flew in the 1960s, Pan Am was in the business of molding women for company purposes. Therefore the company looked for women who were moldable. Makeup was one easy example. She explains: "I think Pan Am hired women who did not wear makeup when they went for the interview, or minimal makeup. Because they wanted to transform you into this person. That's what I believe. So then we had makeup classes, you know with mirrors and everything. And somebody doing this whole thing with you. And you suddenly wore make-up when you'd never worn make-up before" (PAA 1963–69). The malleability of the women into "Pan Am stewardesses" enhanced the standardization and thereby the reliability of the product the airline was peddling.

Another woman from the island of Maui suggests that the airline was looking for the "country girl": "When I heard [Pan Am was] interviewing, I took off from work and I wasn't even ready. I wasn't even dressed nicely. I had an ugly beige blouse and a drab brown straight skirt. And I wasn't at my best, and I went because that was the only day or the last they were interviewing. So I wasn't very confident. Especially when I saw all these pretty, tall, good-looking Japanese [American] girls there. I thought, 'Oh, no chance!' But I don't know what they were looking for. I guess they wanted the country type. Well, I wasn't that sophisticated at that time" (PAA 1963–86). The "country type" suggests lack of sophistication, but it also suggests certain "old-fashioned" traits—loyalty, conservatism, even servitude. Not coincidentally, these are the very traits by which the Asian woman was defined in the 1950s and 1960s (see chapter 1). At a time when white American women may have begun threatening to disrupt gender roles, the Asian woman seemed a welcome throwback.

DREAMS OF FLYING: JAPANESE (AMERICAN) FRONTIERS
BEYOND THE HORIZON OF HOME

But were these Japanese American women such a throwback? What kinds of personal dreams did Pan Am fill for them? Most women whom I interviewed wanted to "see the world."[13] In a public forum on 2 November 2006, two women from the first group, May Hayashi and Masako Tagawa, recounted their experiences: "I thought it was something glamorous. Not that I am a glamorous person, but I just wanted to know what it was like to go beyond Hawai`i" (Hayashi, PAA 1955–57). Tagawa came from a rural area in northern California: "I come from a farming community, a farmer's daughter. And I had never been exposed to anything, period. So when I graduated high school, I went to San Francisco. I was attending a nursing school, and I was at a dentist's office, and here was a Japanese American newspaper saying that Pan Am was looking for girls. And so I thought, 'Oh my god!' I said, 'I get to see the world!' You know, coming from a little farm to this whole big thing. It was exciting, but very scary. The scary part is not knowing what was coming. First of all, to leave a small farming community is scary enough. My exposure in San Francisco was my first time away from the farm. And to think that we're gonna fly the Pacific and we're gonna be on an island" (Tagawa, PAA 1955–58). One stewardess describes herself as a "free-spirited" type of person. She states emphatically, "I knew there was something more than just being here. I didn't want to just work in an office or teach. I wanted to spread my wings [Laughs]" (PAA 1963–86). Other stewardesses tell similar stories of wanting to "see more," including their dreams of class mobility: "Oh, I wanted to travel! Because in those years, people, when they traveled, they wore their finest clothes. They always looked very nice. And so it was just the idea that you'd be doing these things that you wouldn't get here [in Hawai'i]. But it was really because I just wanted to see more" (PAA 1963–69). One stewardess talked of reading many books when she was younger. The world afforded by books whetted her appetite for more: "I wanted to travel, that's all I wanted to do. I looked into going into the military at that time also, but people discouraged me. So I thought of opening a travel agency. I just wanted to travel, see the world, live abroad. . . . I just felt so isolated here. I thought, 'Hawaii's really provincial'" (PAA 1965–86). What these women shared was a willingness, even an eagerness, to test the waters of the unknown, especially if those waters took them to higher places.

Several women spoke specifically of Pan Am as the source of their dreams. During this period flying internationally generally meant flying with Pan Am. "I vividly remember the day when Mr. Bob Nichols from Pan Am called with news that I was hired. I couldn't believe that I was going to join one of the most prestigious international airlines in the world and would be wearing the striking uniform that I had admired from afar. So it was that through Pan Am, my daydreams would be fulfilled" (PAA 1962–65). It was the prestige of the airline—so readily visualized for this woman and many others through its uniforms—that made the whole experience seem like a dream come true.

Several women from the 1950s equated their personal dreams with the aspirations of achievement for the Japanese American community in Hawai'i as a whole. Given the experience of the Second World War and Japanese Americans' subsequent gains in education, politics, and business, Pan Am's hiring could easily be seen as a community accomplishment. "Well, it was a big deal for us. It was something, even the Japanese community picked it up, you know, thinking, 'Wow! The Nisei girls are going to be flying for Pan American!' And Pan Am was considered THE airline in those days" (PAA 1955–58). Pan Am's hiring was thus an accomplishment within the context of a racialized image: breaking through the color barrier confirmed that Japanese Americans had made it to the top, in this field as well as in education and other industries. Only ten years after the end of the Second World War, this *was* a big deal. One stewardess explains: "You know, Pan Am was the top dog in those days. And to be hired by Pan Am—. You know, they were all Caucasian girls" (PAA 1955–58). One can easily infer from this stewardess's comments that Pan Am's hiring gave the women and the Japanese American community a sense of racial parity. This was a new frontier of dreams—of what Japanese American women could be, of where they could go, of whose uniform they could wear. That this was a uniform not shared equally by other ethnic minorities concerned them less than the excitement of their own sense of accomplishment. This was one instance in which it was actually an advantage to be of Japanese ancestry—rather than of Chinese, Korean, Filipino, Hawaiian, or white ancestry. In short, their gaze looked to their own upward trajectory, rather than laterally to others around them.

It is important to historicize this discussion of personal and community dreams, For Japanese Americans in Hawai`i, the 1950s were a particularly promising time of upward mobility for Hawai`i and Japanese Americans within it. Constituting 36.9 percent of the population (down from a high of 42.0 percent in 1920), Japanese Americans made up the single largest ethnic group in the territory, which would become a state in 1959 (Lind 1980, 34).[14] The Servicemen's Readjustment Act of 1944, or GI Bill, paved the way for Nisei war veterans to attend college and enter into the professions, which they did—typically in the fields of dentistry, medicine, and mid-level government. In fact, the proportion of Japanese American men in white-collar professions tripled between 1930 and 1960, to just over 10 percent of the population (Kotani 1985, 145). However, given their numbers, that still left the majority of Japanese Americans in blue-collar industries: they accounted for nearly one-third of plantation workers, one-half of small farmers and fishermen, and three-fourths of domestic service workers

(Okamura 2001, 75–76). In 1950 Caucasians and Chinese were the only ethnic groups overrepresented in white-collar fields; all others remained underrepresented (Tamura 1994, 222, figures 8–9). Over the course of the 1950s, however, Japanese American men began to rise in the white-collar ranks. By 1954 Japanese Americans achieved a notable political presence in what has been called the "Democratic Revolution of 1954," during which Nisei played a significant role in helping the Democratic Party to gain the majority in the legislature for the first time in Hawai'i's history. This turning point confirmed Japanese American gains in the tier of ethnic and racial relations in Hawai'i: the *haole* (white) oligarchy originally based in the plantation economy remained very much on top, but it was followed by rising groups of ethnically Chinese and Japanese, and further down the ladder, Filipinos, Hawaiians, and others (Yano 2006b, 47). As Jonathan Okamura argues, "Ethnicity, as the dominant organizing principle of social relation in Hawai'i society, structures inequality among ethnic groups in various institutional domains, such as education and the economy" (2008, 4). Statehood in 1959 provoked the celebratory statement "We all *haoles* now": this statement, in which "haoles" stood for Americans, cryptically encapsulated locally inflected structures built around race, ethnicity, and nationality (quoted in Chinen and Hiura 1997, 77). As Okamura points out, the effects of this inequality are "cumulative and transmitted from one generation to the next" (2008, 4).

The rungs of the ladder of inequality in the form of education, employment, and politics have not only racialized and ethnicized dimensions but also gendered dimensions (Yano 2006b). As Tamura makes clear, Nisei men and women differed markedly in terms of occupational advancement, with women gaining ground more slowly than men; this disparity reflected the differential status and educational investment in sons versus daughters of the Japanese American family (1994, 221). Both men and women worked outside the home, but women more often than men remained in blue-collar jobs, such as domestic service, barbering, and sewing. Thus a family raising and investing in a daughter who broke out of that mold and into a white-collar profession carried great prestige and significance. White-collar professions signaled class status, among which teaching and nursing were primary, followed by secretarial work.[15] Teaching was considered the foremost profession: "Compared to other occupations, there was little race discrimination in the public school system. . . . And with a standard salary schedule, teaching provided Asians with the same pay as Caucasians. At the same time teaching fit in well with traditional Japanese values, in which the . . . teacher was a respected member of the community" (Tamura 1994, 229). Nursing also provided upward mobility and, given on-the-job training in hospitals, required fewer educational expenses. Therefore a woman who was either studying to become a teacher or nurse or already employed as one of these was considered highly desirable. She represented the "model woman" of a model minority. One stewardess hired in 1955 reminds us of the limited options for women at the time of her employment: "Now remember in the 1950s, the only opportunity, frankly, for a girl was to be a secretary, a nurse, or a teacher. There was nothing really beyond that. That was expected from a girl. And so flying, it was like, wow! It's such a glamorous job. Traveling from country to country. And meeting all these different people. . . . For a girl to be able to travel and, you know, be a part of an international scene" (PAA 1955–58). Becoming a teacher or nurse (or secretary) marked a woman's assurance of middle-class respectability for both herself and her family. Flying as a stewardess, on the other hand, marked her as extraordinary—in her words, "Wow!" Thus her own (and others') dreams of flying can be seen as an achievement of the community, as well as an individual act of resistance against the community's ideal.

Several women whom I interviewed characterize themselves as politically conservative. During the late 1960s, when much of the United States was embroiled in controversies over feminism, race politics, and the Vietnam War, these women expressed little interest. One says, "I guess I'm very conservative. . . . [The late 1960s were] an interesting time, but I never got involved in any movements or protests" (PAA 1968–86). Thus in spite of the Japanese American community's pride in their ethnic "achievement," the women did not see themselves as political activists.

An important characteristic of these women's dreams is that the jobs were configured as temporary aspirations: once having "seen the world," the women would return to their homes, marry, and live a more conventional life. The dreams for the most part thus defined a liminal period in the women's lives: post-education, pre-marriage. Flying for Pan Am was a finishing-school touch that might add gloss to their lives, but never subvert the larger scheme. For the most part the women and their families assumed that they would eventually marry and then quit their flying jobs. The structure of the dreams helped mitigate their irony. If their dreams were to fly only temporarily, then the Japanese American community could have its cake and eat it too: women could fly worldwide for the most prestigious airline alongside whites, and then return to the community's fold as nurses and teachers (or wives) upon marriage. This kind of game plan worked in theory perhaps more than in practice. But it bridged the difference between individual dreams of ambitious, errant, free-spirited women who wanted to "see the world" and community dreams of a stable middle class.

In a panel discussion of eight "Nisei" stewardesses conducted by the Japanese-language newspaper *Hawaii Hochi* in 1956, less than a year after the start-up of the program, the emcee asked Jane Toda, stewardess from the first group, whether she thought she and her colleagues had fulfilled the expectations of Pan Am and the general public, to which Toda modestly replied, "Well, I cannot answer whether or not we met people's expectations, but I think what is certain is that a new door has opened for local women" (quoted in "Sekai no Sora o Iku Nisei Musume" 1956, 2). Although the answer may seem equivocal, what Toda said provides a real foundation for the dreams of these women. The job of international stewardess offered by Pan Am did not even exist in the women's parents' generation. This "new door" offered local Japanese American women the resources with which to dream. What these women dreamed and then ventured was nothing short of a challenge to the social, cultural, and racial frontier, pointing backward to the norms of where they should be as well as forward to the expanded possibilities of what they might become. Most important, the "new door" dream did not risk the community's daughters. Rather, it was acceptable as a temporary gesture that allowed them newly expanded possibilities while still expecting them to retreat eventually to community norms.

GOOD GIRLS FROM GOOD FAMILIES: CLASS-BASED
REACTIONS TO DAUGHTERS' DREAMS

Not everyone dreamed of flying, especially in the early years of the 1950s and even the 1960s.[16] Many women who flew came from upwardly mobile families who had invested in their daughters' education.[17] Some had previous experience in the public limelight, such as on a beauty contest stage (in particular for a specifically Japanese American contest; Yano 2006b) or flying for a local airline. Higher education and public exposure extended the range of possibilities for their futures. Some of the dreams were derived from their social backgrounds, although not all university-educated Japanese American women aspired to fly. Other dreams derived from sheer personal ambition to see beyond their world, to achieve beyond their parents' aspirations. The dreams were fueled by a certain amount of individual wanderlust and willingness to leave the safety and security of home for places and experiences unknown. Some women dreamed with knowledge gained from books; others dreamed simply knowing that they wanted to get away. But what fueled their desire to "get away"?

For some it may have been a desire for the class mobility and sophistication that "getting away" seemed to afford. More than one woman described herself as "country"—whether her home was Maui, northern California, Fukuoka, Tokyo, or Honolulu. One woman laughingly says: "Being real country from Hawai`i, I didn't know anything" (PAA 1964–68). In describing themselves as "country," these women inscribe both a provincial rootedness and a desire to flee from their roots. The ambivalence is key to their designations. These designations have little to do with population density and urbanization but refer more accurately to a particular position away from global centers of power and knowledge. Thus the opposite of "country" is not necessarily "urban" so much as "urbane." These women define themselves against who or what they are not—white, worldly, well-traveled, upper-class, sophisticated, and living in the centers of power. Ironically, calling themselves "country" also linked them to a particular stewardess ideal of the small-town girl next door (see chapter 2). Pan Am's reality may have been slightly different, especially with European stewardesses. One British woman who flew from 1962 to 1963 comments: "I think that many of us who joined [Pan Am] came from international backgrounds like my own. I grew up overseas and many of us grew up in different places, had a true wanderlust." This background—growing up overseas, being white, being already well traveled—was explicitly not that of the typical Japanese American. Through the term "country," "Nisei" stewardesses symbolically distanced themselves from more urbane women in terms of race, class, region, and lifestyle. Their "country" background was simultaneously something foundational to who they were and something from which they fled in wanting to "see the world." These women may have seen the world through Pan Am, but, as the (modified) American adage says, you can take the girl out of the country, but you can't take the country out of the girl. "Country" thus invokes continual rootedness and distance from worldliness, even for those occupying the global stage. For the "Nisei" stewardesses to call themselves "country" reinscribed their desirability as always Asian (American) girls next door.

Very few of the women identified themselves as rebels, although some admitted to being "headstrong" or "free spirited." To Tagawa, "It was exciting, but scary." A willingness to embrace the exciting but scary was remarkable in the Japanese American community, particularly for its women. In an immigrant population known more for its social conservatism than its liberal lifestyle (Yano 2006b), not all Japanese American women were eager for an exciting but scary experience or the "wow" factor of flying. Furthermore, the racism of the Second World War only reinforced that conservatism. Just ten years after internment and Pearl Harbor, the public limelight of global travel may have proved too threatening a position for many women. Thus Tagawa's description of the job as exciting but scary takes on the possibilities of wider dimensions of race, gender, and politics. Forgoing the scary for the safe and familiar limited the number of applicants in the 1950s. But as air travel became more common, as memories of the Second World War receded, and as the unknown became less so through the Jet Age of the 1960s, the number of women sharing the dream of flying increased. What remains important is the changing circumstances of the dreams, and the place they had in the lives of their dreamers.

Parents' reactions to their daughters' dreams were mixed. As a position in the service sector, stewardessing threatened to take on the image of a lower-classed occupation. But by altering particular class practices, airlines and stewardesses assuaged potential class-ridden anxieties. By not receiving tips, the stewardess was differentiated from the waitress and the porter. By dressing in a uniform with military features (at least in the 1950s and 1960s), she was differentiated from the bar hostess. By emphasizing her rigorous training in equipment management and life-saving skills, she was less a decorative feature of the airplane and more an essential safety professional. Overall, by carefully managing a girl-next-door image through selection, training, and structuring of the job, the airlines made the position of stewardess into one that was respectable and middle-class. In the 1950s and early 1960s this image helped to sell seats.

Yet some upper-middle-class parents objected strongly, likening the job to that of a hostess or waitress, and therefore déclassé. One flight attendant from the 1960s had attended an élite private preparatory school in Hawai`i, had graduated from the University of Hawai`i, and was in her second year of teaching elementary school when she successfully applied for a job as a stewardess. Her actions nearly tore her family apart:

> I announced it to my parents and they were livid. They thought I was bringing a great shame on the family. They just said, you know what you've done is just horrible. In those days, it was not only family, but what is so-and-so going to say, you know, all their friends. They thought the career of the stewardess was just a high-class waitress. They were just furious because, especially on my father's side, all his sisters had been school teachers. One of them was even a principal of a Japanese school, so they were just so upset. So what they did was, they actually called my father's sister and her husband, my father's two sisters and their husbands, my uncles and aunts. And they sat me down in a room. And they interrogated me. They asked me why I was doing such a horrible thing. They wanted, actually, to disown me. They were not happy at all. One of my aunts was saying this is just like ruining the family name. They were wishing that I would fall on my face and not succeed. But very reluctantly, they sent me off. (PAA 1964–86)

The thought of quitting the honorable profession of teaching for a perceived dishonorable one was almost more than this family could bear. In class terms, the daughter was opting out of her upper-middle-class position and into a lowly service position. One teacher-turned-stewardess who faced similar opposition recalls: "You see, stewardesses didn't have a good reputation at that time. There were always jokes about stewardesses. So it wasn't something to be proud of" (PAA 1963–69). Her solution to her mother's objections was to explain that she would only fly for two years before returning to her teaching job. Instead she flew for six and a half years, and today she remains one of the most active members in Pan American World Wings International. Here as elsewhere, what made the job barely acceptable to some, as well as highly desirable to others, was the assumption that working as a stewardess would be temporary, not a long-term career.

Some working-class parents in the 1950s also wanted their daughters to stay close to home and not take a job that would send them to distant corners of the world. There was an element of racial clannishness lurking in this: some families were uncomfortable with the idea that their daughters would be in close contact with passengers, pilots, and other stewardesses who were not of Japanese ancestry. Furthermore, working as a Pan Am stewardess would call undue attention to the women and their families. As with the African American women discussed above, there was a certain amount of skepticism that Pan Am—long considered a *haole* (white) company—truly wanted their daughters.

In contrast, other working-class families expressed great pride that their daughters were taking a "glamour job." Some parents threw large parties for their daughters to celebrate their Pan American hire. One flight attendant from 1955 exclaims, "I am a fisherman's daughter. My father was so proud of me!" Her immigrant father kept news clippings of his daughter—the Pan Am stewardess!—from the local Japanese-language newspapers. More than one woman expressed pleasure in being able to make her own parents happy through her job and its benefits: "It made my parents so happy. My father was on one of my flights and he really enjoyed that. So I liked that part—my father especially, what my father felt" (PAA 1955–57). A sister of a "Nisei" stewardess who flew from 1970 to 1986 relates the following story: "After my mother passed away in 1996, my older sister asked me to keep the family *butsudan* [Buddhist household altar]. When I looked inside one of the drawers, I found an old clipping from a Japanese newspaper of a picture of my younger sister when she graduated from Pan Am training school. As I remember it, my mom must have been really proud because my sister gave a speech at the time as the valedictorian of her graduating class." This mother's pride in her daughter flying as a Pan Am stewardess—including standing out at the top of her class—found expression in one of the most lasting repositories of family treasures.

It was the prestige of the airline and the honor of their daughter being selected that impressed many families. What further appealed was the notion that this job would enable their daughters to travel specifically to Japan. Traveling to Japan justified their daughters' employment in a job that would take them far from home. Furthermore, the job came with travel benefits for the families: "The benefits were great. I took my mom and dad to Japan, and that was the first time they went to Japan after the war. . . . In Japan, we were like—gods" (PAA 1955–58). Indeed, these women became "gods" before the Japanese American public in Hawai'i and California, as well as Japanese in Tokyo. This was true especially in the 1950s when war memories were still fresh, and continued in the 1960s as Pan American maintained its empire of the skies. The dreams that animated these women, their families, and the Japanese American communities incorporated that empire into their own sense of identity. For an ethnic community striving for middle-class achievement, wearing the Pan Am uniform bore the imprint of a web of status built upon gender, race, and class. It was exactly this web that defined the job's "wow" factor.

Four

AIRBORNE CLASS ACT
Service and Prestige as Racialized Spectacle

One becomes a woman through race and class, . . . not as opposed to race and class.

KAPLAN 1996, 182

When I started Pan Am one of my pursers said, "You will live like an heiress." And I said, "What?" But then I realized that I was traveling where all these wealthy people were traveling to. And we stayed at the best hotels, the Intercontinental, the five-star hotels that Pan Am owned. We had these beautiful suites overlooking the Mediterranean. And I thought, "I guess we are living like heiresses in a way!"

"Nisei" stewardess (PAA 1964–86)

THE "WOW" FACTOR of the "Nisei" stewardess experience embeds issues of race and class. Pan American occupied a comfortable position as part of the élite haole milieu in Hawai`i. Inviting "Nisei" stewardesses to join the airline's inner sanctum gave a jolt of race and class crossing, and dangled the enticements of having "made it" in the larger world, even if not all families agreed on what this all meant or whether it was desirable. Race and culture formed the basis of the reputation of "Nisei" stewardesses as a group. What is notable is the degree to which they were characterized specifically *as a group* rather than as individuals. Every commendation of Masako or Elaine or Charlotte became part of a group legacy. (Every criticism was also part of their legacy, but criticisms were few.) The group legacy in turn became part of the "model minority" reputation. Pan Am used the "Nisei" stewardesses, as it did other stewardesses in its employ, for promotional

Pan Am promotion for Hawai`i, 1956.

purposes, and they became part of the airline's racialized display: hospitality was central to Pan Am's trade, and hospitality "Asian style" (often linked erroneously to the image of the geisha) was even more valuable for marketing.

In his study of white-collar workers in the United States, C. Wright Mills argues that sales clerks in fashionable stores "borrow prestige" from the wealthy customers they serve (1951, 173–74). This notion of borrowing prestige applies to flight attendants and the airline industry as well. I extend Mills's concept in what I call "proximal prestige," meaning the status that accrues by contagion with one's surroundings. Proximal prestige includes active borrowing, as well as more passive ascriptions of class before an audience of onlookers. As one of the stewardesses recalls, "Wherever we went, people would say, 'Pan Am! Pan Am!'" What those excited onlookers meant and recognized was that Pan American not only flew people in power; it *was* power. That power inhered specifically in class terms. Besides upper-class passengers, the airline often hired stewardesses from the upper middle classes—including some "Nisei" stewardesses from upwardly mobile families. In these ways the experiences of these women were often fraught with the tensions (and pleasures) of proximal prestige and class performance. Learning and practicing upper-middle-class ways filled the "classroom in the air" of the Pan Am cabin.[1]

LEARNING (TO BE) JAPANESE

Many of Pan American's "J-position" (Japanese-language-position) hires were fluent speakers of the language. But many others needed lessons. This irony was not lost on the women. Although all had the "face," they did not necessarily have the linguistic knowledge that Pan Am listed as a minimum requirement. Therefore many of their stories begin with learning (to be) Japanese. Both Pan Am managers and stewardesses describe how company tutors proceeded from a folk theory of language acquisition that assumes the efficacy of grammar and vocabulary. Linguists and second-language-acquisition scholars, on the other hand, carefully point out the rich and complex embeddedness of language within specific contexts—what Ellen Bialystok and Kenji Hakuta, for example, call the "cultural ecology" of language learning (1994, viii). Profit-driven business practices did not accommodate recreating time-intensive methods of "cultural ecology," so Pan Am attempted to provide the basics of "airplane-level" language (e.g. on-board announcements, in-flight service requests) to stewardesses who were purportedly hired for their linguistic ability. One spunky *sansei* (third-generation Japanese American) who flew from 1963 to 1969 recalls: "I didn't speak any Japanese. So when I went to the interview, they asked me if I spoke Japanese and I said, a little [laughs], and they asked me something in Japanese and I answered in English. And so they said, 'Can you answer that in Japanese?' I answered in Japanese and it was very basic Japanese, so they said, 'We're looking for people who can speak Japanese.' So I said, 'During World War II there were many Americans who had to learn German in a very short time and they were able to do that. I could certainly learn Japanese in a short time.'" Pan Am recommended a company tutor, who promptly taught the stewardess all the phrases she would need to know for flight service. She wrote all her phrases on index cards, memorized them, and eventually used these index cards in flight.

Another sansei flight attendant, who flew from 1966 to 1986, felt doubly handicapped—speaking very little Japanese and being underweight:

> When I went for my interview I could only count from one to ten [in Japanese]. You have to understand, they were desperate for Japanese speakers at that time. They had an on-campus [University of Hawai`i] "rep" who was recruiting the girls who were taking Japanese as their major. . . . But I wasn't majoring in Japanese. [The campus rep] told me that they were looking for flight attendants. I said, "I don't speak Japanese." Spanish was my language. And she says, "Go down [to the Pan Am office] anyway and see what they say." So I went, and I guess they must have liked me. But straightforward, I said, "I speak no Japanese." I said Spanish was my language. But they sent me for the physical anyway, which I promptly flunked because I was underweight. I weighed only 86 pounds. And you had to be 100 pounds. I'm 5′ 1½″. Well, I flunked the physical and because of the Japanese, they told me to go get a tutor, which I did. A private tutor for myself, and I had to gain weight. So I went to a gym six days a week and drank supplements. Six months later, I gained the weight. I went up to about 99 pounds. So they accepted me. My Japanese was classified as poor. But they hired me. I think they felt sorry for me because I worked so hard.

It seems that once Pan Am made up its mind to hire someone, it was willing to wait for her to meet the minimum standards of requirement, whether that meant learning the language or gaining weight.

This stewardess was not the only one who spoke another foreign language, but little Japanese. A *yonsei* stewardess (PAA 1968–86) spoke French:

> I was a senior in college in Ohio and at that time Pan Am mainly recruited on college campuses, because they were looking for language and they thought if they went to the college campuses they'd have more of an ability to find language-qualified [candidates]. . . . I had taken five years of French, maybe three years in high school, two years in college. . . . So I interviewed on campus when the recruiters came, and I tested for French. And that's what I was rated on. But they really had a need for Japanese speakers and I guess I was a novelty. "Well, you're Japanese so you should speak Japanese." And I said, "Well, I'm a fourth generation. And I never went to Japanese school growing up." So they said, "Don't worry, we have a tutor available for you so you can learn it." So I got hired by Pan Am, and they said, "We'd really like you to go to Honolulu. We'll get you a tutor. We really think you'll pick up Japanese quickly."

In this case, as in most others, recruiters hired for race and assumed that language was something that could be "taught." They were right, but only because Pan Am did not expect a very high level of Japanese language. All they minimally needed was one who could "perform Japanese"—read announcements, speak at a basic level, and, most important, look the part.

RACIAL AND CULTURAL REPUTATIONS: CREATING AND SOMETIMES RESISTING A LEGACY OF SERVICE

The "Nisei" stewardesses quickly gained a reputation as an airline-industry "model minority"—hard-working, sincere, diligent, dependable, and caring. The women owe some of this reputation to the first group in 1955. As one of them put it, "If we set an example, [we knew] Pan Am would continue to hire [more "Nisei" stewardesses]. So we were the pioneers, and we had to do our best so others can enjoy what we were enjoying" (PAA 1955–57). This awareness of having to set a good example for others to follow is not uncommon, especially for the first among minority group hires. For example, Venus Green writes that when Bell System began hiring African American women in the mid-1940s, the first among them felt that they "'had to set an example . . . to make them be able to hire other black people,' that they 'had to excel' and could not 'be average or ordinary'" (2001, 234). Likewise, as Ernie Albrecht (PAA 1943–85), Honolulu's district traffic and sales manager at the time, emphatically states, "These girls ["Nisei" stewardesses] had to be not only good, but better . . . They had to be more outstanding, and in every way they were." In working hard to "be not only good, but better," the women felt themselves to be on the proving ground of the profession, situated within a racialized frontier. In this way the exemplary reputation of the group came about framed specifically through the processes and pressures of their minority position. Theirs was not simply a job well done but a model-minority achievement.

The women do not talk about these racialized pressures of the job. Instead they talk about their reputation for being "not only good, but better" as a function of sheer effort. One recalls: "You know we were so much in demand, really. You know why? Because we worked hard. They loved to have us on their section. The pursers would go in and they would say, 'Okay, I'll take the Nisei girls.' We were very favored" (PAA 1955–86). Another explains: "The Nisei stewardesses were special because of their dedication, because of their love for their jobs, that they just put themselves out. They never held back, but they went forward to make the passengers comfortable, to let them know that we were their friend, and not just someone who is servicing them on the flight" (PAA 1955–57). This kind of dedication and work ethic became a reputation to uphold: "There was so much respect for the 'Nisei' stewardess. Anytime the 'Nisei' stewardess came on board, they knew they were going to get topnotch help from those girls. Very conscientious, very reliable. It was a reputation to maintain" (PAA 1960–69). Conscientiousness and reliability made the "Nisei" stewardess a team player. These elements—effort, attitude, team player—were the first building blocks of their reputation.

In the words of another stewardess from 1955: "I think everybody loved the Nisei girls. I don't know if it was a novelty. But I think all of us were really nice. I mean, it was something so new, and we really loved our job" (PAA 1955–57). The novelty was felt on both sides. For Pan Am and its passengers, the "Nisei" stewardesses were a wholly new group of employees adding a different look—and perhaps a different level of service—to the airline. For the women, the job fulfilled dreams far beyond their upbringing. Their excitement to be working for Pan Am rested partly in this: having grown up in Hawai`i (or in some cases California) as "country girls," in the words of some, they were now in a glamorous job that took them to every corner of the world.

Leaving home, 1967.

"Nisei" stewardess with grandparents and sister, 1967.

The heady excitement that Pan Am generated undoubtedly helped the stewardesses to approach their jobs with enthusiasm. So many of the women whom I interviewed talked of "loving their job." This may not be entirely unusual among Pan Am stewardesses of the time, but their excitement and love of their job could only enhance the group's reputation and the quality of their service.

Part of the novelty, especially for the Japanese American women from Hawai'i, was interacting with whites: "It was really interesting, because I had never come across Caucasians [growing up in Hawai'i]. I mean my contact here was just strictly Asian Americans. You know, you hardly get to be friends or talk to Caucasians. So it was really a different kind of experience" (PAA 1955–86). Her childhood experience was not unique, and only highlights the degree to which growing up Japanese American in Hawai'i could mean living in an ethnic enclave. Although this woman says that she "had never come across Caucasians" previously, what she meant was that she had never interacted with Caucasians, except perhaps as teachers or doctors. Another Japanese American woman growing up during the same period in Hawai'i explains: "As I was growing up, . . . the whites controlled almost everything. And I could sense that being a person of yellow skin, you were a little bit less than a person with white skin. . . . I could see that the people in power were whites and there were hardly any professionals that were not white. . . . So if you wanted to go to a good medical person, or a good law person, you'd go to a white person, because they had the background, the connections, and the good school that nonwhites did not have" (quoted in Yano 2006b, 103). She, like other Japanese Americans, lived the racial politics of the era, which distanced haole from all others, both because the two groups interacted infrequently and because of the symbolic chasm that accrued from the elevated position of the haole. Notably, the first racial frontier for many "Nisei" stewardesses therefore had little to do with foreign countries: it was their close interaction with whites, beginning in training and extending to the airplane cabin.

Often, interacting with whites meant that the "Nisei" stewardesses encountered their own racialized reputation as Asian women, especially in the image of the geisha or "Oriental doll." One "Nisei" stewardess from 1964 talks about comments made while she was in training: "The mechanics [at the training facility in Miami] commented that we looked like geishas on the catwalk in the hangars with our high heels when we went to lunch"

(Kawada 2004, 6). Such an image quite boggles the mind, but one can only guess that the mechanics were responding to their sense of novelty in the presence of an "exotic" Asian (American) woman. Another "Nisei" woman reacted favorably but also dismissively to the stereotype she encountered: "I think at that time, there was a myth about Japanese women. I was really complimented by hearing about this aura about Japanese women being so feminine, so gracious, and especially to men. I chuckled over that" (PAA 1965–86). Few women express rancor over the stereotype: "Most of the crew members were really nice [to us]. I think what it was, they looked at us as being different. So they treated us—I hate to say this—like little dolls, you know Oriental dolls that they have to take care of. I think they thought we were a novelty. [Laughs] Because we had that image, being Oriental, you know, the Asian impression they have of us—sweet, demure [Laughs]" (PAA 1968–86). These women laugh at being taken as "sweet" and "de-mure." They laugh at having been taken for the "Oriental dolls" that they were not. Their laughter expresses good-natured distance from—and dis-dain for—these misconceptions. Being treated along these kinds of stereo-typical lines was not so common for those brought up in Hawai`i, where Japanese Americans were the single largest ethnic group. Part of the ad-justment for the women from Hawai`i was learning that they were exotic to white crews and passengers.

As for the white crews and passengers, part of their adjustment was learning that the women were not quite as exotic as they looked. One woman remarks: "They would be fascinated that we were Americans and that many of us were not born in Japan" (PAA 1955–57). And yet the women were continually racialized as Asians. A "Nisei" stewardess explains: "The Caucasians would look at you differently because you are Oriental. So you probably attracted their attention more. And if they had questions on things that related to Japan, I think they would speak to you, because you looked different" (PAA 1964–86). Passengers and crew members thus assumed a racialized base of knowledge of Asia from Pan Am's stewardesses of Asian ethnicity. Knowledge, by this, inhered within blood.

In recounting their experiences, several women remember specific in-stances of personalized service that they rendered on board, going beyond the rules to make passengers comfortable. One woman talks about violat-ing rules and offering a pregnant woman sitting in coach class an orange from first class to help with her morning sickness (PAA 1955–57). Thus the women answered needs according to each passenger's needs rather than bureaucratic niceties. Sometimes the personalized service continued on layovers: "The president of this movie studio in Japan, he wanted a Nisei girl on each segment [of his trip]. And one segment he requested me, because he wanted me to do his shopping for his wife in San Francisco. You know, actually we're not supposed to do that, but he put some money in my hand, and what can I say? [Laughs] The money was to pay for her alligator bag and shoes" (PAA 1955–58). Although the "Nisei" did this gladly, one could see where the line between stewardess and servant might easily be crossed in particular situations. Pan Am tried to protect its employees from what it saw as abuse, but it may have been difficult to refuse the request from the president of a movie studio in Japan.

The work ethic that "Nisei" stewardesses brought to the job dovetailed with the kind of service that Pan Am sought in its flight attendants. One "Nisei" stewardess describes Pan Am's training video and her subsequent experience:

> When we were in initial ground school, we all saw this video called "Roses for Routine." Basically, the story was this young girl goes to become a flight attendant and she starts flying, and she does such a wonderful job that she receives these roses. And what our instructor said was, "You do such a wonderful job on board the flight that people appreciate any little thing that you do, and they may not say thank you or you may not get a letter from them, but like this video, you may someday receive a bouquet of roses. And then you'll know that those were just roses for routine. You are just doing your job, and you receive the roses."
>
> I didn't think too much of it, except one day after a flight from London to Beirut, I was in my room in Beirut and I received a big bouquet of roses, yellow roses. And I said, "These are my roses for routine! I can't believe it!" And I had no idea who they were from. I guess it was a passenger on the flight. That was wonderful. (PAA 1963–69)

Other "Nisei" stewardesses received gifts from passengers. Although tips were officially not allowed, some passengers could not resist at least attempting to slip a token of their appreciation to the stewardess.[2] One stewardess received a star sapphire ring from a passenger. Another recalls:

> I had some famous sheik on board from the Middle East. The reason I remember is, they gave us a big tip. And we were not supposed to accept tips, but his

bodyguard, they were all in First Class, as they departed the airplane, they said, "Please take it. His Highness wants you to take it for the wonderful service." And it was all folded, so I thought it was a ten-dollar bill. I opened it and it was a hundred-dollar bill!

And I remember Barbara Hutton. She was such a nice lady. You know, she offered me something out of her jewelry box. This is the kind of passengers we had. She said, "Your service has been most wonderful." And she said, "Would you pick something out?" And I told her, "I don't want to." I told her I couldn't take it. But she was willing to give it to me as a thank-you. (PAA 1968–86)

These gifts represented both the level of service that Pan Am and its "Nisei" stewardesses offered and a historical period when this kind of service was possible.

Pan Am's management and passengers spoke glowingly of the "Nisei" stewardesses. Letters of praise came in. Gene Dunning, one-time steward and part of the Pan Am management team in Honolulu in the 1950s, is emphatic in his praise of the "Nisei" stewardesses: "Passengers wrote letters in, Japanese people flying across the Pacific. They would write letters complimenting us on these wonderful girls. Why? Because when the Japanese passenger got on, they were very polite, and the Japanese were, 'Oh wow, this is nice!' . . . [And the American passengers] felt like I did. They loved them. It was their politeness. Oh, even the haole passengers wrote letters in about these girls. The reputation of Pan Am went up, I swear, twelve points. Immediately. The people in San Francisco, the executive office, would come out and tell me personally about the letters that they would get for the Japanese [American] stewardesses." Dunning emphasizes how polite the "Nisei" stewardesses were and how their exemplary service became part of the company's reputation.

When Dunning and others talk about "Nisei" they inevitably make comparisons with other Pan Am stewardesses; the racial and cultural reputation of the "Nisei" stewardesses lies exactly in those comparisons. Ernie Albrecht, a central part of management at the Honolulu base, explains: "Almost immediately upon arrival at the airplane, that Nisei girl was really delighted to have you aboard. That did not always apply to the other nationalities." He cites their loyalty and their personal conservatism: "They weren't spoiled like so many of the haoles and others, and they had more discipline. They weren't shacking up or something like that on the layovers. . . . They were more conservative. No question about that. And more loyal." Albrecht attributes their success as stewardesses partly to their overcoming their shyness (again, comparing them with others): "Most Nisei girls, most did not have truly outgoing personalities, because they were held back, being on the shyer side, than the Americans or the Germans or anything else. And they knew that, and had to make up for it. So the Japanese girls, they were always smiling, and very wanting obviously to be of help. It didn't take long for them to gain a reputation that was admirable. In fact, it made the whole crew work better. Because of how hard they worked. And how well they did their job." Albrecht, like Dunning, praises their work ethic. But he also perceives a racial and cultural link in the attitude with which they approached service. When asked what made the "Nisei" good stewardesses, he quickly answered, "Their personalities and their—excuse the expression—their subservient attitude."

Interestingly, this is exactly what one of the stewardesses told me when I asked about her on-the-job performance with Pan Am: "I think my cultural background helped me to be—subservient, I would say. You know, to listen to what other people wanted and to do what they wanted. I think my Japanese American background made me a better stewardess. Because being brought up in a Japanese culture, to serve other people—and this is the job of basically, at the time, of the stewardess, was to serve, and of course to be there for emergency, but to serve. . . . Well, as a stewardess, being subservient—I don't mean it in maybe the way that people have the connotation of it now. But subservient is more being polite and quietly doing something that is asked of you to do it. And I was raised that way. I had to do whatever my parents told me. And I was subservient to them in that sense" (PAA 1964–68). She also mentions briefly the "American" side of herself: "And the American side of me, I wasn't afraid to speak up." But it was the "subservience" that helped define and enact her job of serving passengers.

From any kind of feminist perspective (which this stewardess does not necessarily espouse), invoking "subservience" sounds demeaning. However, she uses "subservience" quite literally, to refer to the service that one provides to others, by placing oneself in a lower ("sub") position. She defines "subservience" as "being polite and quietly doing something that is asked of you." In this way "subservience" invokes the "emotional labor" of commercialized host-guest interactions analyzed by Hochschild (1983).

Subservience positions a person in a very specific relationship to authority and power, reifying overdetermined hierarchies: guest over host, male over female, older over younger, white over nonwhite, America over Japan. The overlapping predictability of these dualisms—made all the more powerful when the guest is an older, white American man served by a younger Japanese (American) woman—call out for comment. This loaded situation may be ameliorated by what the stewardess calls her American side, which she characterizes as outspoken and forthright. She thus presents subservience as a Japanese cultural position set against American practices of individuated resistance. Furthermore, subservience provides a racial and cultural model of service inextricably tied to gender as women wait on men. In short, subservience—whether discussed by Pan Am executives or stewardesses—summons the image of the exotic geisha, often erroneously perceived as the ultimate service worker.

Other women speak in similar racial and cultural terms, particularly invoking "Japanese culture" by way of their parents and upbringing. A woman from the first group recruited in 1955 explains (also invoking racial comparisons): "Our parents raised us to be humble. And I think it's not the Americans, but the Japanese who instill that. I kept hearing that nobody could do the job as well as the Nisei girls. And I kept hearing that over and over. Not just our first group, but all the girls that were hired. They said they could tell the difference between the Nisei girls and the *hakujin* [whites]" (PAA 1955–58). Hearing a stereotype "over and over" is exactly where racial and cultural reputations lie—in the self-prophesying realm of expectations. Those reputations ring particularly true when placed within the context of families, upbringing, and the transmission of cultural values. Another woman from the 1955 group recounts: "Our parents taught us so much, mainly to be humble, to just treat each other with respect and honor. No matter how old, you treat them equally, with love. And that's what it is all about. Everything has to come from your heart. And when I do anything, it's from my heart. And if I do it from my heart, I know it's the best I could do for people" (PAA 1955–57). This woman refers both to humility and sincerity—that is, doing something "from your heart"—as a legacy of cultural values. By invoking "our parents," she and others attribute this legacy of service to "Japanese culture."

One woman ties humility to empathy and the interpersonal sensitivity required of empathetic service: "My mother used to always say, 'You got to be humble.' And she says the Japanese people, they notice all these little things that most people don't" (PAA 1955–58). What they notice are other people's needs, at times even before these needs are expressed. This sensitivity to others requires constant vigilance, observing situations, noticing when someone's coffee is getting low, providing an extra pillow to someone who seems unable to sleep. As one Japanese national "Nisei" stewardess explains, "The essence of service is that you don't have to ask for anything" (PAA 1966–86). What she means is that the best kind of service does not merely respond to requests, but anticipates them.

Another woman talks about the lessons of humility and service that she learned when she went to Japan and attended a tea ceremony: "Serving can be very demeaning, especially when you're dealing with people who don't appreciate it. Well, in Japan I went to a tea ceremony, and it just opened my mind. It was the way tea was served. You are the honored guest and everything was so precious. The cup was an antique and it was being offered to you because you are an honored guest. Everything about that tea service made me think this is the way we should all behave on the airplane. It is not demeaning. It is a very honorable thing to serve someone in that way. And that helped me" (PAA 1960–69). She invokes the cultural lessons of Japan to elevate the practices of cabin service. At the same time, she admits to needing that kind of cultural prop to help her deal with the potentially "demeaning" aspects of the job.

Albrecht sums up the women's reputation in fairly crude racial and cultural terms, even as he intends to be complimentary: "All that bowing down. It's typical of Japanese. Respecting old age and power. So they were more subservient. The haoles wouldn't be that way. But the local girls would show their birthright, so to speak. Maybe that's the reason they were liked so much. You could tell they were sincere. They worked hard. Outstanding! They had an outstanding reputation. From the captain of the airplane right on down to people like myself that worked with them." The "outstanding reputation" serves as a racial banner for these "Nisei" stewardesses, adding, in Albrecht's words, their "subservience" to the already gendered service of the flight attendant. Gender and racial stereotypes reinforce one another in the "Nisei" stewardess, the loyal, empathetic, sincere, industrious, uncomplaining workhorse of in-flight hostess duties.

Not all the hostess duties were in-flight. "Nisei" stewardesses, like Pan American stewardesses elsewhere, were frequently called upon for promotional work. If a stewardess was particularly photogenic, she might be called on for publicity shoots in magazines, newspapers, or print advertisements. Given the high-profile nature of the job, "Nisei" stewardesses and others became accustomed to representing the company,[3] the profession, and sometimes the nation. Being placed in a prestigious spotlight as a company representative tended to defuse criticism and instill pride. Some stewardesses were called on for special promotional flights: press and travel agent tours, publicity round-the-world tours, flights with the presidential press corps, or chartered flights by heads of state, such as President Sukarno of Indonesia. Other stewardesses played hostess to travel agents and politicians. One woman flew promotional flights called "West Coast Fly-Ins" to thirteen United States cities in 1968 with sales managers, travel agents, and teachers,[4] during which the airline displayed just "how international" it was in racial terms: "On the flights we'd fly them around, we'd serve them champagne, while they were on board, we did announcements, I did a Japanese announcement. We had a Japanese girl who was in kimono. She was a flight attendant from Japan, and it was just to show how international we were. So the crew was made up of various people that were international. We served champagne, and then we flew around and came back and dropped them off. It was kinda fun. We had a Hawaiian singer on the ground, so while people were waiting to board the flight, he was performing. And there was a hula dancer, too, so she performed" (PAA 1964–86). "Nisei" stewardesses added one more racial element—along with Hawaiian singers and hula dancers—to Pan Am's cosmopolitan spectacle of hospitality.

Although stewardesses in general were part of Pan Am's promotional practices, there was a particular quality to parading Asian (American) women. They became part of an exotic spectacle that gave further proof of Pan Am's mastery of "the world." Rachel Sherman's study of luxury hotels in the United States demonstrates a parallel process, as the hotels displayed the racial diversity of their service personnel (2007, 73). The position mattered: a Filipina maid, for example, did not necessarily enhance a hotel's reputation; however, a well-groomed, knowledgeable Filipina behind the front desk could be a point of corporate pride. It was more than a hotel's or airline's pride that was at stake. By demonstrating the professionalism of its multiracial personnel, a company could claim that it had either been able to hire the best, or that its superior training could transform a person of color into one who could equal even the whitest. Pan Am had a parallel system of prestige, displaying its multiracial, multinational reach in terms of personnel and destinations. In this "Nisei" stewardesses as women "of color but not colored" played a particular role.

Gina Marchetti's analysis of the rise of Asian American female newscasters on American television has parallels with Pan Am as well: "For many in the Asian American community, this figure of the successful female newscaster has come to embody a new bent on racist representations of Asian Americans as the 'model minority.' . . . By making the representative of the 'model minority' female, a continuing specular fascination with Asian women can be coupled with the promotion of this image as both an advance for gender as well as racial liberalization" (1993, 216). Like the Asian (American) newscaster of the 1990s, the jetsetting stewardess of the 1950s and 1960s acknowledged the gaze upon them, but then proceeded to break the geisha mold, looking beyond home and asserting identities no longer tethered to men.[5]

Pan Am's promotional spectacle unfolded on both sides of the Pacific. In the early days of the "Nisei" stewardess program, Japanese media trailed the women like celebrities. One woman from the first group remembers: "I had to go on this shopping spree [in Tokyo for the press]. So I had to put on my uniform and they took pictures of me shopping. I would go and look at these beautiful kimonos and they're taking pictures of me" (PAA 1955–58). This staged shopping spree revealed some of the fascinations constructed by the Japanese press: a Japanese American woman from Hawai`i in the uniform of a prestigious American company engaged in a "typical" Japanese activity—shopping for a kimono.[6] Given the time—ten years after the end of the Second World War—a photograph such as this encapsulated an important moment for the Japanese public. It was a moment that enacted Japan's global worthiness, as well as signifying the bridge that Japanese Americans were supposed to represent, all contained within the Pan Am uniform. Clearly "Nisei" stewardesses presented a complex international photo-op for Pan Am, the United States, Japan, and Hawai`i.

One stewardess who began flying in the mid-1960s explains how Pan Am invested time in local social and educational institutions, from elementary schools to the University of Hawai`i. No school or club was too small to ignore as a potential promotional site. She writes in a letter: "PAA [Pan Am] flight service department, unlike other airlines, was a part of marketing. PAA used us as a marketing tool effectively. I participated in a career workshop, [University of Hawai`i] 1965 with my supervisor. . . . I was also asked with a Filipina from Honolulu to work a 707 flight [Honolulu] to Hilo. It was the opening of the Hilo International Lyman Airport, 1964 or '65. PAA in those days had a very high profile among the airlines serving Hawaii. . . . I used to also give talks at junior high school and elementary school on my travel experiences wearing my uniform and even to some ladies' social clubs" (PAA 1964–68, 1980–86; 19 June 2005). These promotional activities kept women busy even when they were not flying, thus blurring the boundary between on- and off-duty, since it seemed that the women were always on call.

In fact, some were. The sales department kept a list of "house calls"— stewardesses they could call and ask if they would be willing to make a promotional appearance. Women on the house call list were known to be congenial, flexible, responsible, and generally reliable. In the words of one stewardess from Honolulu: "I was on that list, and was called often to appear at various engagements. Once I even flew to Chicago to promote Pan Am and travel to Hawai`i. Another time, while on a five-day layover in Manila, the Rotary Club asked if some Pan Am stewardesses could appear at their function in uniform" (PAA 1968–86). Working these "house call" and other engagements was voluntary and at times unpaid. In many cases the women would be compensated by a free meal, free trip, or some other form of flexible in-kind payment. One "Nisei" stewardess from the 1950s through the 1970s who was called on frequently for promotional work says she was sometimes paid for appearing at events: $25 an hour for a minimum of four hours, no matter how long the event. In her mind, this kind of work was not only enjoyable but lucrative.

Ernie Albrecht, informally (and affectionately) called "Mr. Pan Am" and even "Father" by the stewardesses, describes how he relied upon the promotional services of "Nisei" women as a group: "I used ["Nisei" stewardesses] promotionally. I had a pretty large office in the Pan Am building [in

Honolulu] . . . and I had a boardroom attached to my personal office. . . . And I would invite people like the governor [of Hawai'i] and the mayor [of Honolulu], and generals . . . for luncheon. The commissary at the airport would furnish a first-class meal, and I would have our "Nisei" girls serve it, like stewardesses in my boardroom." Albrecht calls these off-board duties "extracurricular," praising the "Nisei" stewardesses for their willingness to put in the extra time, gratis: "Of those that were willing to do extracurricular duties, so to speak, the Japanese were by far the most willing. Not caring about the dollar, but sincerely trying to help the company. . . . For instance, that luncheon type of a thing. I would have three girls there, and they would do it on their own time. And those that I took around to Japanese [travel] agents and big shots, would also do it on their time. But I also saw to it that our local man, Bob Nichols, would keep them in line as applied to giving them extra time to make up for it." Part of what Albrecht valued about these activities is that they were done in the spirit of cooperation rather than as contractual work. That the stewardesses were informally compensated through other kinds of adjustments to their schedule demonstrates that promotional activities were part of a shadow economy of time, work, flexible perquisites, and a generalized spirit of being a team player, at which "Nisei" stewardesses excelled.

One non-"Nisei" stewardess who describes herself as a "loud-mouthed haole" cynically observed: "The local management [older white men] DEFINITELY took advantage, and assigned ["Nisei" stewardesses] to all sort of local marketing events. And I do mean ASSIGNED" (PAA 1965–86; e-mail, 28 February 2007). She interpreted the treatment and expectations of "Nisei" stewardesses by haole management as exploitation. However, this kind of critical view is nearly absent among the "Nisei" stewardesses I interviewed. What was less important than the labor and time for them was the acceptance of company goals as their own (discussed further in chapter 5). This kind of value system takes work out of a rationalized, capitalist framework and into the realm of subjective commitment, company loyalty, and an assumed level of workers' initiative and agency. Few employees expressed the potential for exploitation in a paternalistic system that might have thwarted their relationship with their employer.

PROBLEMS ON THE RACIAL FRONTIER:
STRESS, DISCRIMINATION, HARASSMENT

All was not necessarily rosy on the job front. "Nisei" women shared with other stewardesses various problems and personal adjustments, from physical illness to loneliness to being away from home to the emotional depletion from days of smiling. As one woman recalls, "Whenever I came in from a flight, my mother would ask me, "Why do you look so glum? You just never smile." And I said, 'Mom, after smiling for all these hours . . .' It was so hard for her to accept, because she heard that we were so friendly. And yet when we came home, we didn't have any smiles left" (PAA 1955–58).

This is the "emotion work" that Arlie Hochschild discusses (1983), compounded by cultural norms of gendered pleasantry and a certain performative "niceness" (Yano 2006). Another stewardess agrees, "The constant exposure to people can be really, really too much after a while" (PAA 1966–86).

Given the longevity of many of the women's careers, most managed to juggle the pressures of such constant public exposure. However, sometimes particularly demanding passengers required a particularly astute—and in one case culturally indulgent—response: "I had one couple in First Class, and the female said, 'Oh, my husband doesn't talk to servants.' So it kind of took me aback. And I went, 'O.K., so what does your husband want to eat?' [Laughs] They were Chinese from Hong Kong. . . . If it's a foreign person, you take it with a grain of salt, and you humble yourself" (PAA 1968–86). The women quickly learned that arrogance is not a white preserve and easily crossed racial lines. In fact, sometimes it was Asian-to-Asian arrogance that became the most demeaning, as I discuss later. In these instances the Asian (American) stewardess could be mistaken for one's personal maid.

Managing the many on-job demands extended to one's home life. As someone concerned with both safety and service, a stewardess had to be in control of the cabin. People's lives depended on it. With this kind of job socialization, some women with families felt the need to retain cabin-like order at home as well. One "Nisei" stewardess confesses: "I went through a period where I suffered from panic and anxiety attacks. And I found out consequent to my episode, that a lot of other flight attendants, even male flight attendants, suffer. It's the lifestyle. I'm convinced it's the lifestyle, because when you're gone for a period of time and you have a family, you have to make sure that things will go smoothly while you're gone. . . . And you become where you organize your life so much. You organize your life ahead of time so that things will go smoothly while you're gone. When I went to see my psychologist, he said, 'Oh, you're a classic A-type personality.' [Laughs] Control, that's exactly what it is. . . . I was always a very laid-back kind of person. But the job made me into an A-type personality" (PAA 1966–86). The "A-type personality" of which she speaks may be endemic to the job—that is, working in a position that runs on tight schedules, requires a high degree of organization, calls for multiple tasking, holds responsibility for other people's lives, and mixes in a certain amount of danger, risk, and unpredictability. This kind of problem is not necessarily specific to "Nisei" stewardesses, but it gains particular poignancy for Japanese American women from Hawai`i whose earlier socialization placed little emphasis or value upon an "A-type" lifestyle. This was not the safe, secure, *heibon* (ordinary) life emphasized by their families (Yano 2006b, 242).

The racialized position of the "Nisei" stewardess came with its own problems. Isolation was structured into the position, as the "Nisei" stewardess alone remained with the airplane circling the globe: "Loneliness was a big problem that we encountered. We used to have thirteen-day [round-the-world] trips, and we were the only ones [that were not part of a changing crew]. . . . And if you're not really sociable, like, oh, they invite you to a crew party and you say, 'Oh, no thank you.' It got really lonesome" (PAA 1964–68). Even after "Nisei" stewardesses made friends with members of the changing crew, the experience of loneliness indelibly sticks in many women's minds. They became accustomed to doing things by themselves— eating meals, shopping, walking around a foreign city. This kind of independence was a particularly big step for "Nisei" stewardesses, given a cultural norm of sociality, especially for women.

One sticking point for many was being assigned to work in the first-class galley, where one would have to cook (and later reheat) food, "plate" the dishes, and generally assume the duties of the kitchen. Although some women preferred such work, others felt that the "Nisei" stewardesses faced an inordinate amount of time assigned to the galley. One woman explains:

> Although we were supposed to rotate duties, we ["Nisei" stewardesses] always
> ended up working the first-class galley. So we became very good at it. But I used

to think, "How can that possibly be? There was another Japanese flight attendant working the first-class galley the leg before!" [Laughs] That was the least desirable position, because it's so much work. Because of the way the presentation of the food had to be, all the different courses and things. We also took care of the cockpit, and it was a lot of work. So in that way, they never were overtly discriminatory, but I think sometimes they were. Because of [the accusation of racial discrimination], they said the Japanese flight attendants were not to work the galley, because they are supposed to be in the cabin conversing with the passengers. I think some of [the non-Japanese stewardesses] resented that—that we were not allowed to work the galley for a period of time. (PAA 1966–86)

Either way, the "Nisei" stewardesses were treated as a group—both when they were repeatedly assigned first-class galley work and when they were not allowed to do "kitchen duty."

The issue of racial discrimination also came up with shared hotel rooms, common for layovers during the 1950s and 1960s. In several cases "Nisei" stewardesses encountered reluctance on the part of other women: "I remember sharing a room in Copenhagen with a flight attendant who was obviously upset because I was going to be her roommate. I could hear her conversation, saying that the beds are too close. She said it should be somebody neater, somebody—. And here I worked with her onboard the flights. I could not believe it. . . . There were some Europeans who felt that the Japanese were a lower class. Or Asians period. Because they were colonial, from those colonial empires" (PAA 1964–86). However another woman admits her own prejudice when faced with the possibility of sharing a room with an African American: "In 1967 or 1968, they started hiring African Americans. It was a big shock to all of us. We still had that mentality, I have to say—'Do I have to room with a black girl, a Negro girl?'" (PAA 1960–69). Thus the racial frontier broached by working for Pan Am challenged the "Nisei" stewardesses in multiple ways.

The one woman who spoke most openly of racial discrimination said that she quit her job with Pan Am because of it. She explains that she was sensitized to issues of race and discrimination—including from other Japanese Americans—from her personal experience of internment during the Second World War, because of her father's position as a Japanese-language teacher: "I think that being in [internment] camp, I think maybe influenced me a little bit. Because we're citizens, we were discriminated on and all, and even when we came back [to Hawai`i], the Japanese [Americans] here discriminated [against] us because we were in camp. We were not desirable citizens. And also, before we went to camp, we had the Japanese [American] people here spying on us, too, 'cause we weren't allowed to speak the language and all that. . . . So I think maybe having that experience, being in camp, coming out, and having people call you 'Jap' and all that. . . . I think maybe that has a lot to do with how I perceive things and how I am maybe a little more sensitive than the others about the way people treat me" (PAA 1957–60). With her keen awareness of racial discrimination, this steward-ess noticed every slight, every slur. So she did the unthinkable: she staged her own personal sit-down: "[The white stewardesses] treated me as though I was sort of a lower, second class. . . . . Somehow they expected me, as an Asian, to do more work. Once I wasn't feeling well and I told the purser, 'I'm not going to be on par, so you'll just have to bear with me.' And then she kept pushing me, pushing me, and then finally I told her, 'You know, I worked all these years. You're treating me as though I don't know any-thing. So I resent that very much.' So afterward, on the flight back from Bangkok, I said, 'You work the flight. I'm going to sit down. I'm not going to work with you.' She never expected that from me, from an Asian" (PAA 1957–60). Interestingly, this stewardess credits Pan Am with teaching her how to be independent and stand up for her rights. "That's what Pan Am taught me—how to be strong. I was never like that before. I was always, 'Yes, okay, fine, I'll be helpful.' And I had to be strong to say, 'No, I'm not working this flight home. You can report me and that's fine.' I knew they needed Japanese stewardesses. They couldn't fly without me; they didn't have enough 'Nisei' stewardesses. . . . And do you know that her whole atti-tude changed after that? I became a person that could do no wrong" (PAA 1957–60). I asked the stewardess whether she felt that she could complain to the union about her treatment, but she said that she felt the union would not be responsive, because it consisted entirely of whites. "We had a union, but they wouldn't have helped me. At that time [in the 1950s], they never dealt with racial things, 'cause they were all *hakujin* [white people], and if I were treated like that on the flight, then I don't see how the union would have treated me any differently" (PAA 1957–60). In the end the stewardess decided to return to nursing, with a bitter parting thought: "I felt like a ser-vant for all, crew and all" (PAA 1957–60). Among all my interviewees, she was unusual for speaking so critically of her experience of flying.

A different kind of racial (and sexual) discrimination occurred with Japanese nationals as passengers. Seeing the Japanese faces of "Nisei" stewardesses, they tended to treat them as they would have treated female servers in Japan: by being highly demanding, to the point of rudeness. Of course rudeness was not a preserve of Japanese men—white men and women could be extremely unmannerly, especially when drunk. But the treatment of Japanese American women by Japanese men took on a particular cultural, even transnational, spin. Many "Nisei" women reacted with patient indulgence: "I had a little difficult time with the Japanese nationals. Their customs are a little different, which I wasn't accustomed to, where you know, the men snapped their fingers. At first I was very offended. But then I said, 'Well, that's the way to get my attention. Well, so be it'" (PAA 1955–58). However, another woman who flew in the late 1950s reacted more like an American: "The Japanese passengers, the men folks, would kind of put you down and say, 'Do this!' and order you around. [She demonstrates by snapping her fingers.] Yes, exactly, and then they never said, 'Thank you.' They would say, 'Peel this for me,' and 'Do this,' and 'Do that.' They never had to peel oranges before, and so they expected me to peel it. And I would say, 'Well, if you're going to America, you're going to have to learn how to peel your own orange. And this is how you do it.' [Laughs] Well, they had never had anything like that happen before, and they said, 'Ohhh.' They were shocked, I'm sure" (PAA 1957–60). One woman from the 1960s and 1970s cries out in exasperation, recounting the demanding, sexist behavior of a Japanese passenger: "He wanted me to peel his grapes for him. That was because the image of the Japanese geisha type. His friend said, 'He wants you to peel his grapes,' and I looked at his friend and I said, 'Excuse me, I don't do grapes. Is he serious?' And he said, 'Well, it could be just like a geisha house in Tokyo'" (PAA 1966–86). In fact, true geisha did not "do grapes" either. However this kind of anecdote highlights how the geisha stereotype—here invoked by a Japanese man—filled mythic fantasies far exceeding the realities of the role. The aircraft was obviously not a geisha house, and at least some women refused to make it into one. They refused to be geishaed, by Japanese nationals or anyone else.

One "Nisei" stewardess explains how Japanese men treated women differently, depending on whether they looked ethnically Japanese. For these men the Japanese American stewardess became the in-house sounding board—or worse—to which they could take all their complaints: "The Japanese businessmen knew we were Japanese [ethnically], and they took it out on us, any of their problems. They were really nice to the non-Japanese, but they would take it out on us. You know, if they complained about something, instead of complaining to the person who offended them, no, they would want to talk to us. And then they would rant and rave. I didn't like that. I heard stories where the passenger [a Japanese national] was angry at the Japanese flight attendant. He stuck his leg out purposely. I knew he put it out purposely. To hurt her, because he was so mad. The girl almost fell over" (PAA 1968–86). The flight crew seemed to know what to expect of belligerent Japanese businessmen, so some even manipulated the situation accordingly. A Chinese stewardess recounts:

> Yeah, Japanese [American] girls were harassed by the Japanese passengers. The Japanese passengers are usually guys, and so in those days, when the Japanese passengers harassed the Japanese [American] flight attendants, the purser would say, "Alright, get me a couple of yellow-hair, blue-eyed girls down here." And then once the blonde [stewardesses] come back [to the area], the whole manner of the Japanese passengers changed. It was so funny to see. They became very docile and they would do whatever you asked them to do. And if you said, "No more drinking, stop now," they would stop. But if it's a Japanese [American stewardess, the Japanese male passengers] would give her a tongue lashing to the point where the girls were in tears. Sometimes they think I'm Japanese, so I would write "Chinese" in *kanji* [ideographs] and tape it to my apron. And then the Japanese [American] girls would say, "Oh write for me too, please." [Laughs] They would tape it on their aprons. It was so funny. (PAA 1961–64, 1977–86)

Thus the worst thing for a stewardess was to be mistaken for a Japanese (American) woman. If "Nisei" stewardesses could have donned a blond wig, then their problems would have been solved.

The mistreatment by Japanese male passengers often devolved into sexual harassment: "The Japanese [male] passengers tend to be the ones who would sexually harass you more [than white male passengers]. Especially being a Japanese [American] flight attendant. They always touched our backside to get our attention. I think that's maybe just their mannerism. But initially, it's such a shock. It's like, 'Don't do that! You can't do that!' [Laughs] Yeah, they [gestures] . . . on the bottom, trying to get your attention. Yeah, they're tapping us on the butt. That used to upset me, but after a while, it was like, you know, 'Oh, you idiot.' [Laughs] A lot of times you just think, 'Well, they're just ignorant or uneducated. Country people.' Of course we had it more on the Osaka trips. You know, the older person from the country. As opposed to being from Tokyo where people are a bit more sophisticated" (PAA 1968–86). The woman's response—"Oh, you idiot"— emasculates the "butt tapper," whom she dismisses as a country bumpkin. In these ways she delimits sexual harassment as the mark of an older, rural, unsophisticated man from Japan.

When I interviewed "Nisei" stewardesses I always asked about sexual harassment, especially given the coffee-tea-or-me notoriety of the profession. But aside from a few responses—including stories of Japanese butt tappers, of a near-rape in Beirut, and of an occasional straying (older, white) married pilot—most stewardesses claim to have experienced little or no harassment. One story emerges about the notoriety of older, white pilots: "I was really shocked. After the flight the pilot came to my room and he was lying on my bed. I don't know what he was expecting. Finally I said, 'You have to get out of here.' I was so scared" (PAA 1957–86). But a story like this is rare.

Of course issues such as sexual harassment must be historically constituted. As many of the women said laughingly, "We never even heard that expression in those days." The women rationalized joking innuendos, the playful, leering glances by pursers, the captains' after-flight cocktail parties, the supposed girdle checks by pursers and pilots (discussed in chapter 5), and the flirtations of drunk passengers as simply "the way things were." The women laughed off these incidents as "innocent," and for the most part they were—that is, in general the women's safety was not threatened and neither were their jobs or their advancement within the company. However, the everyday sexual practices that one era considers innocent are considered unacceptable in another, more conscious era. As Albrecht says, the "Nisei" women in general were "conservative"; they "weren't shacking up or something like that on the layovers."

Whereas the women tended to normalize heterosexual advances—playful or not—they demonized homosexual ones. These are the ones that stuck out in women's memories. Of the thirty-four women I interviewed, five mentioned lesbian harassment. For the most part, the encounter was with a European, either a fellow stewardess or a purser. What is more important, in every case the encounter was a total surprise to the "Nisei" herself; most were slow to even recognize the advance as a lesbian one. Here is one woman's story:

I was so naïve at that time. I was still on probation and on probation you can be fired any time. The purser was Scandinavian and I noticed during the flight, she kept on brushing up against me. And I thought, you know, I was so young then . . . But it didn't hit me, and she kept on. And after the flight—this was in San Francisco—she said, "Let's have dinner together." And I said, "Are you kidding? I'm just a bit tired. I'm going to go to bed," because I was flying out the next morning. And I didn't think about it. I got to my room, and there was a bouquet. It wasn't a teeny one. It was huge! I remember it was purple, lavender, and it was huge, sitting in my room. And I thought, "Is it my birthday? No, it's not my birthday." It was from her! And I thought, "Gee, I must be a great stewardess. Wait until I go home to tell mom about this. I must be really good. I'll get an A+," because the pursers had to write reports about us. So when I came back to Honolulu, I talked to some of the other flight attendants, and they just laughed and said, "She's a lesbian." I said, "What??? No wonder she gave me that bouquet and wanted to have dinner with me!" And that was it. I never saw her again. (PAA 1965–86)

Several other flight attendants commented anecdotally on the number of gays in the business (see chapter 1). One former steward from the 1940s notes: "I can't speak for other industries, because I don't know, but there were a pretty high percentage of homosexuals in the airlines. And incidentally, not to just talk about the [male] pursers and stewards, but in the cockpit too." He does not recall hearing of any kind of discrimination against them; rather, he says that as long as they did their job, the airline did not care about their sexual orientation.

"Nisei" stewardesses seem to have taken the lesbian advances in stride as another eye opener in the new "frontier" world in which they were now flying. In the minds of the "Nisei" women, lesbianism and the freer sexuality that it encoded may have seemed not only "perverse" but also slightly "sophisticated," given that the women making the advances were typically Europeans. However, this was not the kind of sophistication to which "Nisei" aspired. Sexuality was a different kind of borderline that reinforced the separation between them (Europeans) and us (Japanese and Japanese Americans). Like the practice of sleeping in the nude, which several women observed among European stewardesses, homosexuality may not have been part of Japanese (American) upbringing, but it opened the eyes of "Nisei" stewardesses to cultural difference. Like some of the foods they tried while flying around the world, homosexuality may not have been quite to their taste, but it suggested the variety of practices around the world, and being exposed to it made them more worldly. It reminded them that practices, knowledge, and foods are embedded within a global hierarchy of cultural capital and prestige. Within that hierarchy, things European carried their own unmistakable stamp of worldliness.

PROXIMAL PRESTIGE: LEARNING, BORROWING, TRYING ON RACE AND CLASS PERFORMANCES

For many "Nisei" stewardesses from Hawai`i, flying for Pan American was the first time that they were in such close and continuous proximity to white culture and the wealthy. The leaps for some were manifold: they were leaving behind Hawai`i or their hometowns, establishing close and continuing contact with American white culture, traveling outside the United States, forming connections with Europeans and nonwhites, including Japanese nationals, and becoming part of Pan Am's corporate culture. Each of these leaps offered lessons and required adjustments.

These leaps gave the "Nisei" stewardesses the opportunity to learn, borrow, and imitate—as well as reject—racial and class performances that seemed to spell prestige. What they gained was "proximal prestige." Pan Am enabled them to act like jetsetters, not necessarily by acquiring wealth but by exposure to the customers they served, the lodging where they were housed, and the off-hours lifestyle of their overseas layovers. Proximal prestige further complicates their purported "subservience": even as the job disciplined these women to embody hierarchical service (that is, to place themselves below those whom they served), that service became the source of their own status elevation.

Through Pan Am the women learned about first-class foods that some had never eaten: caviar, rack of lamb, squab, turtle soup, oysters Rockefeller, baked Alaska, Cornish game hen, moussaka, and an assortment of cheeses (most only previously knew of American cheese). They did not necessarily like everything they tried, but eating fine food gave the women a taste of whiteness and the upper classes. One thing they knew was that this was not the food of their homes. They marveled at Pan Am's array of hors d'oeuvres. One stewardess exclaimed: "Hors d'oeuvres! It seems so common now, but hors d'oeuvres were so—. When we took out the cart of hors d'oeuvres, there would be just a whole assortment of the most delicious things on it" (PAA 1963–69). Another stewardess sums it up: "It just opened up my eyes . . . I lived such a sheltered life that flying just kind of opened a whole new world to me. Flying to the different countries and meeting different people, seeing how they lived. Even the food they ate was different. It was an eye opener. Not only that, but at that time, Pan Am was *the* airline. So when we went through training, we had to know that red wine goes with meat, and vodka goes with caviar, and white wine goes with fish, and the different types of cheeses, and caviar. I'd never heard of caviar before I worked for Pan Am. So it was just tremendous learning" (PAA 1964–86). The women talk about exotic foods, peoples, and experiences as key elements of their own new frontier, moving beyond a "sheltered life" to "a whole new world." This was a world defined by the intertwined hierarchies of race and class.

Some of the lessons were learned by casting sideways glances at first-class passengers. One flight attendant from the 1960s learned how to eat an orange by watching a first-class passenger cut off the ends of the fruit, score it, peel it, then eat the segments. By watching passengers she and others learned how to hold and use a fork and knife in the European style, how to take bites of the right size, how to refrain from making noise while eating, how to carry on a table conversation, how to pace oneself while eating, and how to maintain the correct posture. There may have been acceptable cultural differences in all these practices, but the lessons that mattered were those coded as (European) upper-class practices.

The woman also learned how to drink, or at least about the culture of "first-class" alcoholic drinks. For the most part the women did not know much about alcohol, except beer and Japanese sake. One stewardess from 1964 recalls: "To this day I do not drink, so for me the hardest part of training was remembering how to mix drinks" (PAA 1964–86). Another woman humorously describes her first encounter with alcohol: "I was still in training [in San Francisco] and we went out to dinner downstairs in the restaurant, and the waiter asked, 'Cocktail?' So I said, 'Oh, yeah.' And then he's standing around and waiting, and he said, 'Well, what would you prefer?' And I'm thinking he meant fruit cocktail. [Laughs] So he said, 'Would it be a Manhattan or martini?' So I trusted him and said, 'One of those.' I wasn't used to liquor. I took a sip and I said, 'This is it?' I would have preferred the fruit cocktail" (PAA 1955–57). The lessons of alcohol service were difficult for women who drank little or not at all. Many of them hardly knew or tasted what they served.

As one stewardess succinctly put it, "It was like a classroom in the air" (PAA 1964–86). The "teachers" were primarily white, first-class passengers: "People, particularly in first class, everyone was well groomed. No sandals, no slippers. Most of the men wore suits, and the women wore maybe a suit or a dress, hat, and gloves. Traveling was expensive, so it was only an élite group who could afford in most cases to travel. So they dressed really nicely. It was really first class" (PAA 1964–86). Stewardesses could learn some practical lessons: "I wasn't exactly watching [first-class passengers], but I would notice them. Once we had this movie star on board and I noticed how she—I can just picture her—how she slept on that flight. She had her head up and she just slept like this [imitates someone sitting upright]. And I thought to myself, 'So that's how you're supposed to sleep'" (PAA 1963–69). What gave these lessons particular force was the relative class position of the passenger-teachers. Although many of the stewardesses came from middle- or upper-middle-class families, the first-class passengers were from an even higher, moneyed stratum. Furthermore, unlike the "Nisei" stewardesses the great majority of first-class passengers were white. Thus eating an orange, holding a fork and knife, or sleeping in a particular position represented not only one way to do something but the "supposed-to" way derived from social class in combination with race. These were lessons from people in power, and were thus lessons *of* power. One stewardess sums it up: "It opened up a totally new and different way of life. Especially to see the first-class service and first-class passengers, because this was nothing that I would have ever seen if I had just stayed in Hawai`i. It was really mind opening" (PAA 1964–86).

Lessons came from other flight attendants as well. Several women noted that many of their co-workers were from wealthy East Coast, European, and later Asian families: "I met some wealthy young ladies from Europe who said, 'I guess I have to do something because I can't go skiing all year round. So I decided to join Pan Am.' And I thought, 'My goodness! I had to work. We lived on a budget, we had hard times, and here I'm sitting next to these gals who had servants and who decided to fly for the fun of it, for the experience of it'" (PAA 1965–86). She remarked upon the disparity between her own class position and that of well-to-do stewardesses, seemingly biding their time until they got married and quit. The worst offenders were some

of the wealthy Asians who flew in later years. One woman relates incredu-
lously: "When we opened the Singapore base in the 1980s, the gals that
were hired at first were all from very wealthy Chinese families, and it was
really funny because after a few months, they decided that this is servant's
work. [Laughs] Like what their maids do in their homes—some of them had
personal maids. And one of the trainers told me, I couldn't believe it, one of
the [Singapore] flight attendants said, 'If I can't make it on my flight, can I
send my maid over, because I let her try on my uniform and it fits perfectly.'
We were just so floored" (PAA 1965–86). What apparently surprised some
of the upper-class hires was that this was a serious job that required more
than fitting a uniform.

The attitudes of "Nisei" women toward European stewardesses in general bears some analysis. Although being European in itself does not con-
note a particular class position, for Americans during this period European
culture—distilled as a unitary set of practices and beliefs from a variety of
cultures in Europe—epitomized "class." The "Pan Am Way" incorporated
this assumption through food, wine, and the hiring of European women.
Thus for many "Nisei" (and others), European stewardesses were seen as
a site of sophistication. To one stewardess who grew up in a rural area of
the island of O'ahu, "Oh, the European girls were supremely sophisticated
and you learned a lot from them, about clothing and food and just manner-
isms, the way they ate, you know, with the fork and the knife, and I wanted
to emulate that. And their mentality. I just admire them. There's something about the Europeans, especially the Swedish girls, and a core of self-
confidence that they had. It's a different mind set, I think. They just seemed
to be more aware of things happening in the world" (PAA 1960–69). The
European was thus a model not only for clothing, food, and manners but,
more important, for psychological well-being, confidence, and maturity.
This went beyond class to "a core of self-confidence" and an awareness
of the world; in short, European women acted like "sophisticated adults."
Given the many embedded leaps that "Nisei" stewardesses had made (from
Hawai'i to the continental United States to Europe and Asia), their own cul-
tural distance from European women seemed vast.

Class positions became further blurred with the possibility of interpersonal connections between cabin crew and passengers. During this period
of air travel, and especially before the arrival of the jumbo jets in 1969,
passengers and stewardesses could engage in far more personalized inter-

action, which sometimes resulted in true friendships, particularly with re-peat customers: "I have some very good friends that I met [while flying]. I was their stewardess on a flight from Japan to Hawai`i, and they're my friends 'til today. In fact, I'm part of their family. They're Jewish from Los Angeles, and they used to come to Hawai`i often. They would invite me to dinner. After they got off their flight in Hawai`i and went through Cus-toms, they said, 'We're staying here. Why don't you come out to dinner with us?' So I went, and we were friends from then on" (PAA 1964–86). She was not alone. Other stewardesses I interviewed spoke fondly of forming long-lasting friendships with passengers (including romance, which I discuss below). One can only reflect poignantly on that possibility given the imper-sonal nature of contemporary air travel.

Forming friendships with customers could result in class ambiguities. The job allowed stewardesses to rub shoulders with the élite whom they served. Class confusions between server and served were sometimes real. One stewardess recounts incidents while working on separate charters with the imperial family of Japan and President Sukarno of Indonesia: "They had charters—President Sukarno, the king and queen of Siam, the royal family of Japan—and I was always on the flights. We went to Istanbul with the royal family of Japan, and they—the Istanbul people—gave a party. These people thought I was one of the royal family. [Laughs] I thought that was the fun-niest thing that ever happened. But they were very, very nice. I said, 'No, I'm just a stewardess.' [Laughs] So everybody got invited. And with Presi-dent Sukarno, we went to Indonesia, we went to their palace and stayed at the palace. Yes, in Bali. He had a beautiful palace in Bali and we were there for a week. As a stewardess! Would you believe? [Laughs]" (PAA 1955–86). The stewardess laughs in disbelief that she, a stewardess from an immi-grant family, could be hobnobbing with emperors and presidents. This kind of blurred boundary was something that Pan Am cultivated and encour-aged. It added to the airline's prestige that its stewardesses could be seen socializing with the élite of the world. And the stewardesses often did. One "Nisei" stewardess recounts a humorous tale: "When we were in London, our crew decided that we would go and see a play. And after the production, we decided we would have dinner. And a very nice man came, a gentleman joined us, and asked if he could buy us dinner. And I'm still a young, inno-cent girl from Maui, and I thought, 'Oh, I don't know if this is really right to do.' And so I asked one of the girls, I said, 'Do you think it's safe to have dinner with this old man?' And she said, 'Don't worry, he's an M.P.' And I thought, 'Oh, that's right. There's nothing to worry about. He's a military police.' So we were having a very nice dinner, and he gave us his card. And it was at that point that I learned he was a member of Parliament, and that's what M.P. was in London [Laughs]" (PAA 1963–69). Thus members of Parliament joined emperors and presidents in surrounding themselves with Pan Am stewardesses, and "Nisei" were among them.

These blurrings raise the question of the women's interpretations of their own class position. Did they believe that cavorting in palaces made them, in effect, princesses? Did engaging in the practices of the upper class seduce them into believing they were a part of it? For the most part, the women I spoke with had no such beliefs. Here is one woman's reaction: "Pan Am taught me how to be in a better society, you know, really polished. You get into a society that you don't normally go. You get to know the other side of the fence. Not that you want to belong there, but you get to see it, and I think it gives you a little bit more confidence to get into the world, to be able to talk to people, and not to be so withdrawn. . . . High society people. I don't really care to be one. I just like to stay the way I am. . . . [The other people] think I'm rich, and that makes me laugh, because I'm not. I like good clothes. I always did. But yeah, they think I'm rich" (PAA 1955–86). In this woman's interpretation Pan Am gave her access and the social tools to feel comfortable interacting with the élite. But she readily admits that she is not one of the élite and would not even like to be one of them. By enjoying some of the perquisites of the élite (nice clothes, good food, international travel) while rejecting the identity and its responsibilities, she asserts her own agency in the midst of powerful seductions.

One question remains: How much leeway did these women have in handling the race- and class-lessons of the airplane? The Cuban sociologist Fernando Ortiz proposes the term "transculturation" for the process by which a subordinate group does not merely adopt the norms of the dominant group but selects and sometimes invents materials from a dominant group (quoted in Pratt 1992, 6). To a certain extent, the women who flatly reject the identity of the élite engage in a form of selective appropriation— that is, transculturation. For most "Nisei" women, however, the standards of the dominant group were integral to a job that paid them to acculturate to a new class position. More accurately, the job required them to perform that acculturation before an audience of management, other stewardesses, passengers, and the general public. They did not necessarily perform as "heiresses" but as accomplished servers or even hostesses to heiresses (and heirs). This audience assessed the women's performance of the race- and class-lessons of the airplane, limiting the possibilities of transculturation to her off-duty life.

SKY HIGH ROMANCE: MARRYING UP, MOVING OUT, OR STAYING PUT

What blurred the boundary of class positions even further were the many instances of hypergamy—stewardesses "marrying up." By this practice some stewardesses did indeed become "princesses." It is this possibility of upward mobility that make class distinctions truly ambiguous. Hypergamy also blurs race and class: when I talk to stewardesses about "marrying up," many assume that I mean "marrying out"—in other words, marrying whites.

The most famous instance of a "Nisei" stewardess marrying up is that of Elaine Okamura (PAA 1964–66), who married the entertainer Wayne Newton in 1968. Newspaper accounts of the wedding, marriage, and subsequent divorce in 1985 unfailingly identify her as a "former Pan Am stewardess." Okamura met Newton when she was twenty-one, a new stewardess working on only her second trip. The Pan Am flight, returning to the United States from Vietnam, carried Newton and others after they had entertained American troops. Okamura had been working in the first-class galley when Newton asked for her telephone number. As Okamura related in an interview on 3 October 2005: "I was very shy, so I was hiding in the galley, and he kept sending his manager to ask if I would give him my number." Okamura refused, but he got it anyway from someone else. Eventually she agreed to have dinner with him on her next visit to California, and two and a half years later they were married. What is perhaps more interesting than their story is the way it was handled by the press and Pan Am. According to Okamura, the press "sort of made up a fairytale story on their own." It had all the elements of one: a Cinderella-ish, small-town Japanese American girl flying for Pan American meets a big-time (white) Hollywood star-prince, who whisks her away and marries her, albeit not happily ever after. These were the same elements that also made it a good story for the airline. According to Okamura, Pan Am viewed her marriage to Newton as good publicity: "[Pan Am was] were very excited. Marrying Wayne was a very big deal and they got a lot of publicity for that." The airline viewed highly public hypergamy as good imaging: it proved the excellence of the company's selection and training that one of its stewardesses could and did "marry up" to a Hollywood star. The story spectacularized the airline's reputation of glamour and cosmopolitanism. At the same time the story provided other women with a fairytale dream of their own: by working for Pan Am, they might find their own happy-ending prince.

Of course it was more than the headlines about the wedding of Okamura and Newton that fueled this reputation. "Marrying up" did not necessarily mean marrying a celebrity. Stewardesses married pilots, well-to-do businessmen, politicians, doctors, lawyers, and many others; "Nisei" stewardesses married white men, as well as Japanese and Japanese American men. Both fairytale and reality rested in the notion that the job placed women in a highly public position where they were noticed, and that many women capitalized on it. Although most of the women I interviewed recalled a more circumspect off-duty life, one "Nisei" stewardess, Peggy Tanaka, admits to the female equivalent of the sailor's "girl in every port" in a series on career women published in a Honolulu newspaper in the 1960s: "[Peggy] does have boyfriends at most of her stops, and feels that stewardesses have a real edge over girls who are permanent residents of any one city. 'The fellows tell us to call them when we get in, and we do. I'd never do that if I weren't in the traveling position which I'm in,' said Peggy" (Patterson 1961, 17). Tanaka admits to a different set of practices and perhaps ethics within the liminal time and space of layovers. According to the article, she was willing to engage in less restrictive, unorthodox behavior within the context of traveling.

This may have been particularly true when the stewardesses were traveling to foreign countries whose customs of seduction differed from those prevailing at home. Thus the public position of the stewardess provided an opportunity for some men to cast their net. I deliberately use the heteronormative language of hunter and prey to replicate some of the attitudes of the time, recognizing that in many situations romance resulted as well from women casting their own nets. But not always: "In the Philippines they used to send us flowers. These guys would hang out in the hotel lobby waiting for our crews to come in. They were rich, young Filipino kids, or some were in their forties, but their family had money. They would hang out in the lobby, waiting for us to arrive. Sometimes, I understood, they paid off the front desk clerk for our room numbers, and so they sent us flowers" (PAA 1968–86). Airline crew members provided ready targets for those seeking foreign liaisons. Their public position made stewardesses easy targets, and provided them with a useful vantage point for meeting men (or in some cases, other women).

The possibilities of marrying up colored the occupation, raising expectations in some cases, amplifying disappointment in others. If hypergamy was a stereotype of the profession, then the non-hypergamous marriage may have caused more of a stir than it might have done otherwise. Even more pertinent than these few instances, however, are some of what I call the marriage-related unintended consequences of flying for Pan American. The women who were selected to fly were considered some of the most desirable from the Japanese American community. Many were educated and on a track to becoming teachers or nurses. Many were attractive. Many were personable, sociable, and outgoing.

However, in the process of flying globally they unintentionally became career women. What was supposed to be a temporary job of a few years became a lifetime profession for many of those I interviewed. In the process, some of them postponed or relinquished one realm of life choices — marriage. Among the women I interviewed, several married in their thirties or forties, one married in her sixties, and several never married at all, including some who flew from the 1950s onward. One who married at the age of thirty-two explains: "I was having too much fun at the beginning to really get married" (PAA 1966–86). Another who married after the age of sixty says: "Some of us who married much later, we were an oddity at that time. In those days, when I was growing up, if you were twenty-five and not married, something was wrong with you. So by the time I was thirty, my parents were really worried. [Laughs] And I would hear them talking, 'Something's wrong with her'" (PAA 1964–86). Many of these women did not have biological children; some adopted children. Of course the option to marry was always there. However, given the strong emphasis on family, the life course of the stewardess contradicted cultural expectations. In terms of community norms and values, these once-ideal marriage candidates ended up leading "unorthodox" lives. None of the women I spoke with expressed any regret for the life choices they made. But none of them spoke of deliberately rejecting marriage either. Rather, in the process of flying for Pan Am, many of these women found tremendous fulfillment and veered off the path that they might have expected to follow. None of the women I interviewed entered the job with intentions of making it a lifelong career, but for some women this was one of its major unintended consequences. These women flew headlong into unexpected dreams, spun from the fibers of race and class, and made them their own.

Pan American's "Nisei" stewardesses—like others—indeed *became* the women that they are through the idioms, assumptions, and practices of race and class, as noted by Caren Kaplan, whom I quote at the beginning of this chapter. Just as *becoming* is an ongoing process for an individual and a group of people, so too are the changing conditions of race and class. What their careers with Pan Am gave the stewardesses is what sets them apart from those who never left home—distance and the perspective that it affords. The changing conditions of race and class for these women were dramatized by the many leaps they made: from "country girl" to round-the-world traveler, from local to global, and, in their words, from "naïveté" to worldliness. Even after retirement and returning home—some to live not far from where they were born—the experience of those leaps shaped them indelibly. Thus race and class within the context of global travel continue to provide the ground from which these women produce themselves.

Five

BECOMING PAN AM

Bodies, Emotions, Subjectivity

My heart is with Pan Am. It's like your first boyfriend. All the experiences to have, we had with Pan Am.

"Nisei" stewardess (PAA 1963–86)

This is our lifetime love affair! Pan Am treated us so well. What job pays you to go shopping and eat good foods? Pays your hotel bills, pays for transportation, pays for the trip in and out, gives you per diem?

"Nisei" stewardess (PAA 1966–86)

I think flying was one of the big highlights of my life. Had I never flown, I would not be what I am today.

"Nisei" stewardess (PAA 1964–86)

PRODUCING SELVES out of corporate materials was part of what both Pan Am and the women did best, though not necessarily easily or without consequences.[1] The quotations above from "Nisei" stewardesses highlight the ways the corporate and the personal intertwined, both as company design and as a means by which the women took the company as their own, for their own purposes. Indeed, these women "became Pan Am." For some the period of employment was a brief few years until marriage; for others employment with Pan Am lasted through the company's decline until it finally relinquished its Pacific routes to United Airlines in 1986, and eventually shut down completely in 1991. I do not assume that every "Nisei" stewardess (or every employee) necessarily "became Pan Am." But among the women I interviewed—admittedly a self-selected group—most express an inordinately strong attachment to the company and to how Pan Am defined who they are. Some worked for other airlines (for smaller airlines before their Pan Am hire; or more typically, United Airlines from 1986, or Delta Airlines, which took over Pan Am's Atlantic routes in 1991), and say that the experience pales by comparison with that of Pan Am. Of course part of that experience is historical: the women worked for Pan Am at a time of luxury travel and the beginning of the Jet Age, and flew with other airlines as flight attendants under the changed conditions of deregulation after 1978. However, what is important is the way the women configure their Pan Am experiences as unique to an era and to an airline. By doing so, they configure themselves as participating in Pan Am's specialness. Here is corporate exceptionalism as a guiding principle that links women's subjectivity to the work-as-play world of Pan Am.

Much of what I analyze could as well be said about other Pan American stewardesses and employees. During the airline's heyday, many employees shared the headiness of the job, the rigors of job training, and the enticement of the lifestyle. However, here I argue for the particular significance of corporate personhood for the "Nisei" stewardesses. It was the position of the women as racial minorities from a distant outpost of the United States with a recent history of wartime racial hysteria that gave their Pan Am experience personal and lasting significance. Working as international stewardesses for a prestigious company signified a move from the margins to the center, which undoubtedly contributed to their enthusiasm in "becoming Pan Am."

TRAINING TO BECOME THE PAN AM STEWARDESS NEXT DOOR: UNIFORMS AND UNIFORMITY

Let me begin by quoting a training manual from the 1950s, entitled "You Are Pan American": "The most important point you will have to keep in mind from the time you start training is that you personify Pan American. . . . The impression you make upon them . . . is . . . the real and lasting impression that they get about the entire company. So, you see, what you do . . . on duty and off . . . is very important to all of us. You are Pan American!" (*Horizons Unlimited* 1959, 57). Becoming Pan American began with a six-week training program and a six-month probationary period that women began as "unfinished" raw material and from which they emerged as "finished" Pan Am corporate products. The makeover was more than superficial: it was critical to the women's performance as "Pan Am people." Rules, regulations, and training helped to guarantee the reliability of the industrial product. One woman exclaims, "It was like the army. They were strict about our hair. It had to be right here [points to the nape of her neck]. They measured it with a ruler" (PAA 1964–86).

Like the military, Pan Am aimed to transform both the bodily and psychic selves of its recruits. Another woman recalls, "I remember at Coral Gables [the Pan Am training center in Miami], we all went to the same hairdresser and she cut all our hair the same way" (PAA 1968–86).[2] The airline emphasized this and other transformations: "before" and "after" visual representations served as popular corporate evidence of the airline's ability to produce Pan Am women. David Palumbo-Liu's comments on American postwar exceptionalism demonstrate some of the parallels between the airline and the nation: "Unlike every other country, America was claimed to be able to work a particular transformation upon its immigrants, and this ideology of course was accessed frequently and loudly throughout and after the war in order to put forward the American cause in the postwar refiguration of the world" (1999, 223). So too Pan Am's "exceptional" ability to transform its trainees to exacting standards became a point of corporate pride. This was especially true of Asian women, whose transformation could be so vividly depicted through side-by-side photographs that showed them successively in native dress and Pan Am uniforms (see chapter 3).[3]

Several women talk about their height in relation to that of other trainees. Pan Am had lowered its height minimum especially for the "Nisei" women, from five feet two inches to five feet one inch, and many of the women just barely made that. Being shorter than many of the other stewardess trainees affected how the women thought about themselves: surrounded by taller (white) women, it was difficult not to think of "being short" as a shortcoming. It is not as if all Japanese American stewardesses were short. Of the ones that I interviewed, some were as tall as five feet six inches. Rather, shortness became part of the bodily reputation of the group. In her study of Japanese American imagery in literature, Traise Yamamoto discusses body size and its impact on identities. She argues: "What is most significant here is that exoticization, dehistoricization and infantilization occur at the site of the (small) Japanese body, which . . . is variously though consistently constructed as the site of irreducible difference" (1999, 17). Difference of course occurs within a particular context. When placed within a racialized context of taller, white women, the height of Japanese (American) women's bodies could be interpreted as an obvious marker of difference—contributing to the image of Japanese (American) women as geisha, dolls, or children (as discussed in chapter 1).

Pan Am left nothing to chance. A training guide from 1959 explicitly states the gendered nature of its lessons. Although all new trainees received the same classroom instruction in grooming, conduct, and safety, women received a special set of lessons in "grooming training," conducted in the early years by modeling schools (Grooming Program 1959). Many "Nisei" stewardesses speak of the demanding professionalism that was an eye opener for them—from applying mascara to wearing gloves, most for the first time. I provide some of the details here, not only to historicize a particular era of gendered training, but also to demonstrate how the careful control of health, grooming, and beauty were intertwined with the presentational requirements of service. Thus a stewardess's service depended on her femininity, which in turn depended on policing "body odor, superfluous hair, [and the] physical let-down that comes with menstrual period[s]" (ibid.). The triple axioms—"Sit like a lady, stand like a model, walk like a queen"—regulated posture and movement. The woman's best friend in this was the full-length mirror, and many advertisements for the stewardess profession depicted a woman standing before a mirror, checking her appearance, adjusting her uniform. The doubled image—the woman and her reflection in the mirror—implicated the woman's body, as well as public scrutiny, in measuring her on-the-job performance.

Hands received special attention. The grooming guide for women reminded trainees: "Much of a person's character can be read in his hands" (Grooming Program 1959). Besides rules for hand care and tips for chipped nails, the guide suggested "hand slimnastics"—exercises to improve circulation and wrist flexibility. This was not only because stewardesses would be using their hands when serving passengers. (Stewards had previously done the same thing, but no manual provided them with "hand slimnastics.") Rather, hands were a window into social class, with the most elegant hands looking as though they worked the least. There was another rationale: hands (and other body parts) could be seen as markers of individual effort in contributing to on-the-job performance and the airline's goals.

Thus trimming one's cuticles was not a mere option; it was one's corporate responsibility.

There were other windows upon social class. During the 1950s and 1960s Pan Am issued "grooming newsletters" to all female pursers and stewardesses, updating women on the latest grooming rules and regulations. An employee manual from 1966 cautioned against "an exaggerated appearance . . . [resulting] in a 'hard' or jaded look" ("Flight Service Indoctrination" 1966, 63). "Gaudy or unusual colors" were subject to particular disfavor. One grooming newsletter included a brief article, "A Psychiatric Evaluation of Odd Colors": "A group of psychiatrists recently made a survey on the habits of women regarding choice of colors in make-up and nail polish. An interesting point found in all cases of women who used outlandish shades [and] . . . startling colors . . . was that it usually indicated some unsatisfied personality need or even an emotional disturbance" (Grooming Program 1959, 2). According to the article, choosing brightly colored makeup and nail polish was not merely an aesthetic preference but a sure sign of female neurosis, a common concern in America of the 1950s and 1960s (Herman 1995; cf. Miles 1991). I argue that this gendered "neurosis" was thinly veiled coding for social class: it was purportedly "cheap" women who wore those bright colors.

The policing of social class extended to hair. A flight service bulletin from 1960 explicitly stated: "Hair color is to be natural: dyes, bleaches and/or rinses are not permitted" (Grooming Newsletter 1960). At the same time, permanent waves that produced curly or wavy hair were an assumption for Japanese American and other stewardesses whose hair was naturally straight. Another grooming guide from 1966 prohibited "noticeable false hair coloring, such as streaks, brassy and theatrical tones," as well as "French twists, extreme bouffant, excessive back combing, pixies, braids, shaggy in appearance and long hair" ("Flight Service Indoctrination" 1966). Pan Am issued "hair exceptions" to women who felt that short hair was unbecoming to them, but these exceptions were granted grudgingly; thus grooming newsletters published names of women who were granted exceptions and allowed to wear their hair in a chignon or French twist.

Stewardesses' off-duty wardrobe received as much attention as their on-duty uniform: one set of training notes explained, "You will be in the limelight when you are off duty." A Foucauldian corporate gaze extended to the general public, reminding women that they were Pan Am representatives, day in and day out. In effect the women were being trained in performance as specifically public women, on and off the job. The specter of the neurotic woman loomed large, as a training manual on wardrobe cautioned: "A scatterbrained wardrobe, which is full of unrelated clothes and accessories, is like a neurotic female. It doesn't make sense. No matter how much is spent on this kind of wardrobe, the wearer always looks as if she stepped out of a mixmaster [a brand of electric mixer]. She is self-conscious, always in debt and never looks smart." The manual thus links psychology, personal finance, and fashion. It divides fashion into two types—"your style" and "high style"—which encode social class. "Your style" is "based on classic lines. It is not fickle and is inclined to be conservative and standard in pattern" (ibid.). "High style," by contrast, "caters to novelty and the mode of the moment, and changes with the whims of each new social trend" (ibid.). "High style" clothes, in other words, are fads that will come and go; "your style" clothes are "classics" that by Pan Am's definition will always be "in style." In urging its stewardesses to dress in "classics" during off-duty hours, Pan Am was molding women to the upper-middle-class image that it desired. The woman called "you" thus belonged to the sorority of Pan Am. The manual gives explicit instructions for women on color, accessories (pearls), and "things that detract," warning that a "messy" impression "can be an indication that your mind is a mess" (ibid.).[4]

The manual provides a prime example of a "smartly dressed woman": Wallis Simpson, the duchess of Windsor (1916–86). Ironically, Pan Am's choice was a woman admired in an America fascinated with British royalty and romance, but also mired in real-life controversy: Simpson was a twice-divorced American for whom Prince Edward, duke of Windsor, relinquished the throne in 1936, and who was later suspected of being a Nazi sympathizer. She was thus an American (divorcée) who charmed her way into British royal circles through style rather than birth. In many ways hers was the ultimate "marrying up."

Why did all this attention to appearance matter so much? It mattered because stewardesses were Pan Am's most public signature commodities. They were the airline's interface with the passenger and integral to its marketing. Trainees were instructed on the value of company promotional work. A training guide from 1959 discusses public relations in the following categories: (1) importance to Pan Am; (2) behavior in connection with press, radio or TV interviews; (3) selection of personnel for assignments; and (4) promotional assignments of equal importance as flight assignments (Grooming Program 1959). With promotional work considered part of their job, stewardesses became accustomed to acting as the public face of the airline, especially in front of media—as many "Nisei" stewardesses did. One stewardess manual from 1966 explains: "It all comes down to this: *You are Pan American.* You will represent those people behind the scenes because your job will put you out in front—meeting the customers others rarely see. To passengers, you are Pan American for the typists in Lisbon, mechanics in Monrovia, weather men in Buenos Aires, baggage handlers in Tokyo, radio men in Rome. In a very real sense, the future of our company—our future—is in your hands. . . . *The Image of a Stewardess is the Image of Pan Am"* (*Horizons Unlimited* 1966, 70, 73). Thus the stewardess stands for all of the company's employees, "behind the scenes," in remote parts of the world. Even more explicitly, stewardesses were part of marketing and regularly called upon to do promotional work, such as public appearances, media spotlights, and any kind of photo opportunities. The first group of "Nisei" stewardesses in 1955 gained front-page headlines in Honolulu newspapers and were subsequently called upon by the airline to appear in photo spreads as a group. Promotional work fostered women's belief in the company and their essential place within it. As one "Nisei" stewardess explains: "I believe that working for Pan Am—such a great airline— that we had to be ambassadors. We had to sell the airline. And this was my purpose" (PAA 1955–57). This assumption contributed to the women's representation of themselves—then and now—as "Pan Am people." Concern for one's appearance was very much part of the job, both in and out of the cabin. As summarized in a newsletter in 1960 (emphasis in original): "AN ATTRACTIVE, WELL-GROOMED APPEARANCE IS A SOCIAL EXPRESSION OF GOOD WILL AND A GESTURE OF FRIENDSHIP TO THE WORLD" (Grooming Newsletter 1960, 3). In sum, failure in being "attractive and well-groomed" was nothing less than a social affront—and even potentially a diplomatic faux pas.

It was not all makeup and hair. Training also included "self-improvement" in the interest of enhanced interaction with passengers. One training guide suggested "language classes, hobbies, keeping up with current events, keeping well informed on the various countries, . . . developing friends in other fields to avoid a one-sided personality" (Grooming Program 1959). The goal was to develop oneself as a person and thus more effectively interact with a range of people who had diverse interests. Pan Am's almost evangelical approach to self-improvement provided a self-reinforcing loop: Who could argue with the goal of developing oneself as a well-rounded person through education, hobbies, and a wide range of friends? That one might do so to become a better hostess and thus enhance the passenger count of an airline faced little challenge. Training in self-improvement seemed to benefit everyone.

Conversational skills were suggested as one of the desirable in-flight attributes for a stewardess. If, as Ernie Albrecht said, "Nisei" stewardesses were more reticent than other stewardesses, then Pan Am's training in "polite and gracious conversation" could ease them out of their shell. Pan Am did not invent its instruction manual but compiled it from various sources, including *Vogue's Book of Etiquette* and a course offered by the Dale Carnegie organization, based on Carnegie's book *How to Win Friends and Influence People* ("Hints on Polite and Gracious Conversation" 1966). Thus the instruction came within a framework of public self-help lessons on interpersonal relations.

Analyzing some of the instructions given during stewardess training provides a clear picture of Pan Am's goals for its service personnel. According to the guide, the onus of responsibility rests with the stewardess, who must first have something interesting to say, and then know how to say it while drawing people into the conversation. To have things worth saying the stewardess must both "become more observant about people, places and things"—in other words, be sensitive and empathetic—and study "current events, current fiction, the entertainment world, sports, arts in general," and Pan Am's publication *New Horizons* was suggested as a source of conversation material. The guide gives specific advice for starting, conducting, and ending a conversation. It addresses social class: "Keep slang at a minimum in your conversation." It also addresses the psychology of passengers, attending to their "fear, anxiety, and boredom." Finally, it suggests topics to avoid, including anything controversial: religion, politics, other passengers, Pan Am or other airlines, and flight disasters. The guide emphasizes the role of the stewardess as hostess, whose goal is to sell the airline. This corporate emphasis on verbal interaction placed added pressure on any "Nisei" stewardess whose own cultural values may have deemphasized speech and who may have been, as Albrecht put it, "quiet" and "reserved."

Pan Am made explicit the ideal career trajectory for stewardesses: to

limit flying and become a wife and mother. Its "Flight Service Indoctrination" from 1966 provided a list of advantages of the profession, including the following: "Last and perhaps most important—being a Stewardess
is excellent training for a future as a wife and mother. Good grooming,
hostess ability, good conversationalist, cooking, food appreciation" ("Flight
Service Indoctrination" 1966). Thus Pan Am's training professionalized
the skills of the homemaker—looking good and making others feel good,
through verbal interaction and culinary excellence—at the same time as
the position was clearly designed as a stepping stone to becoming a homemaker.

Training emphasized the interlocked nature of physical appearance
and social performance. A stewardess manual summarized the company's
philosophy: "Well, we know that there is a definite relationship between
a well-groomed appearance and a well-groomed personality, and it is exemplified in good service aboard our Clippers. A girl who knows that she is
presenting her most attractive manner and appearance automatically gains
confidence and adds to her charm. Her gestures are more natural. She is
more tactful in her dealings with other people. . . . We cannot emphasize
this enough. A neat, attractive appearance automatically gives one a 'lift.'
It creates a favorable impression and, unconsciously but very definitely, it
reflects on the service to guests" (*Horizons Unlimited* 1959, 57). The "lift"
of good grooming thus rests in self-confidence, which affects one's outlook, including how one treats passengers. The links make sense. What the
manual does not say is that these aspects are gendered—that is, it matters
more that women are well groomed and attractive, because physical appearance helps define them. This is not to suggest that grooming is unim-
portant for men (stewards), but physical appearance does not determine
men's ability to carry out their job. Pan Am was not alone in making these
assumptions, but the thoroughness of its training suggested that it was expert at putting the assumptions into practice.

Donning the Pan Am uniform at the end of six weeks' rigorous training signaled to "Nisei" women their birth as stewardesses and their transformation—a sublimation of racial difference for the polished corporate
product. Elaine Kim discusses the significance of uniforms for members
of minority groups: "Fastening on clothes and roles . . . is part of the desire
to be invisible and acceptable at the same time, just as U.S. Army uniforms
have made men from minority groups feel more 'American' and less Asian,

Black, or Chicano. Through clothes and roles, invisibility can become acceptability, since attention is drawn not to the person but to the image in the braided uniform or white gown" (1982, 87). The Pan Am uniform reduced the differences between Japanese (American) woman's bodies and others, and thus marked assimilation as a corporate and individual achievement. "Invisibility" through the Pan Am uniform meant nothing short of professional parity—at least in theory. The Pan Am uniform did not erase racial difference, but the juxtaposition of the uniform within racialized practices and hirings made the "Nisei" stewardess appealing as testament to Pan Am's training and the women's efforts. In the minority's realm of "not only good, but better," the message of the Pan Am uniform speaks most clearly. The uniform containing racialized bodies within the visual language of corporate assimilation, symbolizing both the newness of the frontier and the longstanding history of its colonization. Here was a different kind of Cold War containment, enacted in corporate terms.

PROCESSES OF BECOMING: RULES, PRESTIGE, FAMILY, WORKER SUBJECTIVITY

Pan Am used techniques other than training for inculcating workers' identities: a family idiom, including a well-defined worker hierarchy and a pattern of treating employees well; the instilling of company pride by emphasizing selectivity and prestige; rules of comportment; internal newsletters; constant evaluation of employees, including letters of commendation; and voluntary organizations and social events, such as sports teams, clubs, retirement groups, and parties. Pan Am shared many of these techniques with other large corporations. What set the airline apart were the global resources in image, personnel, and cosmopolitanism from which it could draw. These global resources enhanced the attractiveness of the company. Thus the company's training manual quoted at the beginning of this chapter, "You Are Pan Am," functioned most effectively when employees could likewise proudly say, "Pan Am is me."

The link between Pan Am and its workers was the image of the family. Like many other corporations, Pan Am's use of the family metaphor reinterpreted worker's bonds as affective rather than contractual. The obligations run on both sides—the company will paternalistically take care of its employees, and the employees will uphold the smooth running of the company. Individual and organization exist as mutually beneficial and cooperative rather than confrontational. Interestingly, paternalism here is deeply dependent on a nurturing female enactment of service. The family metaphor also suggests clear-cut internal organization, typically along hierarchical lines. Pan Am used a paternalistically benevolent hierarchy to bind its workers vertically (with management, superiors, and subordinates), as well as horizontally (with co-workers).

The family metaphor is a powerful device for inspiring in workers a sense of company obligation, loyalty, camaraderie, and identification. Conveniently, Pan Am had as its head a charismatic founding father figure in Juan Trippe. The company's image, prestige, and global domination rested in the person of Trippe, who was continually portrayed as a visionary with both corporate and humanitarian ambitions (see chapter 2). Several women I spoke with mentioned their admiration for Trippe, coupled with their admiration for the airline.

Pan Am's place as a pioneer in commercial aviation (discussed in chapter 2) gave its workers a sense that they were at the forefront of technology and an entire industry: "Everybody knew of Pan Am. At the time we were the top, so whenever they heard you were with Pan Am, it made you feel really proud. Yes, it did. I was happy to be associated with it. 'Oh, she's with Pan Am.' It was a big deal" (PAA 1955–57). One "Nisei" stewardess from 1955 writes, "Thank you, Pan Am. Because of your reputation as being a FIRST CLASS AIRLINE, we who were stewardesses for you, are looked upon with much respect and gratitude" (PAA 1955–57; capitalization in original). The sense of participating in history by being the first, the best, and the most made workers proud. Riding the wave of "proximal prestige" because of a corporate status that included humanitarian endeavors helped Pan Am flight attendants to take pride in their service. At times those endeavors drew upon "naturalized" abilities of women as maternal caregivers (see accompanying illustration).

Part of that pride was also personal: one stewardess from 1956 was told that she was selected from a field of over three thousand applicants. She calls working for Pan Am a "privilege," and "the best thing to happen" in her life. One woman from the 1960s writes, "Because we were a select few we all knew how special our jobs were." Newspaper articles on "Nisei" steward-

Shhh.
Stewardess at work.

She's off duty now, but she's working. As a Pan Am volunteer.
On this trip, Mimi Narita is escorting two children who have just been discharged from the Honolulu Shriners Hospital for Crippled Children. She'll see them home to their parents in Western Samoa.
Unusual?
No.
With Pan Am people, this sort of thing goes on all the time.

●PAN AM
You call it the world.   We call it home.

"Nisei" stewardess in Pan Am ad for its humanitarian endeavors (date unknown).

esses likewise emphasized the company's selectivity. With so many other women vying for the job, the woman selected considered herself privileged, and thus less likely to approach work with a critical attitude. As one "Nisei" stewardess put it, "It was like winning the lottery!" (PAA 1960–69).

The many rules that Pan Am instituted encouraged each employee to identify with other employees as well as the company. The rules could be seen as a common denominator of restriction and conformity to corporate modeling. There were seemingly rules for everything, from what one said to how one said it, from the length of one's hair to the color of one's underwear, from on-duty checks to off-duty behavior. One stewardess explains, "There were so many things that you learned, but it became second nature to us" (PAA 1963–69). Pan Am's training and rules involved precisely that—the making of one's "second-nature." Pierre Bourdieu's notion of habitus—the inculcation of bodily practices through long-standing repetition—is useful (1977). Pan Am's creation of a corporate habitus, particularly with the professionalism of its stewardesses, extended from grooming to serving to safety. The professionalism of Pan Am stewardesses suggested both corporate control and individual agency.

Agency did not rest solely in the hands of servers. Rather, Pan Am established a system of surveillance, with pursers and grooming supervisors (and sometimes pilots) reporting any infringements. Other stewardesses did not participate so much in reporting infringements, partly from an unspoken code of solidarity with each other. The six-month probationary period for all flight attendants was most critical in this close scrutiny; however, a stewardess could be "written up" by a supervisor at any time in her career. Furthermore, Pan Am paid attention to letters from passengers. Both compliments and critiques went into a stewardess's personnel file, subject to management review. Thus pursers, supervisors, and passengers formed a "panopticon" of surveillance—a broad, all-seeing base of observation from which to police employees' adherence to rules (Foucault 1977).

Pan Am's regulation of the body bound its stewardesses. Weight was a constant issue for some, although less so for "Nisei" stewardesses, who tended to be underweight.[5] Policing weight was built into evaluations of job performance: if a woman was found to be approaching or even exceeding her "limit," she would be placed on a weight-check regime of more frequent measuring, with the possibility of eventual dismissal. Later in the 1970s the company loosened weight restrictions by using a body-frame approach. Based upon the measurement of a woman's elbow, she would be classified as a small-, medium-, or large-frame, each with a maximum allowable weight.

One convenient symbol of the containment and molding of women was an undergarment common during the 1950s and 1960s and less so today—the girdle. Most of the women I interviewed spoke animatedly and sometimes vehemently about the girdle, a requisite part of the uniform. Wearing a girdle had little to do with the weight of the women—most of the Japanese (American) women were thin, some even too thin. It had more to do with the control of women's bodies and the production of the look: a smooth, chaste body that showed no seams, wrinkles, or bulges. One woman explains: "It was kind of for modesty for one, and to give you a sharper, smoother look. There wouldn't be ripples in your skirt" (PAA 1964–86). At some airports a grooming supervisor performed a "girdle check," patting derrieres to ensure that the undergarment was in place. One woman was reprimanded for not wearing a girdle even while in training, being told, "Go back to the hotel and wear your girdle and come back. If not, you are welcome to go home" (PAA 1965–86). The enforcement of girdle regulations gave license to unofficial checks by company men—office staff, pilots, and pursers. One woman who flew from 1957 to 1960 recalls: "Before we boarded the flight, we had this flight checking thing where you had to know where all of the equipment is. And what the captains would come and do is pat you to see whether you were wearing a girdle or not. And if you weren't wearing a girdle, you're off."

The girdle was not the only element that was policed. One flight attendant from the 1960s gives a rundown of the company's checklist: "Before we got on the flight, we'd have to go to a briefing office, and in the briefing office would be a grooming supervisor . . . Your hair had to clear the collar. You'd have to have either red lipstick or if you had nail polish it would have to be red nail polish. No pink lipstick. It had to be red. You could not have any dangling earrings or anything like that" (PAA 1964–86). Another remembers other rules: "There were things you could not do like wear dark glasses inside a building. If you were going from the building to the aircraft, you could wear your dark glasses. Never in the plane. If you were in public view in the terminal, you always had to have your white gloves on, depending on the season. There were seasons when you switched to black leather gloves" (PAA 1963–69). The women took these lessons—from girdles to hair to gloves—primarily as finishing-school tutorials, learning the ways of (white) upper-class debutantes. The lessons stuck as bodily regimens of the performance of class and—especially for Japanese Americans who might have been sensitized to racial issues during the Second World War—white, Euro-American culture. These lessons were thus made all the more valuable for their associations with positions of gendered power and privilege. Becoming Pan Am meant participating in the power and privilege of the airline.

Part of becoming Pan Am lay in the nature of the work: long, stressful hours flying in an enclosed space, bound by the requisite performance of serving passengers, and always doing so with a smile. Working within the liminality of the airplane cabin—with a suspended sense of where one was or what time it was—brought members of the flight crew together. The constant busyness of the job required multitasking, managing passengers' demands, and working with a team: "Being a Pan Am stewardess . . . taught me how to be gracious, even under the stress of a few rude and demanding passengers. It was my first experience at multitasking and learning how to politely rush through meal service and cleanups. I learned a lot about people's idiosyncrasies, eccentricities, and other personality differences. Flying with five to six other attendants was my initial exposure to teamwork. . . . It was the only job that I can truly say was a 'fun job'" (PAA 1962–63).

The "fun" aspect of the Pan Am position helped stewardesses to form bonds with each other and with the company. Several women I spoke with talked about the partying by the crew that went on after the flight, often initiated by the captain: "We used to have crew parties. So whenever, say, we landed in Beirut, then they would say, 'Come up to the Captain's room.' So just for relaxation, we would get together, and we would have drinks" (PAA 1964–68). Some women welcomed the after-hours relaxation that inevitably involved drinking; others felt coerced—especially given the exalted position and sometimes sexualized reputation of pilots; and a number of the "Nisei" women I spoke with declined to attend the parties. One woman explains that the "Nisei" stewardesses were often excluded from the parties because they worked alone rather than as part of a set crew on the around-the-world flights (PAA 1958–86). In fact, their abstemiousness during off-duty hours set the "Nisei" stewardesses apart. Most of them drank very little or no alcohol. One woman explained: "We were not the party kind. We didn't drink. In fact, I never went to any parties. We weren't raised that way" (PAA 1957–86). Another agreed: "We were pretty low key and a lot of us didn't even drink. We led a pretty sheltered life" (PAA 1968–86). There were practical aspects as well. One woman remembered that when the crew went out for meals, other members would order numerous alcoholic drinks, while the "Nisei" stewardess would order only one soft drink.

Grounded in a snowstorm, "Nisei" stewardess posing in a jet engine, 1968.

Thus when it came time to split the bill, the "Nisei" stewardess paid more than her share for the party. After a while she learned to refuse to join the others (PAA 1958–86). This no-partying, no-drinking "Nisei" behavior became generalized as part of a racialized reputation. Some "Nisei" did join the party, but they were the exception.

From speaking informally with other white flight attendants, it became clear to me that Pan Am off-duty life was characterized by many as a party culture, often fueled by drinking. Although not everyone partied, socializing in this way during off-duty hours was not uncommon. When I attended three Pan Am events in one weekend in December 2006 in Miami, including two evening events with alcohol, I fell asleep exhausted at 1:00 a.m. on the drive back to my hotel. The two flight attendants giving me a ride remarked jokingly, "We can tell she's not Pan Am. She doesn't know how to party!" My brief interactions with the former flight attendants now in Miami helped me better understand why "Nisei" stewardesses stood out for their relative conservatism.

Off-duty hours were not all about parties. Pan Am regulated the behavior and dress of its crew on layovers through official rules and unofficial mentoring. As one "Nisei" stewardess put it: "I remember in training they always said, 'Remember that you represent our company in this foreign land. So you must always dress appropriately.' And of course we had the older flight attendants who kind of mentored us on layover. So when I joined, they all wore suits, high heeled shoes, and a matching handbag. And so we just did the same thing" (PAA 1968–86). That "same thing" meant dressing the part on layovers, maintaining the Pan Am image even when off duty. This blurring of on-duty and off-duty dress and comportment demonstrated the degree to which Pan Am expected stewardesses to perform their corporate role at all times.

The demands of traveling to countries whose language and customs were foreign also brought the crew together—in the luxury enclave of Intercontinental hotels. In fact, Pan Am's routes were *only* international, so employees regularly compared their global stage with that of all other American carriers. On this stage the obvious differences between "them" (foreign residents) and "us" (Pan Am crew) made the Pan Am employees draw closer together in work and play.

The bonds between crew members became particularly significant for "Nisei" stewardesses, since some of their interactions with Pan Am—both training and flying, with passengers as well as other employees—were among their first and closest dealings with whites. In the words of one woman who flew from 1955 to 1986: "Flying for Pan Am was the first time I really had anything to do with Caucasians." Her admission demonstrates the separation of the ethnic enclave, even growing up in so-called multicultural Hawai`i in the 1930s and 1940s.

The work-as-play with whites and nonwhites in distant ports of call around the world defined the "Pan Am Way" as not merely a job but a lifestyle. This was a huge leap—from Kalihi (a blue-collar section of Honolulu) to Paris and New Delhi—for women who had previously only interacted with other Japanese American friends and family in tightly circumscribed neighborhoods. Several women told me, "It wasn't like a job!" One who flew from 1964 to 1986 exclaimed: "I was paid to travel! It was wonderful!" (PAA 1964–86). As for another, who flew from 1966 to 1986: "What kept me flying was because it was just the whole lifestyle. I would never have been able to do that on my own."

The shopping, restaurant going, and sightseeing became part of the Pan Am Way. The world was the stewardesses' mall. The World Wings International calendar of 2006 includes this caption for its photograph for July: "Who better to conduct a lesson in shopping than a Pan Am stewardess? Pan Am Flight Attendants were World Class shoppers who were expert at getting discounts and bargaining in bazaars and gold markets wherever in the world Pan Am took them" (*World Wings International 2006 Calendar* 2005). Shopping was contagious and bargain hunting exciting, with stewardesses comparing purchases and prices during layovers and recommending stores and items to each other. The result of this was often standardized places to shop, and even standardized items to buy. Thus the Oriental Bazaar became the Pan Am stewardess stop for mementoes in Tokyo; Mr. Wong became the place to have clothes tailored in Hong Kong; Bangkok became the place to purchase jewelry. By purchasing similar items in layovers around the world, many stewardesses built similar collections of mementoes. Walking into various women's homes, I sometimes encountered the same objects, often bought during layovers. There was thus built a Pan Am trove of material culture shared by stewardesses.

The same held true for restaurants and even particular dishes. For example, in Singapore many Pan Am stewardesses would go to the Peninsula Hotel for orange pancakes. It also held true for grooming: several women mentioned getting their hair cut at Vidal Sassoon's in London, the premier, trendsetting salon of Britain's "swinging '60s." It also held true for sightseeing: more than one woman showed me a photo of herself seated at a bench in front of the Taj Mahal. These patterned purchases and experiences too became part of the Pan Am Way.

Of course Pan Am stewardesses shared these shops, restaurants, and sights with other tourists, but their worldwide and patterned collection of souvenirs and experiences became a trademark of their profession, status, and corporate identity. Furthermore, what separated them from tourists who may have made similar round-the-world stops is the frequency with which they traveled. Women whom I interviewed told me that they traveled around the world fifty or more times—working, but also sightseeing along

Pan Am stewardesses in front of the Taj Mahal, ca. 1968.

the way. For them Tokyo, Bombay, Beirut, and London were everyday stop-overs.

The particular mix of work and play—including ambiguous forms of work that looked like play—marked the profession of international stewardess. Because Pan Am was the premier American employer in this field, the work-play mix in global ports of call marked the Pan Am Way.

The mix of play and work can be clearly seen in the scrapbooks that many of the women kept and showed me. The scrapbooks, which memorialized both on- and off-duty activities, demonstrate the blurring of boundaries in the profession. On the one hand, if stewardesses were supposed to act as hostesses, with the airplane's cabin as their living room, then the flight could be configured as one long party. The job entailed far more than that, of course, but the hostess image was useful to the airlines in emphasizing the pleasure of the flight and managing the quality of service. It was a job in which work was meant to look like play. On the other hand, off-duty dress and behavior were the concerns of the airlines. If stewardesses represented Pan Am even on layovers, then their play time was indeed work time.

By examining the highly detailed scrapbook of one "Nisei" stewardess (PAA 1964–86) one can analyze her career trajectory, and how she gave meaning to her employment. Her scrapbook, entitled "My Flying Career with Pan Am," fills a blank book intended specifically for flight attendants:[6] with dividers marking off sections for training (with details on places, dates, courses, dates when wings were received, and descriptions of uniforms); graduation photos; diplomas; first flight (with details on the date, time, destination, type of aircraft, speed, altitude, and crew members); airline routes; "hospitalities enjoyed" (hotels, restaurants and cafes, theaters, shows, sights); aircraft; V.I.P. passengers; cities and countries visited; crew photos and memorable flights; and "The Day My Wings Were Clipped" (date, reason, total hours spent in the air, miles flown).[7] The categories spell out the phases of life of a stewardess, from training to retirement.

As the scrapbook makes clear, a stewardess's life is only partly about flying. The rest is about "hospitalities" and visiting far-off places. The book also makes clear the importance of glamour in the profession, including meeting important people. Even without embarking on the career, a potential stewardess knew what awaited her, including the job's inevitable end.

Humorous illustrations decorate the scrapbook and underscore many of the assumptions of the profession. The drawing accompanying "The Day My Wings Were Clipped" shows a heart and a male cupid shooting an arrow through the hat of a stewardess in uniform. The message is clear: the primary reason to stop flying is to get married. Another drawing accompanying "V.I.P's aboard My Airplane" depicts an older, white, slightly portly gentleman, smoking a cigar, carrying a cane—providing a stereotype of exactly who might be a "very important person."

The scrapbook contains all the stewardess's letters of evaluation throughout her career. When the result of labor is interaction rather than a physical product, the only way to judge quality is through observation and evaluation. One form of evaluation is the official report submitted by flight supervisors or pursers. The report covers appearance, passenger relations, crew relations, and procedures.[8] There are commendations from higher-ranking employees such as pilots, pursers, and flight supervisors, as well as from passengers. What each of these addresses is outstanding job performance. It is not enough to simply do a job well to receive a commendation; one must exceed expectations. A letter from a passenger sent to Pan Am's senior vice-president in marketing reads: "On the 6th of Dec. 1969 I rode Pan Am from Honolulu to Saigon. The cabin crew in steerage (tourist) were so exceptional that a 29-year veteran of flying military and commercial aircraft feels motivated to commend them. The attention to their duties and the kindnesses extended by [names three women] to the passengers merits your attention. . . . [They] were exceptional." These documents build a reputation, duly entered into an employee's personnel records, as well as this stewardess's scrapbook. Accordingly, the scrapbook contains all letters of promotion—from stewardess to trainer to purser. It also contains details of the stewardess's reemployment as part of Pan Am's "returning mothers" program, which the company began in 1974, when it offered employment to those women who had quit because of pregnancy.

A large portion of the scrapbook contains photographs and mementoes of the stewardess's travels. We see her in the gardens of Japan, shopping in Delhi, at the Temple of Dawn in Bangkok, and viewing Kensington Gardens in the spring. In the photos she wears regulation outfits, including white gloves. In group shots with other crew members she is typically the only Asian (American).

In scrapbooks such as these one can read a life built around Pan Am. It is a life documented as a series of milestones recorded in photographs, certificates of commendation, and newspaper clippings. It is also a career of privilege, a career spent traveling in the footsteps of the élite, placing one's face within the upper-middle-class frame of a jetsetter. The scrapbook records these travelogue memories as the actualization of a dream. And indeed, for many "Nisei" stewardesses their years of flying for Pan Am were just that. What the scrapbook does not record are the corporate terms of that dream and the inbuilt limitations based in assumptions of gender, race, and class.

The scrapbook also does not record some of the techniques of resistance that the women employed even while living the dream. In the course of their employment with Pan Am the women found within themselves the agency to assert their will. For the most part this did not come easily. Structual constraints worked against them—besides being young, junior, and female, they were not white. One woman recalls: "We were so unexposed, so whatever anybody wanted us to do, especially if it was a haole person telling us something, a crew member, 'Can you do this?' 'Sure, I can do this.' Now I learned, 'No, you do it yourself.' . . . I think they did [take advantage of us], because they knew that we would do it" (PAA 1968–86). Complying with orders followed neatly along more generalized racial hierarchies, echoed by culture and geography. The upbringing of many of the women reinforced obedience to authority as a form of respect behavior. Furthermore, the geographic isolation of Hawai`i placed the women even further at the periphery of power and control. These multiple layers of inequity made saying no that much more difficult for the women.

The areas of resistance centered around those realms that the women found most oppressive. One of these was the girdle, discussed earlier. Although the rule for wearing a girdle gave the women no leeway, even in training, several found ways to squirm out of it: "I always remember the girdle, because it was so uncomfortable. Some of us would just stick the girdle in our bag and before we'd go to the [grooming supervisor's] office, we would put the girdle on, and then we'd go there and get our weight check, and then we'd get on the plane and we'd take it off. A lot of us cheated like that" (PAA 1964–86). Another woman claimed what resembled reasons of health: "I was a rebel. I would wear the girdle through the flight check. But the minute I got on the airplane, I took it off. I'll be honest—I was the only "Nisei" girl that didn't wear a girdle. Because what I found when I first started flying was I got airsick. And I discovered if I took off the girdle, I wasn't sick. So I got really sloppy and didn't wear it" (PAA 1960–69). This stewardess apparently did not realize how widespread the girdle rebellion was. Given the number of women who detested wearing it, as well as the strictness of company rules, the girdle became a particularly volatile issue. Thus grooming supervisors patrolled specifically for it as they did with no other undergarment. As noted earlier, girdle checks conducted by supervisors (and, jokingly, by other male employees such as pilots and pursers) became notorious. The girdle's containment of women's bodies simultaneously encoded their physical and emotional discomfort. The struggle over the girdle symbolized a struggle of surveillance, control, and ultimately resistance.

Most forms of resistance and agency were discreet. The stewardesses pilfered small bottles of alcohol and took them home to friends and family as souvenirs. Having grown up with canned tuna and sardines, these women now ate caviar by the spoonful—leftovers from first class. One woman recalls: "This was Iranian caviar, you know. I mean, nobody [at home] eats Iranian caviar, right?" (PAA 1963–69). Home became a constant backdrop for these small acts. But it was more than gorging on expensive leftovers that titillated the stewardesses' fancy. Peering backstage gave them access to further transgressions. One stewardess remembered sneakily trying on a passenger's ermine coat; she said that all the flight attendants on board took turns trying it on. Trying on an ermine coat was only a refracted version of what the flight attendants were doing off the job on layovers in different ports of call: trying on the lifestyle of the élite.

Most forms of resistance—including refusing to be "geisha-ed," talking back to passengers, staging a sit-out while in flight, even declining an invitation to party—were individual rather than organized. Most—though not all—were done with a smile. These were women who were invested in the position and the smile. By contrast, Ien Ang asks, "Are we [Asian women] accepted, or tolerated, only when we display our girly smile—the stereotypical submissive smile of the exotic oriental woman traditionally so enchanting and pleasing to Westerners?" (2001, 149). Ang speaks from the perspective of another generation of women and a different intellectual outlook. For the most part these women found that playing the highly gendered, smiling role of hostess got them farther than shouting their demands. Feeling privileged to be where they were, they tended to be less demanding. So as a rule they did as they were told. They stood up for themselves when something obviously offensive came along—for example, they would refuse to peel grapes—but otherwise they managed to play a low-key role in the cabin. For this they garnered ample praise, which became a source of their own professional worthiness. In short, theirs was the model-minority flight pattern.

Confronted with racially based practices, such as the assigning of "Nisei" stewardesses to galley positions, the women quietly asked for changes. They asked quietly, in part because asking quietly was their cultural mode of interaction, in part because their minority position made them aware of the potential for reactions and claims of preferential treatment. They noted social snubs based in race, but they found their own activities and made their own friends. By this they gained independence. They chose to ignore racial intolerance more often than they challenged it, and thus exerted a de-gree of agency. Because of their job-worthiness they were offered and took positions of leadership, such as positions as trainer or purser or recruiter, sometimes relocating to other cities such as San Francisco or Miami to do so. They also found a mouthpiece in the union, which ultimately led to the end of Honolulu as a closed Asian-language base—a process I detail in chapter 6. I do not mean to homogenize their experiences nor to downplay their differences. But working as a Pan Am stewardess between 1955 and 1972 provided a shared context within which the women developed their own subjectivity, often in the glare of a high-profile, racialized position. That subjectivity gave rise to its own individuated forms of agency and re-sistance. The most "successful" of these women—the ones with the positive experiences, the ones with whom I spoke—are those who found in Pan Am employment the personal resources to make the job their own.

The concept of consent is useful here. Rachel Sherman borrows the con-cept from Michael Buroway's study of blue-collar workers, as she addresses the attitudes among the luxury hotel workers she researched (2007). What both studies emphasize is the worker's agency in choosing to participate in the work environment, and thus accept certain norms and conditions. The key, as Sherman puts it, is the workers' "active investment in work" and thus their use of "agency to participate in work rather than to refuse to par-ticipate" (2007, 16). In placing agency within workers' consent as much as in resistance, we can address their autonomy and accept company loyalty and affiliation as critical expressions of individual choice.

As the quotations with which I began this chapter indicate, expressions of loyalty and affiliation with Pan Am overwhelm this research. In their emotional fervor these expressions go well beyond the loyalty of obedient employees and enter the realm of testimonials. In interviews, letters, e-mail messages, and cards that I received, the women express overwhelming gratitude toward the airline that changed their life. "I am forever thankful" (PAA 1968–73 and others), they say, to Pan Am opening up a world to them and providing them with opportunities. They refer to Pan Am emotionally as a "first boyfriend," more than one woman saying "I'll always love you!" (PAA 1955–57) and "Pan Am will always be #1 in my heart!" (card, November–December 2006). Their expressions of emotion are dramatic: "My life began when I joined Pan Am" (PAA 1969–86). They are philosophical: "Pan Am was my 'finishing school in life!'" (PAA 1966–86). They are emphatic, and sometimes have the immediacy of the present tense: "Pan Am is the best part of my life" (PAA 1958–86). They are all-encompassing: "Pan Am gave me the world" (card, November–December 2006). And of course, given the airline's demise, they are poignant: "I miss you, Pan Am!" (card, November–December 2006).

One gets the sense of a highly personal relationship with the airline, going well beyond the typical relationship between employer and employees. One woman explains the emotional nature of the relationship: "It's like loving a person. The emotional feeling and connection. It's not just me, and not everybody, but so many of the girls . . . Most of us have this connection and affection. Well, it's almost like Pan Am had certain qualities that you can love like a person. I mean, what it did for us. The experience, . . . I mean, opening up routes, and their romantic early beginnings of flying. It just had, you know, a context that you loved. So many good things about it. The history and the people. And with Pan Am stewardesses, too, you don't really have to have known them. But just to know that you had this common experience. There's this bond. And there's a mindset that you share" (PAA 1960–69). In our conversation I asked this woman, "If Pan Am were a person, would it be a man or a woman?" To which she answered, "Probably a man. I'm picturing that it would be like a man in his 60s or 70s. It's not a romantic figure or a sexual figure" (ibid.). She surmised that it would be more like a father figure. In many ways, gendering Pan Am as an older (white) man is not surprising, especially since management and top officials with the company were all older, white men. So too were most of the pilots, although they may have held a different image for these women who had to fly with them and interact with them on the job. The company image was more distant, carrying with it the authority of corporate decision making and history. According to this woman, Pan Am's achievements—including its firsts—added to the stewardesses' "connection and affection." Of course the man most closely associated with Pan Am's frontier of firsts was Juan Trippe, a distant authority figure who not coincidentally fits the description of this woman's "Pan Am." Not that the women necessarily expressed any kind of displaced attachment to Trippe, but he provided a convenient emblematic figure on which to hang their dreams. For them Trippe's Pan Am was the frontier of their lifetime.

The woman's personal link to Pan Am also links her to other stewardesses, because of their shared experiences. This horizontal link adds another homosocial dimension to the corporate bond. However, the complexities of that link structure certain aspects of the women's attachments to the company. First, the link is racially inflected, partly through the Asian-language position that the "Nisei" women occupied. They were known by other crew members as "J-girls"—occupying a Japanese-language position as much as a racial category. That they occupied a language and racial position handled in particular ways set them apart from other stewardesses. Second, the link was geographically inflected through its tie to the Honolulu base. Although the "Nisei" stewardesses flew on round-the-world flights, they were indelibly associated with Asia and the Pacific—if not racially, then through their connection to Hawai`i. This placed them apart from others—for example, those based in New York, which was focused on Europe. The geographic positioning of Hawai`i (and the Pacific-Alaska division of which it was a part) placed the women at the exoticized peripheries of global American power. These elements ineluctably shaped the bonds and attitudes of the "Nisei" stewardess.

The emotional attachment of the "Nisei" stewardesses to Pan Am made for many vivid memories. The varied nature of the stewardesses' job, the places to which they traveled, the prominent people they met, the spotlight under which they worked and played—all these provided a wealth of experiences that etched their Pan Am lives in high relief. When I asked flight attendants to write down some of their memories of Pan Am, many of them quickly and easily provided a litany of places and things. One woman wrote, "There are so many memories all over the world," after which she enumerated the following:

London: walking on Trafalgar Square and going to see a play
Rio de Janeiro: Going up the Corcovado on a tram
Tokyo: walking on the Ginza and eating at Torigin
Beirut: Dancing on the rooftop restaurant Phoenicia
Kharachi, Pakistan: Sailing with Captain Pan Am on his boat
Hong Kong: I miss Mr. Wong, who used to sew for me
(Card, November–December 2006)

Others provided similar lists—with the same places, the same experiences. That the places named—Trafalgar Square, Corcovado, Ginza—were some of the best-known icons at each locale reinforced the headiness of the global encounter, safely packaged into the space of a layover. The off-duty life of the stewardess made the world a whirl of commodities, sights, and relationships. According to the women, doing their job was like traveling with a guidebook and hitting all the must-see, must-do, must-eat highlights. And Pan Am took them there to do it.

This is part of the shared lifestyle of the Pan Am stewardess—the lasting memory of the cabin, but more important, the world beyond. This is the stuff of scrapbooks, memorializing travel as part of a paid job. And this is the seduction of the "local girls" (Japanese American and Asian nationals) gone global, whose job with Pan Am afforded them such riches. This is the story often repeated by the women I interviewed, each with her individual refractions, but following a similar plot line. It is a story of a world grown larger—filling a blue globe—its very expansiveness routinized by familiarity. It is a life story nurtured by agency, then filled with the emotion of indebtedness.

LASTING EFFECTS: PAN AM LIVES

According to the women, that indebtedness arises from the ways Pan Am changed their lives. The lasting effects of the Pan Am lifestyle range from the mundane to the profound, from knowing how to "plate" food to shaping one's personality. One woman talks about learning the presentational skills of upper-class, cosmopolitan foodways, and later extending these to her home life: "Pan Am always did things very well. Cordon Bleu was our training for our galley, how to prep the meals, how to plate the meals and things like that. How to serve it: you always put the entree at 4 o'clock, you put the starch up here, the vegetable here. Everything was very specific. You had to follow a standard; the level of expectation was very high. And you never had a messy plate. If there was gravy spilled somewhere, you always wiped it down. There was always parsley on the plate, that type of thing, because that's how it's done. You know, fine dining. And I think because we were exposed to so much as far as eating in places all over the world and eating really good food. Because of that, I was exposed to so much as far as dining and food, I think at home, I cook a lot more multicultural than if I had stayed home in Hawai`i" (PAA 1966–86). This stewardess extended the lessons of food presentation ("plating") to her home life, integrating her knowledge of where different foods and silverware should go on a well-set table: "The Pan Am stewardesses, they all do that. It's just ingrained." This notion of practices becoming "ingrained" is key to the contagion of the performance of class. Whether flight attendants always "plated" by Pan Am's entree-starch-vegetable standards or not, what they minimally took with them was knowledge of these standards. Thus an unadorned plate of food was forever a plate missing parsley, like lamb chops without mint jelly or caviar without vodka. What these women learned through their Pan Am training were the standards of upper-class, Euro-American life. The conditions of work created a web of expectations and practices shared with passengers, as well as other Pan Am flight attendants. These became lived as the Pan Am Way.

Not all the lessons were positive. At a time when cigarettes were commonplace and the United States surgeon general was not yet requiring printed warnings on cigarette packs on the deleterious effects of smoking, one woman learned to smoke: "We had little sample cigarettes for first class. And you could never stand and smoke. You had to sit. So one of the reasons I smoked, everybody used to take smoking breaks. Because you had to sit when you smoked, right? [Laughs] So I used to smoke. I learned to smoke when I was in the training class. You had to keep awake for so long, so smoking was one of the ways to keep awake, and drinking coffee was another. It was hard to stay awake all the time" (PAA 1963–69). Smoking was far more commonplace in those days, and this woman learned it as part of a lifestyle of long working hours, seated smoking breaks, and free cigarettes.

Plating and smoking were minor lessons. What mattered far more was the exposure to different cultures. Even for women from Hawai`i—a place known for its multiculturalism—travel was an eye opener. One woman reflects: "For me, it was really growing up. I mean, it got me out and away, which I don't think anybody in my family envisioned" (PAA 1955–57). The process of "growing up" according to Pan Am meant learning lessons of difference from each port of call. As one woman put it: "It made a total difference in my life, becoming a Pan Am flight attendant. It took me out of Hawai`i and exposed me to a world out there that I never knew before starting to fly for Pan Am. I think it broadened my horizons. It gave me an appreciation for other people, other cultures, other lifestyle which I would never have had if I stayed in Hawai`i. So I think it's made a vast difference in my life. I would have been a totally different person" (PAA 1966–86). It was not enough to simply know that difference existed "out there." The first-hand knowledge of these different worlds—the "broadened horizons" of international flying—became a self-reflexive lens upon one's own identity.

Working for Pan Am fostered an appetite for travel itself. Most of the women came to the job with some wanderlust. However, in working international routes they became accustomed to regular flying to distant places: "My curiosity with travel came from my traveling with Pan Am. And this is why I go to Turkey almost every year. I was introduced to Istanbul as a young girl with Pan Am, and this has been my favorite country to visit every year" (PAA 1964–68). Note that in this woman's narrative she refers to "traveling with Pan Am" rather than "working with Pan Am." If one did not know that she worked as a stewardess, one might think that she was a passenger on the airline rather than one of its staff. These are the kinds of subtle work-play blurrings endemic to the job.

For some women traveling to different countries generated an interest in reading more about those places: "You know, when you're exposed to all of [those different countries], you try to learn as much as you can. I was never much of a history buff, but when I started flying to Japan, I remember a passenger asking me a question. And then it dawned on me that I should read up on my countries because you're asked questions. So it makes you realize that you have to know these things, and I have to admit

I wasn't much of a reader then, but I started to be" (PAA 1956–58). Learning more about the countries was part of the job. Pan Am urged women to read newspapers and books to be better conversationalists. The women complied. One woman explains her own process of learning as a pragmatic part of on-board service: "Coming from an insulated place like Hawai`i, and then exposing yourself to these businessmen, I found that I had to grow up a lot, fast. Because the conversation with them was not what I expected, being raised in Honolulu. You had to keep up with the news. They would talk about economics, they would talk about what's going on in the world, they would talk about their country. It was a learning experience to see how people lived in different countries and how they thought" (PAA 1968–86). Like others, this woman continually contrasts the insularity of Hawai`i with the expansive world that Pan Am presented. In effect, she reifies some of the problematic dynamics by which Hawai`i is stereotyped. She and others read because they were urged to do so; but they also read because their compass now included distant cities of the world. Rather than abstract, exotic names, places like Beirut, Tehran, and New Delhi had real experiential meaning for them.

Those places also had real meaning through consumption—shopping, eating, sightseeing. Among the lasting effects of Pan Am in these women's lives were the material objects and cultivated tastes that they acquired. One "Nisei" stewardess writes in a letter (15 June 2005): "Our home is decorated with Japanese and Chinese objets d'art and travel memorabilia. PAA [Pan American] introduced me to Indian, Thai, Vietnamese, Lebanese, South American etc cuisines. . . . PAA exposed me to the arts, culture of Europe. I enjoy French, German and Italian foods, European opera, symphonic and chamber music" (PAA 1964–68, 1980–86). In the process of her Pan Am work-play travels, she had become a consumer cosmopolitan.

Some women recognize the very intimate nature of the transformation that Pan Am effected. One woman says that her personality itself changed: "The person I was before Pan Am was very quiet, very introverted, just toed the line. But the person that I became because of the exposure went in a different direction. I had a huge life change at age twenty-eight. I decided being introverted, being quiet, being real submissive was not working for me, and so I did a turnaround. Even my handwriting changed. [Laughs] I think I matured and realized that I was capable of a lot more than I thought I was. I think Pan Am made a huge difference in making the lifestyle change. I became more independent, more outgoing, more assertive. I became a different type of person" (PAA 1966–86). She continues, explaining the specific ways in which Pan Am forced her change in personality: "For me, the confidence that Pan Am gave me came through just little things, like being able to go to a restaurant in a foreign country, sit there by yourself, and eat a meal. You know, you're forced to do things like that. And just dealing with people of different cultures that you're really not familiar with. It was all the little things that we were exposed to" (PAA 1966–86). This woman became more sociable because of the conditions of work and more independent because of the conditions of after-work hours.

Many women talk of their Pan Am experience by telling similar stories of transformation: they were small-town girls now exposed to the world of urbane jetsetters. The rhetoric of maturity and its processes explains why so many of the women I spoke with consider Pan Am foundational to their lives. Pan Am was the source of lessons and experiences that transformed them into adults. (One can only wonder what they feel they would have become had they never flown for Pan Am. Would they have remained "immature" or would they have grown up into different kinds of adults?) The concept of "maturity"—interpreted as worldliness and cosmopolitanism in specific terms of race and class—is critical when considering the place of Pan Am in these women's lives.

The women say this repeatedly: Pan Am made me who I am today. They acknowledge the critical role of their families and hometown environment, but credit their work-play lives as stewardesses for the molding processes of maturity. In short, Pan Am was the transformative agent, both forcing and enabling them to "grow up." They position themselves as passive recipients of Pan Am's largesse—not only economically but, more important, experientially. But this is incompletely put. I argue that the women were active agents in making themselves through Pan Am. They transformed themselves, appropriating the lessons of the air into their lives. They chose the paths they took, the work they put into that path, and the pleasures they enjoyed, as well as the lessons they incorporated into their lives.

The double meaning in the phrase "Pan Am lives" that I use above is intentional. Pan American World Airways continues to live through the actions and sentiments of these women, other fans, and aficionados, and through the ongoing commercialized nostalgia that is cropping up in unexpected places. The phrase "Pan Am lives" also refers to the women's stories about their own lives, molded by the company—about "growing up" Pan Am. These are lives with yearly, monthly, and some daily reminders of the airline. The women have indeed "become Pan Am"; at the same time, Pan Am continues to become through them.

Six

FRONTIER DREAMS

Race, Gender, Class, Cosmopolitan Mobilities

> The notion of boundary is an ambivalent one: it both separates and unites.
> It is always the boundary of something and so belongs to both frontier
> cultures.
>
> LOTMAN 1990, 136–37

FRONTIERS DEFINE BOUNDARIES to be surpassed. But as Yuri Lotman
points out, a boundary—including a shifting one—"both separates and
unites." Pan Am (and Juan Trippe) inscribed a corporate frontier as a grand-
scale technological, ideological, humanitarian, capitalist, and inevitably
racialized endeavor. "Nisei" stewardesses who flew for Pan Am envisioned
their own frontiers in the making, incorporating themselves within the Pan
Am vision and thus transforming their lives. Let us examine more closely
the nature of these intertwined corporate and personal airborne dreams
and the boundaries they shared. And expanding our outlook more broadly,
let us examine how race, gender, class, and cosmopolitan mobilities defined
the separating and uniting boundaries that helped shape globalism in the
postwar era.

The personal and corporate histories and aspirations unfolded in the
burgeoning postwar cosmopolitanism of the Jet Age. They created a sense
of frontier that mixed new technology with changing economics and old
concepts of race in the development of large-scale global tourism. In the
1950s and 1960s Pan American and Juan Trippe defined that frontier for
the world through the airline's position as a premier trendsetter. But Trippe
could not do it alone. His dreams of frontier and empire could be realized

only with the infrastructure of government and industry, as well as the incorporation of individual workers. The genius of Pan Am lay in how it inculcated worker identities to mesh corporate dreams with individual ones. The quiet daring of the "Nisei" stewardesses lay in how they took Pan Am's corporate ambitions—including celebrity—and carved out their own sense of self within its framework. Given the conservatism of their communities and families during the postwar period, this was daring. Their career paths went outside the model-minority, gendered ideals of teacher and nurse and took to the skies instead.

FRONTIER WOMEN: TRANSGRESSIONS AND CELEBRATIONS OF RACE, CLASS, AND PLACE

By doing so, the "Nisei" stewardesses created and surpassed their own personal frontiers. Let me focus on the Japanese Americans, who formed the core of the group. Some defied the middle- and upper-middle-class aspirations of immigrant families to become "waitresses in the air." They left the ethnic enclave of Japanese Americans to join a mostly white company. They fled the stability of nine-to-five neighborhood jobs and sought out the instability of bidding for routes and flight times. Each month was different. Even more transgressively, the job took them away from home for days at a stretch. This was not the lifestyle to which they were raised. For a group of middle-class Japanese Americans highly concerned with job security and retaining the comforts of middle-class life, the notion of their daughters as "traveling women" could be seen as an embarrassment, even an affront.

And yet the community as a whole celebrated these "frontier women" as marks of prestige for themselves, their family, and Japanese Americans in general. In accepting and even glorifying Pan Am's "Nisei" stewardesses, the community demonstrated its part in incorporating a rapidly expanding frontier to continually redefine itself. The class stigma of working in a service industry did not impinge upon the celebrity of the women. Their job was reconfigured from that of "waitress in the air" to that of a working cosmopolitan with more than a hint of glamour. The prestige of the airline, the wealth of its clientele, and the inclusion of Japan in its routes played a crucial part. Stewardesses and their families viewed the job not merely as work with travel benefits but as round-the-world travel through work.

Even Hawai`i took part in this glorification. The media spotlight on the women became a media spotlight on Hawai`i—by way of Pan American. The women continued to be called "Nisei" long after most of them were well past the second-generation Japanese American designation, long after Pan Am's group included women from China, Japan, Singapore, and the Philippines. The "Nisei" label hung on the coattails of Japanese American war veterans lionized in postwar Hawai`i as heroes. The public relations moment of 1955 was not lost upon institutions such as the Hawaii Visitors Bureau, which could parlay any news of air traffic in and out of the islands as a gesture toward tourist promotion. The fascination was thus not only with the "Nisei" stewardess as a daughter of Hawai`i but on Hawai`i as a tourist destination. The stewardess joined the hula girl as a lure for the tourist dollar: two female bodies, dressed in opposite fashion for the same purpose, one demonstrating the straight lines of domestication, modestly cloaked within a quasi-military uniform, the other demonstrating the curvilinear form of tropical exoticism bared through a hula skirt.

Media in Japan too took notice. From the perspective of Japan, the women demonstrated a startling racial testament of the country's own transcendence: out of war defeat, through the American occupation, and into rocketing postwar economic accomplishment. The "Nisei" stewardesses of the 1950s were not Japanese nationals, but their in-between status as Japanese Americans made them both a biological proving ground and a novelty of citizenship. That they could wear the Pan Am uniform with such aplomb took the Japanese public by surprise. They became prodigal daughters in Japanese media coverage, depicted as doing Japanese things, even while wearing American uniforms. That those uniforms belonged to the most prestigious airline in the world made the Japanese media all the more proud. The frontier of the "Nisei" women thus extended past personal, family, and community boundaries to Asian aspirations as well. They performed a racialized bridge that helped smooth the hitherto confrontational mood between victor and vanquished.

None of the women could have foreseen the extent of what was meant to be a temporary period of their lives. They all expected that once they saw the world they would move on to a life of marriage and children. They did not foresee the seductions of the air. Although many women did fly for only a short time, some found it difficult to quit the lifestyle. Besides the shopping, celebrities, and fancy food, the very act of traveling, including its unpredictability, grew into a desirable way of life. The women inadvertently became footloose—globetrotting cosmopolitans who performed themselves as Japanese (American), American, and always Pan American. Their engagement with the frontier became ongoing; their dreams were in a constant state of becoming.

The element of social class was always part of the fabric of the job. Pan Am training assured that the stewardesses learned the best of everything, at least according to an élite Euro-American definition of the best. They were also to look their best, both on duty and off duty, in colors, styles, and accessories that spelled upper-class tastes. The stewardess profession may have traded on a girl-next-door image, but the neighborhood of Pan Am consisted unapologetically of the wealthy of the world. This gave a tinge of performance glamour to the Pan Am stewardess that suited the theatricality of the role. Race and class were inextricable: passengers were not only rich but for the most part white. Even the nonwhites who flew Pan Am either shared a global élite culture or expected it onboard. The lessons of the cabin for "Nisei" stewardesses thus lay in race and class. The women could train to learn the foodways and dress of the rich. They could even marry up and enter the gates of that wealth. But they could never become white. Race was the ultimate frontier.

I find subtle parallels between transnational Filipina nurses and Pan Am's "Nisei" stewardesses. In Catherine Ceniza Choy's analysis of the nurses, she argues that Filipinas, most of whom were élite by birth and upbringing, found moving to the United States for nursing training and jobs both "liberating and exploitative": the work presented new opportunities abroad, but these opportunities were structured within a larger American colonial framework that racialized the nurses (2003, 20). Likewise, Pan Am's program of "Nisei" stewardesses provided opportunities to middle-class and relatively élite Japanese American (and other) women that many found "liberating," allowing them to leave their homes in a glamour job that transported them to distant places. At the same time, these opportunities were built upon racialized assumptions in hiring, route assignments, and on-the-job practices.

There is more to Choy's analysis than the larger American colonial agenda (in parallel with Pan Am's imperial agenda). The other side of each picture is that the women were "liberated" from a dearth of choices by this new expansive possibility in their lives. Unlike the Filipina nurses, the women who flew for Pan Am took the opportunity as only a temporary phase in their lives. And many of them did stay on the job for only a few years before marrying and retiring. What matters, however, is not the length of employment but the meanings that these women give to their Pan Am years. What I found continually striking is that many of the women who worked for Pan Am for only a few years in their twenties remain some of the airline's biggest champions. Clearly the process of "becoming—and remaining—Pan Am" was not contingent upon long-term employment.

What "Nisei" stewardesses share with other former Pan Am flight attendants is the opportunity to work in a prestigious company, fly to different parts of the world, rub shoulders with the rich and famous, learn about service in exotic environments with exotic peoples, and do so in a period when the company was at the top of its form and could treat them very well. This kind of experience is difficult—some would say impossible—to replicate. Many Pan Am flight attendants from this era have stories of loyalty and gratitude that are similar to those of the "Nisei" stewardesses. Their shared experiences flying for Pan Am circumscribe a particular time and place in postwar America.

However, the Pan Am workplace for "Nisei" stewardesses was different from the rest, and this gives these women's strong sense of attachment a distinctive cast. The differences occur in the areas of race and place. The racialized nature of their hire always conditioned the workplace—even when they became pursers and trainers, even when they became union representatives, even when they were praised as hard-working, gracious, and sincere. In all these instances individual actions added to racial reputations. Their drive to be "not simply good, but better" was interpreted along model-minority lines, amplified by the racialized focus on the women. The gaze of management, other personnel, and passengers was unrelenting— They were criticized if they did not wear a girdle, praised for outstanding service. Others too received criticism and praise, but the criticism and praise that the "Nisei" stewardesses received redounded to the group as a whole. Knowing this placed pressure on the women to behave, because they knew that their actions would inevitably affect others. This was an essential part of inhabiting Pan Am's frontier: the frontier would continually inhabit them as the internalized gaze upon race.

Because many of the "Nisei" stewardesses were from Hawai`i (or an Asian community in California, or Japan or another Asian country) also conditioned the workplace and their experiences of it. Today the stewardesses position themselves as "country girls"—women from areas peripheral to world power. They speak of their naïveté as part of the "country" conditions of their upbringing. They assert these qualities in parallel with class-based conditions, even if some came from families with sufficient wealth to send their daughters to universities.

These conditions of race and place position "Nisei" stewardesses at a remove from the people and context of their employment with Pan American. Their distance from the world that Pan Am employment presented contributed to the huge impact upon their lives. One stewardess says: "The opportunities they afforded me as a little girl from Honolulu who had only been to the mainland twice before, was phenomenal. We went shopping in Beirut, and sat watching all the beautiful people overlooking the Mediterranean!" (PAA 1966–86). A statement such as this places the distance in concrete terms and dramatically illustrates its impact: the stewardess was a "little girl from Honolulu" now traveling the world along with "the beautiful people." Pan Am afforded the "Nisei" stewardesses that distance, opening their eyes even as they were subjected to the constant measure of difference. Both distance (race and place) and its upward trajectory (class) are important to "Nisei" women's talk about Pan Am.

But the subject is not only travel. The rhetoric of maturity informs stewardesses' narratives of "becoming" through Pan Am. When women say, "I had to grow up a lot, fast," they invoke the distance ("a lot"), the speed ("fast"), and the urgency placed upon them. Their act of "growing up" was not always by choice: circumstances forced and enabled the process. In crediting Pan Am with their "growing up," what did they envision themselves becoming? They may have had in mind the people who traveled Pan Am in the 1950s and 1960s—those "beautiful people," the jetsetters, who modeled sophistication and worldliness. For the postwar era these travelers symbolized the cosmopolitan adult. As many of the women say, they themselves had no sense of who or what they could be: they only watched the "beautiful people"; they did not become them. But they had aspirations, and seeing these models up close, imbibing the proximal prestige of the airline, overlooking the Mediterranean like "heiresses," lit a path toward cosmopolitanism, the path of the worldly adult. That this path was enabled and defined by Pan Am suggests the interplay of individual dreams with corporate ones.

The beginning of the end of the closed Asian-language base of Honolulu—and thus the specific program of "Nisei" stewardesses—came about as a result of questions concerning promotion to the rank of purser, a position of responsibility and added pay. In 1970 the newly elected union representative Minnie Nishi noted a discrepancy between the two closed-language bases of Honolulu (Asian) and Washington (European): stewardesses in Washington could become pursers, while those based in Honolulu could not. The situation smelled of racial discrimination to Nishi: "I was new at the time with only two years' flying and wasn't quite up to the rules and regulations, so I made a trip on my own to the San Francisco union hall to research the situation, and in doing so I found out that Washington, D.C., was 'crewed' with European language speakers only, but had their own pursers. Honolulu was an Asian-speaking base without pursers. After returning home, I contacted my parents' attorney, who assisted me in drawing up a letter citing racial discrimination. I then mailed out to each flight attendant a copy of the letter with a stamped, self-addressed envelope. Once I received a fifty-one-percent-of-the-base-signed draft, I then contacted Ernie Mitchell in New York and we presented the bundle to then-president of Pan Am, Halaby. In 1971 we got our own pursers" (personal communication, 28 March 2007). In August 1972 the first group of eight Honolulu-based stewardess-turned-pursers celebrated their promotion with a photo in the local newspaper. The eight women—Grace Fujisawa, Evelyn Hiroshige, Ruth Migita, Joyce Harada Patrick, Jeanne Sakakihara, Frances Okazaki Sigler, Cynthia Tsujiuchi, and Charlotte Yamashiro—represented an achievement for Asian (American) women in an American corporation. Pan Am also decided to change the Honolulu base to open status, ending the closed unit of Asian languages and effectively the racial and ethnic enclave of the operation.

This decision marked the end of an era for Pan American, Honolulu, and the "Nisei" stewardesses. The opening of the base meant that they shared it with other non-Asian-language hires. It also gave further opportunities for women in Honolulu. But while operating as a closed base, Honolulu represented a node of racial and cultural exclusivity that was not duplicated afterward. In fact, it is this exclusivity that the women fondly recall: the same boundaries that limited promotion were boundaries of familiarity and intimacy. Those boundaries may have locked the women in and kept them from agitating for more, but they also kept others at bay.

During the years 1955 to 1972 "Nisei" stewardesses acted as a site of what I call "translational identities"—identities whose very in-betweenness are convenient bridges, translating experiences from one realm to another. The stewardesses bridged images of the Asian woman with their own sense of themselves as Asian and Asian American. They bridged the whiteness of the Pan American cabin with an evolving concept of who and what they were. In doing this they engaged with their own representation by negotiating the terrain of their performances. In the process they learned the power of consent and resistance. Their work on board the airline demanded constant translation, brokering racialized, gendered, classed, and regionalized identities with individuated ones, and back again. The process was and is continual. As Stuart Hall asserts, identity is "a 'production' which is never complete, always in process, and always constituted within, not outside, representation" (1990, 222). "Nisei" stewardesses' interaction with their own representation characterized the frontier.

These identities are generational. Those who flew for and with Pan Am during its heyday of the 1950s and 1960s constitute a postwar crowd who were there at the birth of the Jet Age. This Pan Am generation is a crowd defined by social class, as much as jetsetters were. Even if one was not truly a jetsetter, one could still participate in the Jet Age through media representations and personal aspirations. In this Pan Am was supreme, grabbing the spotlight whenever it could.[1]

On 26 April 2005 more than one hundred "Nisei" stewardesses gathered at a country club in Honolulu to commemorate the fiftieth anniversary of Pan Am's program. They came from as far away as Tokyo and Paris to join in a nostalgia-filled luncheon of celebration. For the event they created a *mon* (family crest) imprinted on t-shirts and bags: two fans, one representing their Asian heritage, the other with the famous Pan Am logo. Senator Daniel Inouye sent his greetings: "With their grace, intelligence, bilingual fluency, and devotion to service, [the "Nisei" stewardesses] were unofficial ambassadors for not only Pan Am, but also for the United States and Hawaii." They displayed their uniforms, bags, pins, and photographs. Most of all, they displayed themselves and each other. Their shared role in Pan

American's development of air travel in Asia and the Pacific was only the underpinning for the collective memories of their personal experiences.

Their memories may be refracted in different ways. For them Pan American was a "first love," a "teacher in the air," a key agent that they used in transforming themselves from "naïve, island girl" to "worldly adult." In the process of working within Pan Am's corporate dreams they interpolated several of their own. They surpassed their own novelty, amused (and made incredulous) by how others racialized them. They created dreams on their own terms, learning upper-class ways that would allow them to switch modes at will, often refusing the parties that surrounded them, sometimes "marrying up," sometimes not. I do not want to overstate their agency. Nor do I want to say that all "Nisei" stewardesses who worked for Pan Am felt the same way. The ones who spoke with me tended to be among those most strongly devoted to the airline and their Pan Am selves. Yet judging from what they say and what others said about them, they were hardly unique in their experiences and collective memories. They were employees in a large, prestigious airline that needed their image and quality of service to help realize corporate dreams. They worked within corporate hierarchies encoded by race, gender, age, class, and region. But many also learned to work the hierarchies to their own advantage, displacing stereotypes or confounding them with their own individuated practices. They smiled all the way to their own first-class seat.

BEYOND ASSIMILATION? MARKETING PRACTICES OF COMMODITY CITIZENSHIP

It is useful to compare "Nisei" stewardesses' experiences with those of the Nisei WACS mentioned in chapter 1. Both the United States military and Pan Am offered training in assimilation to women, whether overtly in the lessons of the classroom or covertly in the shared space of American white culture. Many of the Nisei WACS talk of how "military service facilitated their goal of attaining the American dream" (Moore 2003, 151). That American dream rested in "full citizenship rights" for their families as well as in the upward mobility that military service afforded them. I argue that part of that upward mobility may be attributed to the shared space of whiteness of the military experience. Nisei WACS, like "Nisei" stewardesses, worked alongside white professionals. They worked alongside other people of color as well, but in general whites held the power that structured the institution. They also traveled to distant places, meeting different peoples, while in the uniform of the United States. These same elements defined the experience of "Nisei" stewardesses.

However, the stage for "Nisei" stewardesses was fundamentally different. Theirs was a commodified, performative role, often interpreted as a glamour job. Their place on the national stage took on a different tinge—less legitimized perhaps than the critical wartime function of the military, but no less important for the postwar role of the global travel industry. That place could be called "commodity citizenship"—membership in the larger group in capitalist terms. Of course they shared other kinds of belonging with other citizens. But in addition, as Aihwa Ong argues, "mobile individuals who possess human capital or expertise are highly valued and can exercise citizenship-like claims in diverse locations" (2007, 7). I use Ong's analysis of a later neoliberal order to argue that "Nisei" stewardesses possessed the cultural capital that allowed them to make tenuous claims to membership among the jetsetters. This cultural capital had its own set of limitations and problems: trade in this capital rested in the stewardesses' own commodification. I call this complex of cultural capital, market trade, and belonging commodity citizenship. In an age that predates multiculturalism, the place of the "Nisei" stewardesses in the Pan Am cabin demonstrated just how global—and national—the travel industry could be. The industry's globalism rested not in any profound intercultural, international exchange but on commodified images and bodies. Pan Am hired Asian (American) women to compete in a market of global travel primarily because its management thought that what the "Nisei" stewardesses brought to bear—Asian languages and the image of the Asian woman—would sell. What the airline had to sell was the "Family of Man" in the air, and more specifically the racial frontier of Asia as the exotic domestic (or the domesticated exotic). This historicized brand of cosmopolitanism—the "orientations and competencies" of global consciousness founded in race, class, and gender—earned "Nisei" stewardesses their berth.

"Nisei" stewardesses share structures and practices of the racial frontier with other women of color. Ien Ang's essay on gender and multiculturalism in Australia of the 1990s finds parallels here. What prompted her essay was an Australian governmental poster of a young Asian-featured woman with the caption "Come and join our family." For Ang this poster inscribes the "complex and profound" ambivalence surrounding multiculturalism on two levels: at the structural level, where difference is simultaneously benign and conflictual, and at the more personal level, where there are continuing tensions between majority-minority subjects (2001, 143). "If the ambivalence of multicultural discourse creates a space, . . . then it is a space in which minority subjects are both discursively confined and symbolically embraced" (Ang 2001, 147). This is the in-between state of being confined and embraced that the "Nisei" stewardess inhabited. What Ang writes of Australian multiculturalism could be said of the Pan Am cabin as well: "In contemporary Australia, . . . Asians are no longer excluded . . . , nor are they merely reluctantly included *despite* their 'difference,' but *because* of it! What we have here is acceptance through difference, inclusion by virtue of otherness" (2001, 146). That difference is gendered and racialized—within Australia's multicultural, multiracial desire of the 1990s, as well as in the structuring of the Pan Am cabin of 1955. Habits of the heart, it seems, are difficult to break. Those habits find other parallels, as may be seen in Arlene Davila's study of the marketing of Latino culture in the United States: "The commodification of U.S. Latinas involves their re-authentification by association with the 'right' way to be an 'ethnic,' which requires them to be 'exotic,' that is, cultural different, but to stay within normative patterns in which the traits of upward mobility are always associated with an aspirational Anglo not Latina world" (2001, 98). The "exotic" for Latinos in the United States keeps them within a "frontier" (Anglophone sense), but outside of a more profound *frontera* (from the Spanish; a frontier of their own making) (Saldizar 1997). The difference lies in who gets to control and define that aspirational world that we might call cosmopolitanism.

These other examples make clear the connections between the "Nisei" stewardess program and the "acceptance through difference" that formed the backdrop for the "right way to be an ethnic." The lessons of the Pan Am cabin constitute the multicultural ideal of the assimilated minority. The "right way to be an ethnic" parallels Pan Am's program of "Nisei" stewardesses: simultaneously exotic and domesticated through rigorous training in corporate blue. The underlying assimilationist message was clearly written under the raced and classed banner of professionalism and a nascent multiculturalism by which the Pan Am Way carried the prestige of the world.

The right way to be an ethnic is also importantly gendered. It is quite clearly women who are the conduit of desire and service. However, this is not simply the story of a white male corporation looking upon Asian women as sexual objects. There is too much talking back, sitting down, and turning around to paint such an overdetermined picture. Even as they smiled corporate smiles, the "Nisei" stewardesses ate leftover caviar, tried on ermine coats, gained competence and education, and experienced the challenges of the new. The Asian (American) women understood the right way to be an ethnic, even as some of them fled model-daughter jobs as teachers and nurses, then ran from or delayed model-daughter lives as wives and mothers. They were "right ethnics" doing some "wrong things."

Other Asian Americans at the time were practicing the "wrong way to be an ethnic." In 1964 Patsy Takemoto Mink became the first Asian American woman elected to the U.S. Congress. A firebrand liberal, Mink would go on to sponsor what eventually became the pathbreaking Title IX Amendment of the Higher Education Act (later renamed the Patsy T. Mink Opportunity in Education Act). Meanwhile, the longest student strike in American history, co-sponsored by the Asian American Political Alliance at San Francisco State College in 1968–69, resulted in the establishment of the first school of ethnic studies (Umemoto 2000). These Asian Americans were "bad ethnics" by assimilationist standards—having little to do with exoticism and overstepping the bounds of enclave aspirations.

In many ways the "Nisei" stewardesses and these bad ethnics were miles apart. The "Nisei" smiled, while the others lobbied and staged strikes. They seemingly accepted the terms of the American contract, while others challenged it. They acquiesced while others demanded a voice. The differences may be easily seen as polar opposites in terms of goals, methods, and modes of interaction. But does one really negate the other? Is there no common ground? I argue that there is, in the concept of frontier—in the newness of the endeavor, in expanded goals, in the redefined terms of the encounter. The "Nisei" stewardess program encompassed frontiers on many levels, from the corporate to the personal. The stewardesses' frontier was a particular racial frontier that promoted Asian women while denying the promotion of, for example, African American women. The "Nisei" grew up as corporate persons, leaving homes and becoming the persons that some never intended to be. They redefined the terms of the encounter by their longevity and by taking positions of responsibility. If Pan Am ever had Madame Butterfly in mind, they did not expect her to become a union representative and to challenge racist policies. Theirs was a commodity frontier of global tourism, answering to a rising Asian market, but more importantly placing the Asian (American) stewardess in service to the jetset traveler. Undoubtedly the "bad ethnics" sought to work against these very corporate strategies and images, but in doing so they failed to recognize the agency of the women who seemed so very complicit in the airline's strategy (at least on one level). The frontier for the bad ethnics lay in explicit empowerment and political action. Their American assimilation could be seen as far more complete than that of "Nisei" stewardesses, as they embraced the foundation of the politics of representation in a thoroughgoing manner. In many ways both "Nisei" stewardesses and bad ethnics invested themselves in endeavors of representation—one for commodified purposes, the other for identity politics.

PAN AM'S OWN EPILOGIC NOSTALGIA

The Jet Age encompassed not only rising ethnic expectations but also falling corporate realities. Pan Am's failed business dealings of the 1970s and 1980s—a loss in revenue from higher fuel costs during the energy crisis of 1973, a misguided merger with National Airlines in 1980, an inflexible corporate culture that could not respond to changing air travel—paved the way for the airline's eventual downfall in 1991. By that time it was clear that Pan Am was an airline out of step with the culture of budget travel prompted by the Airline Deregulation Act of 1978.

The end of Pan Am on 4 December 1991 prompted a flurry of emotion from employees and management, as well as from passengers who fondly remembered the airline's most successful years. In 1992 company executives established the Pan Am Historical Foundation, whose goal was "to preserve the history and accomplishments of Pan American World Airways, and the people who worked to make her the World's Greatest Airline" (http://www.panam.org).[2] Besides the Pan Am Historical Foundation, employee organizations create continuing ties to the company. One of the most vibrant of these, and the one which best expresses Pan Am's public ethos, is World Wings International, a nonprofit service organization of retired flight attendants.[3] In 2007 World Wings International had over two thousand active members in thirty-four local chapters and members-at-large in twenty-three countries.[4]

The slogan of the group—"Pan Am brought us together; World Wings keeps us together"—accurately describes the role of the organization for active members. Another slogan—"Gone but not forgotten"—expresses the spunky, even defiant, spirit of former employees. The organization "keeps its members together" through meetings (a yearly international convention and local chapter meetings), newsletters (*Jet Wings*, the official newsletter of World Wings International, as well as separate newsletters of local chapters), charitable activities (working with CARE to help women and children in developing countries, and taking part in local service projects),[5] and social activities. The centerpiece event for the organization is its annual convention, held yearly since 1970, usually in the United States but also in Europe, Asia, and more recently aboard cruise ships.[6] World Wings International also sponsors an oral history project, housed at the University of Miami, Richter Library; maintains a uniform collection; and publishes a yearly calendar. If a woman is an active World Wings member, she is likely busy with the organization—and thus with Pan Am—frequently throughout the year.

Other Pan Am organizations include Clipper Pioneers (for retired pilots), a retired employees' association, and special groups that commemorate historic flights (e.g. the fall of Saigon flight, the Korean orphan baby lift, the Dooley Foundation flight).[7] Many other veterans of Pan Am do not necessarily join groups but socialize informally with other Pan Am people. In doing so these and other former employees of Pan Am demonstrate the strength of their ties to the airline nearly twenty years after its demise.

Pan Am memorabilia fuel nostalgia for the former airline. One former employee now in her eighties, Mary Goshgarian, sells memorabilia at the Pan Am AWARE shop, at the Pan Am International Flight Academy in Miami.[8] The AWARE organization was begun over thirty years ago as an employee-run support association for the airline. In 2007 goods sold at the AWARE store include videotapes, model airplanes, tableware, bags, clothing,[9] jewelry, calendars, bumper stickers, and license plates bearing legends such as "We're back" and "Gone but not forgotten," along with the Pan Am logo. One may thus embellish one's everyday life with proclamations of Pan Am. The proceeds from sales "go to AWARE's work to keep the name and history alive for future generations" (http://www.panam.org).

Nostalgia for Pan Am extends to the general marketplace, through on-line retailers such as eBay, antique, consignment, and secondhand shops, and specialty shops devoted to airline memorabilia. Whereas the goods sold by AWARE are marketed under the informal auspices of the Pan Am Historical Foundation, other Pan Am merchandise is not under official control. For example, in April 2007 in SoHo in New York City, at Marchand de Legumes, a hip vintage store run by Japanese (whose website is primarily in Japanese, www.marchanddelegumes.com), I found numerous Pan Am nostalgia items, from old in-flight bags ($58, $68), to replicas of bags ($48 to $75), to replicas of vintage postcards (set of twenty for $16.99), to notecards (set of sixteen for $18.00), to travel magnets ($9.00).[10] All the replicas are from a company called GoPanAm. The tin of notecards reads: "Pan Am has defined modern air travel by shaping airline services since its early days. Pan Am perfected the craft of offering passengers the ultimate flying experience from the late 30's to the mid 60's. Pan Am was the benchmark in luxury travel and coined the term 'jet setting.' During this time Pan Am represented the sophistication & class that only the world's premier airline could offer." Another fashionable travel boutique in three locations in New York City also carries GoPanAm items, and makes oblique reference to the airline through its name, Flight 001—Pan American's renowned round-the-world westbound flight (www.flight001.com). A British consumerist website, "Retro to Go: A Guide to All Things Hip and Retro," also displays these Pan Am items as "vintage reissues" (www. retrotogo.com).

GoPanAm is a subsidiary of Machine Project, Inc., which acquired the Pan Am license in 2006 and began marketing Pan Am products in 2007. In an interview Irving Glazer, the company's communication and sales director, and Anthony Lucas, its brand planner, explained that their marketing is aimed not so much at baby boomers who might have flown Pan Am as to people in their twenties and thirties, for whom the airline is a distant icon (personal communication, 17 May 2007). This younger generation has no direct experience with Pan Am, but through the company's marketing efforts it is becoming acquainted with an image of the airline that brought the Beatles to the United States. They learn about the image through goods and a label—Pan Am jetsetter commodities, now a source of retro fetishism—sold to the material child, for whom any lifestyle, sentiment, or era may be purchased.

Meanwhile, another Asian company produces and sells imitation Pan Am bags for sale in department stores of Tokyo, as well as the bazaars of

Phnom Penh, suggesting that nostalgia for Pan Am crosses as many continents and oceans as the airline once did. Tracing Pan Am's current global trek is dizzying. Even a high-fashion designer such as Marc Jacobs has got into the act (through GoPanAm), releasing his own version of the Pan Am bag in 2007—one side says "Pan Am," the other "Marc Jacobs."

This dual-sided object invokes nostalgia for postwar America and its era of domination. But what is the object of nostalgia? What is Marc Jacobs's intervention on Pan Am? Or perhaps more to the point, what is Pan Am's intervention on Marc Jacobs? I argue that this nostalgia repossesses postwar America through selective visions of a past that subverts the tensions of internal race relations and Cold War global configurations onto a tropical idyll to be contained within the luxuries of first-class service. The "home away from home" of the Pan Am cabin domesticates difference into sensual pleasures of dancing hula maidens and demure geishas. Even during the Jet Age, these images were old and evoked luxury travel of a previous heyday. The exact years of the images matters less to present-day consumers who see in the postcards and bags a past age—modern, yet old—refracted through nostalgia.

There is more. Since the airline's demise in 1991, there have been new incarnations of the Pan American brand. The first of these was short-lived: an airline by that name flying from 1996 to 1998 between the United States and the Caribbean. The second was run by Guilford Transportation Industries, a company in New Hampshire headed by Tim Mellon, from the wealthy banking family. This "Pan Am" operated from 1998 to 2004, flying primarily charters in the eastern United States and the Dominican Republic, and subsequently scheduled operations in New England, Florida, and Puerto Rico. From November 2004 the business, still controlled by Guilford, was operated by Boston-Maine Airways, in February 2005 it took the name Pan Am Clipper Connection, and in March 2006 Guilford Rail System changed its name to Pan Am Railways and redecorated its railway cars with the Pan Am name and colors (www.guilfordrail.com). "Pan Am," it seems, cannot die.

Pan Am nostalgia takes yet another turn in performances by the Australian comedienne Caroline Reid, also known as "Pam Ann." Using the familiar blue globe logo and font, but with the name "Pam Ann" replacing the airline's, she has gained popularity in Britain and elsewhere as a "bitchy, overly made-up air hostess, all lipstick and white gloves" (Lewisohn 2003).

In an interview Reid explained that she chose Pan American as the source of her comedy precisely because it was the premier airline in the 1960s and 1970s, evoking style, class, glamour, jetsetters, and James Bond (personal communication, 6 June 2007). Reid's humor is ribald and outrageous, with overt gay ties (her website shows a passport labeled "GAY.COM"). In 2004 she performed in New York for twenty former Pan Am stewardesses: "I have only gotten a great response from my audiences and if you can make the real crew laugh, you are doing a good job" (ibid.). Pam Ann's comedy only toys with nostalgia, but her barbs are a sign of the continuing popularity of the airline and the notion that there will never be another airborne empire quite like Pan American's. The logic of Reid's camp works on this shared assumption.

That there are so many manifestations of Pan Am in the twenty-first century speaks to the durable legacy and visuality of its image. The color, font, and design of the company's blue globe evoke an era. Edward Barnes could not have predicted the longevity of his design in 1955. Pan Am nostalgia for the general public rests in the notion expressed by GoPanAm of "jet-setting," "luxury travel," and "sophistication & class." Even in a spoof such as Pam Ann's, the airline's image remains intact. The spoof only works because the image is so strong.

RETYING THREE STRANDS OF A JET AGE TALE

Let us return to the three strands of this story—Japanese Americans, Pan American World Airways, and the Jet Age. Pan Am and its "Nisei" stewardesses are each a lens through which the other can be viewed at a particular period in American and global history. It is important to situate the story as a form of postcolonial cosmopolitanism, highlighting both the intimate nature of the enterprise—bodies, smiles, girls next door—and the grand scale of the endeavor—corporate legacies, advanced technology, empire. In Ann Stoler's words, these are "tense and tender ties," embodying contradictions and cachet (2001).

The cover of the 2007 calendar of World Wings International depicts two Pan Am stewardesses, Carol Woodward (white) and Lois Okamoto (Japanese American), seated and in uniform, holding flags of the countries served by Pan Am's round-the-world flights 001 and 002. Against a superimposed background of a map of the world and a Pan Am jet,[11] Woodward's

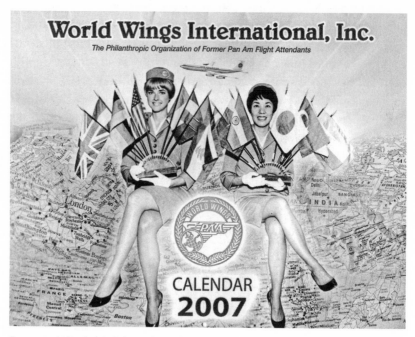

East meets West (original date unknown).

bank of flags includes those of the United States and Britain; Okamoto's flags prominently include that of Japan. The photo depicts two of Pan Am's girls next door in a neighborhood defined as "the world." For the time the world was indeed Pan Am's. One "Nisei" stewardess estimates that in the seven years she flew with Pan Am, from 1963 to 1969, she circled the globe fifty-five times. If one could quantify "worldliness," one might say that she had logged more distance crisscrossing the world than nearly anyone else. (After all, it was "Nisei" stewardesses who remained on the round-the-world flights while other members of the crew changed.) Pan Am's poster girls speak well to the claim of the airline in calling the world their neighborhood, a claim symbolized by the twinned, racialized images of the girls next door. But it is worthwhile to pause and look again at the images. One takes for granted the white, Euro-American girl next door. She is our assumption of the airline standard. The extension of Pan Am's postwar image rests elsewhere. That image and that claim to the international world rest in the invocation of the Asian (American) woman. She is the authenticating presence to Pan Am's claim. Sheathed in the iconic Tunis blue uniform of professionalism, she does not simply complete the picture; she defines it through the metaphoric site of her body.

In many ways it comes down to this: bodies as metaphors, uniforms of professionalism, claims of "the world." The linking of these elements, small and large, demonstrates the intertwining of airborne dreams, personal and corporate. If Pan American was going to retain its dominance in the postwar era, it would have to compete with upstart competitors such as Japan Airlines. More important, it would have to wield the tools of that competition, which increasingly involved its image as an airline that could do it all and had it all. Placing the Asian (American) woman on board helped prove Pan Am's point.

At the same time, the Asian (American) women whom Pan Am placed on board discovered their own dreams in the making. These dreams went far beyond the wary expectations of their upbringing in postwar America. The racialized specter of the Second World War, Cold War confrontations in Asia, heated race relations, a burgeoning American and global popular culture, and images of Asian women formed a distant backdrop. A more immediate backdrop included family, friends, and the Japanese American community. The "Nisei" women knew they would be traveling to Asia and the rest of the world. But they had no idea that they would be traveling uncharted territory inward, taking up positions of power within themselves. Crossing this frontier surprised many of them. The cosmopolitans that they became enthusiastically embraced their new status as "Pan Am people," but they also celebrated their own emergent selves as women whose airborne dreams brought postwar riches into their lives.

To return to the question I posed in the introduction: How are frontier and cosmopolitanism intertwined in this multi-stranded story? The answers lie in the concepts of mobility that fueled the era. The Jet Age may have been founded upon the technology that gave the period its name, but the airplanes themselves were only part of the story. As jets symbolized new possibilities of shrinking distances, lightning speed, and mobile populations, so too did they become a metaphor for the social changes that accompanied these hyper-modern attributes. The personal and group mobility afforded by new professions newly opened to women became part of the Jet Age. "Nisei" stewardesses' smiling Asian faces contrasted with other nonwhite faces elsewhere amid sites of racialized conflict, both domestic and foreign. These kinds of rapid social changes acted as prompts for nostalgia. Thus Pan Am as a site of group and personal nostalgia indexes both the establishment and passing of an era. That era wedded the conceptual and material possibilities of the Jet Age, reconstructed as a golden period of travel and exoticized fantasy. The trick of the Pan Am uniform lay in making the "Nisei" stewardess both desirably exotic and believably familiar. The practices of the Jet Age fantasy lay in other larger processes of "assimilation" as well, taken broadly and metaphorically: from the margins to the metropoles, from ethnic enclaves to the multicultural cabin, and even further to the multinational world. Here lie the transformations of empire that link frontier and cosmopolitanism in a postcolonial setting.

Pan Am's "Nisei" stewardess lived amid the contradictions of the period: "good ethnics," "bad ethnics," and the mixings of these; the display of women "of color but not colored"; Cold War meddling in Asia and incendiary racial tensions at home; Jet Age glamour and one-world exploitation; the hyper-sexualization of the stewardess profession and feminist-led union activism; Sinatra cool and younger Elvis heat. She flew in the latest jets, embodying newer "borderless" freedom in an industry built upon older, racialized femininity. Sinatra's Jet Age hit "Come Fly with Me" painted jetsetter lives aloft, "where the air is rarefied," en route to Bombay, Peru, and Acapulco Bay.[12] For the American public Sinatra's voice evoked the desires of an era and transformed dreamy, far-off places into household words, even if many listeners could not find them on a map. This was the context for Pan Am's hiring of the "Nisei" stewardess, bringing into the cabin "Asia" and the exotic girl next door. As she moved beyond home and into the spotlight of globalism, the "Nisei" stewardess discovered a stepping stone to her own emergent cosmopolitanism, built upon the race, gender, and class assumptions of the era. Her leap from "country girl" to Jet Age cosmopolitan can be configured as an American postwar story fraught with the complexities of the times.

This, however, is not her story alone. It is also the story of an airline that defined the terrain of postwar empire. That Pan Am was meant to be an "empire of the air" reinforced the notion that its "world," and thus its worldliness, were limitless. Pan Am advertised itself as the expert of the world to the world, as the first and foremost cosmopolitan pioneer. By this position it inhabited its own self-proclaimed frontier as a purveyor of dreams. The "Nisei" stewardess joined the ranks of other Pan Am "dream girls," part of a multilingual, multicultural, and now multiracial display. This display defined Jet Age cosmopolitanism, performing difference as a gendered and racialized commodity. The dreams were for sale. That these airborne reveries have become the stuff of nostalgia in the twenty-first century suggests an unabated, reconfigured hunger for that old sense of the new. Sinatra's invitation to "Come Fly with Me" sings of nothing less than the seductions of Jet Age swing—mobility as a pendulum that arcs back to the familiar, even while appearing to glide forward.

CHRONOLOGY OF
PAN AMERICAN WORLD AIRWAYS,
1927–1991

Events particularly pertinent to the subject of this book are in boldface.

1927   **Pan American Airways, Inc., begun, headed by Juan Trippe as a subsidiary of Aviation Corporation of the Americas.**

1928   **Pan Am hires its first male steward, Amaury Sanchez (native of Puerto Rico).**

1929   Trippe tours Latin America with Charles Lindbergh to secure landing rights. Offers flights down west coast of South America to Peru.
Pan American-Grace Airways (Panagra) is formed; gains further routes in South America.

1934   First Clippers: Sikorsky S-40 flying boats to Panama.

1935   **First scheduled trans-Pacific flights.**

16 April 1935   Historic trans-Pacific flight to Hawai`i from San Francisco Bay (landed in Pearl Harbor, taking 18 hours and 37 minutes); returned to San Francisco five days later with fourteen thousand pieces of U.S. mail.

22 November 1935   Beginning of first scheduled air service over a major ocean route: Pan Am's China Clipper, headed for Manila, Philippines (landed and refueled in Honolulu, then Wake island, then Guam, then Manila).

1939   Boeing 314 Flying Boat Clippers purchased by Pan Am.
First regular transatlantic air passenger service from New York to Europe.

1940   President Franklin D. Roosevelt secretly awards Pan Am contracts to build airports throughout Central and South America to counteract German air power, defend Panama Canal, and transport supplies to Allied powers in the Mediterranean and Asia. In August 1941 these efforts are extended to Africa, where Pan Am pilots transport airplanes and materials to British forces in Egypt and the Mediterranean.

Pan Am quickly develops Pan American Airways-Africa, Ltd., to aid allies in Second World War.

1943 Roosevelt uses Pan Am to become first president of the United States to fly overseas.

1944 **Pan American Airways hires first stewardess.**

1945 Pan Am's ground service employees unionized under Transport Workers Union (Air Transport Division); later flight service personnel are also included.

1946 **Pan Am hires its first European flight attendants.**
Faces airline competition for the first time from other carriers in the United States: TWA, American Export, Northwest Orient Airline, Braniff.

1947 **First commercial round-the-world flight (not sustained).**

1948 Pan Am introduces "tourist class."

1949 Double-decker Boeing Stratocruiser introduced.

1950 **Name changed to Pan American World Airways.**
Introduction of trademark slogan "World's Most Experienced Airline."
Pan Am establishes round-the-world Flights 001 (westbound) and 002 (eastbound).
Pan Am recruits its first Hispanic stewardesses to fly to Latin America.

1955 **Pan Am orders largest fleet of commercial jet airliners, ushering in the Jet Age.**
New blue-globe logo, created by the New York architect Edward Barnes.
Beginning of "Nisei" stewardess program, based in Honolulu.
"Hiroshima maidens" transported from Japan to the United States for plastic surgery.

1958 **Pan Am flies first fleet of passenger jets (Boeing 707).**
Pan Am's flight from New York to Paris is first scheduled commercial jet flight by a United States airline.

1959 **Jet service begins to Hawai'i and Asia.**
Pan Am is first airline to offer sustained round-the-world jet service.

1960 Pan Am builds Worldport, Terminal 3 at John F. Kennedy International Airport. Terminal symbolizes the Jet Age with its "flying saucer" roof.

1962 Pan Am creates Panamac, the first global electronic reservation system; becomes the model for all other airlines' reservation systems.

1962 Pan Am acquires Inter-Continental Hotels.

1963 Opening of Pan Am building and headquarters in New York on Park Avenue.
Company hires six stewardesses in the Caribbean: two from Haiti, two from Guadeloupe, two from Trinidad.

1964 NAACP **accuses Pan Am of discriminatory hiring practices; company points to its Caribbean stewardesses.**

1965 **Pan Am hires its first African American flight attendant.**

1966 **Pan Am starts to hire Japanese nationals to fly in the Pacific Division.**

Pan Am orders new wide-bodied jumbo jets (Boeing 747).

1968   Juan Trippe steps down as CEO of Pan Am; Harold Gray takes over.

1969   Pan Am issues symbolic tickets to the Moon.

1970   Najeeb Halaby takes over as head from Gray.

Boeing 747 begins flying, christened by First Lady Pat Nixon. First commercially scheduled 747 commences, flying from New York to London.

1972   **Celio Diaz Jr. sues Pan Am for sex discrimination under Civil Rights Act of 1964.**

1973   Worldwide oil crisis greatly affects Pan Am.

Pan Am Flight 110 is target of terrorist attack in Rome by Palestinian group; thirty people killed.

1976   Pan Am's Clipper Liberty Bell (Boeing 747 SP-21) breaks commercial round-the-world record with a time of 46 hours, 50 seconds, New York to New York, with stopovers in New Delhi and Tokyo.

1977   Pan Am's Clipper New Horizons (Boeing 747 SP-21) sets new record for a commercial aircraft flying around the globe over the equator and two poles with a time of 54 hours, 7 minutes, 12 seconds, San Francisco to San Francisco, with stopovers in London, Cape Town, and Auckland.

Pan Am's Clipper Victoria (Boeing 747) involved in Tenerife disaster, the worst disaster in aviation history; Pan Am plane collides on the runway with a KLM 747. Total of 583 persons killed, 335 aboard the Pan Am airplane.

1978   Airline Deregulation Act.

1980   Pan Am tries to gain domestic routes by merging with National Airlines. William Seawell takes over as head.

1981   Juan Trippe dies.

1985   **Pan Am sells all its Pacific routes to United Airlines.**
Edward Acker takes over as head.

1986   Hijacking of Pan Am Flight 73 in Pakistan; twenty passengers and crew members killed.

1988   Bombing of Pan Am Flight 103 above Lockerbie, Scotland; 270 killed.

1991   **Pan Am declares bankruptcy; Atlantic routes sold to Delta Airlines.**

Notes

INTRODUCTION

1 The postwar Japanese American magazine *Scene*, based in Chicago and published from 1949 to 1953, also extended the use of the term "nisei" to mean second-generation Asian Americans, especially in its later years when the magazine included articles about Asian ethnic groups other than Japanese Americans to broaden its readership (Lim 2006, 116–17).

2 This is a popular claim among commercial airlines, premising quality upon experience. In 2008 Qantas Airline adopted the same slogan, "World's Most Experienced Airline," making the claim on the basis of having a longer record of continuous operation than any other airline. Other airlines that have made similar claims include Finnair and Mexicana.

3 The history of anti-Asian immigration laws in the United States begins with the Chinese Exclusion Act of 1882, followed by the Gentlemen's Agreement of 1907–8, extending exclusion to Japanese and Koreans. The Immigration Act of 1917 further excluded Asian Indians from entry. The Immigration Act of 1924 effectively banned admission of Chinese, Japanese, Koreans, and Asian Indians. The Tydings-McDuffie Act of 1934 then added Filipinos to the list. These restrictions upon Asians emigrating to the United States lasted until the landmark Immigration Act of 1965 that dismantled national origins quotas and banned discrimination by race, religion, or national origin. This act effectively ended systematic racial discrimination against Asians and transformed the immigration picture from a primarily European movement to one in which Asians constituted a major part (Ong and Liu 2000, 155, 159). As a result of the Immigration Act of 1965, Pan Am was able to begin hiring Japanese nationals and eventually other Asians to fill the Asian language positions.

4 Pan Am was part of the very fabric of life in a place such as Hawai`i. For example, in 1936 the yearbook of the main public high school in Honolulu, McKinley

High School, included a multipage photo and narrative spread on the historic role of Pan American Airways and its Clipper ships to Hawai`i.

5   Although BOAC offered the first jet passenger service in 1952 with the Havilland Comet, this experiment failed, and crashes led to the suspension of flights in 1954. Thus Pan Am's order for passenger jets in 1955, and its highly successful trans-Atlantic flying of them from 1958 on, may be considered the effective start of the Jet Age.

6   BOAC's early Asian hires were not full-fledged stewardesses but "assistants" whose "exotic" dress contrasted with the military-inspired regular stewardess uniforms. According to BOAC literature, they were viewed as an "eye-catching, publicity-winning innovation" (quoted in Mills 2006, 160).

7   By 1953 the Japan Civil Aviation Bureau certified the first two Japanese as flight navigators and one Japanese as a DC-4 co-pilot. In 1954 it hired its first two Japanese certified as DC-4 pilots, and in 1955 it hired its first two Japanese certified DC-6B pilots—that is, the first Japanese pilots on international routes (www .jal.com/en/history/history/). As a side note, in 1953, even before it began flying internationally, it opened sales offices in New York and Honolulu.

8   Pan Am's hiring of "Nisei" stewardesses in 1955 was not the first accommodation made to attract the Japanese-speaking passenger. An article in 1953 in the employee newsletter the *Clipper: Pacific-Alaska Division* explained: "The growing number of Japanese-speaking passengers flying between Japan and the United States had created a problem. Rather than teach all flight crews and traffic personnel Japanese, a quicker solution was hit upon" ("Pan Amerikan Koukuu-gaisha" 1953, 8). That solution was a twenty-five-page illustrated handbook for the Japanese customer, including English phrases and words, as well as explanations in Japanese of plane routes, in-flight information, and other points of interest.

9   Using "frontier" evokes the field of border theory pioneered in Latina/o cultural studies by scholars such as Gloria Anzaldúa in her innovative book *Borderland / La Frontera: The New Mestiza* (1987). Drawing upon her own experiences of the border between Mexico and the United States, Anzaldúa argues that liminal spaces such as these can be analyzed both as a physical location and as a symbolic resource indexing cultural meeting grounds fraught with tensions and violence—what she calls "intimate terrorism" (1987, 20). Anzaldúa proposes a new borderland subject—not the fear-laden subaltern but the "*nueva mestiza*," the new woman of hybrid spaces. The "Nisei" stewardesses are not *nueva mestiza*. But their experiences negotiating the spaces in between as part of the "frontier" of trade in postwar American racial politics can be interpreted as a new mix that holds forth possibilities for agency and change. Herein lies the overlap between frontiers and borderlands (*"la frontera"*).

10 Internment targeted primarily Japanese Americans on the West Coast but extended eventually to Canada and South America.

11 The stereotyping of Japanese Americans as highly assimilable stands in direct contrast to earlier pre-war characterizations of Issei (first-generation Japanese Americans) as exactly the opposite—that is, "unassimilable." For example, during one of several Congressional hearings between 1910 and 1930 focused on keeping more Japanese from immigrating to the United States, Mr. V. S. McClatchey, secretary of the California Joint Immigration Committee, testified: "The Japanese are unassimilable with our civilization and our people" (quoted in Bell 1978, 384 n. 19).

12 The critique continues into the twenty-first century. The interactive website "Model Minority: Asian American Empowerment" comments on the myth: "While superficially complimentary to Asian Americans, the real purpose and effect of this portrayal is to celebrate the status quo in race relations. First, by over-emphasizing Asian American success, it de-emphasizes the problems Asian Americans continue to face from racial discrimination in all areas of public and private life. Second, by misrepresenting Asian American success as proof that America provides equal opportunities for those who conform and work hard, it excuses American society from careful scrutiny on issues of race in general, and on the persistence of racism against Asian Americans in particular" (http://www.modelminority.com; accessed 29 May 2008). The website serves variously as a watchdog for media stereotypes, a forum of postings by Asian Americans on a variety of topics (e.g. "Is Islam really homophobic?," "What does being Asian mean to you?") and news clippings (e.g. "Facebook Racism," "For Asian Women 'Fetish' Is Less Benign"), and a compendium of scholarly and popular press writings on the subject.

13 The continuing place of Nisei war veterans is nowhere better expressed than in the establishment by the Colleges of Arts and Sciences at the University of Hawai'i of "Universal Values for a Democratic Society–Nisei War Veterans Forum," a series of public discussions and talks on the subject of "universal values." Its first keynote speaker in January 2000, to a packed and enthusiastic audience that included numerous Nisei war veterans, was Senator Daniel K. Inouye.

14 It is worthwhile to note that the word "cosmopolitan" was also used to mean mixed-race, and particularly part-Hawaiian, in beauty contests in Hawai'i from 1941 to 1971 in which women competed by ethnic group (Yano 2006b, 60–62).

15 Beginning with the Chinese Exclusion Act of 1882 (the first to restrict immigration on the basis of race), and continuing through the Gentleman's Agreement of 1907–8 that halted Japanese labor migration, the Immigration Act (Asian Exclusion Act) of 1924, and the Tydings-McDuffie Act of 1934 that disallowed Filipinos from working in the United States, anti-Asian racism has dogged their every step.

16 For example, Japanese Americans in Hawai'i led strikes in the plantation fields in 1909, the first major labor dispute in the history of the sugar industry in Hawai'i, and another major strike in 1920; decades later Asian American stu-

dents participated in a strike at San Francisco State in 1968 that led to the establishment of the first school of ethnic studies in the country.

CHAPTER 1: 1955

1   For a compelling account of nationalism and aviation in Germany see Peter Fritzsche's *A Nation of Fliers* (1992). The Nazi slogan "We must become a nation of fliers" may have been intended to generate public support for a military buildup during the Second World War, but it also expresses the bold imperative of German aviation (Fritzsche 1992, 5).

2   The United States was not the only nation in which domesticity played an important role in the 1950s. Germany shared a home-as-nation ideology ("Heimat") during the same period, although in a differently nuanced historical context. Von Moltke explains: "The Heimat topos combined the longing for home, restoration, and stability with an affinity towards the economic and geographical mobilization of postwar Germany. It provided a ground for wistful backward glances and a headlong rush towards the future without monopolizing either one of these impulses" (Von Moltke 2005, 133).

3   Kroc's restaurant was actually the ninth in the McDonald's franchise, begun in 1940 in San Bernardino by Dick and Mac McDonald. However, Kroc took the McDonald brothers' formula and business to a new level that has since become synonymous with fast-food practices and American-based globalization.

4   During the postwar period there were a few scattered examples of hiring minorities, but primarily for specific routes. For example, in 1949 United Airlines embarked on a program of hiring men from Hawai'i (called "Hawaiian" although they were not all of Hawaiian ethnicity) to add "local flavor" to their flights to the islands. These "Hawaiian stewards" flew only the Hawaii-bound run, adding racialized "authenticity" to in-flight service (Barry 2007, 115).

5   The racial hierarchy could vary by region, especially as the pecking order intersected with issues of labor migration and other forms of competition for resources (e.g. Chicanos versus African Americans versus Asian Americans in California). The label of "honorary white" parallels Japan's positioning of itself as the "whitest" among Asians during the colonial rule of the Second World War (Ching 2001).

6   The phrase "family of man" was reputedly borrowed from a little-known speech given in 1861 by Abraham Lincoln (Sandeen 1995, 177). One fundamental and critical difference between the exhibit and the book was the latter's exclusion of an image quite central to the former: a photo of the explosion of a hydrogen bomb at Bikini atoll in the Pacific in 1954. The bomb image placed the exhibit within the context of mankind's technological destructive capability, exemplified by the bombing of Hiroshima and Nagasaki. This was part of Steichen's point. However, the omission of the bomb image gave the book a far more benign, apolitical message. "The exhibition spoke directly to the audience of 1955

and was destroyed. The book, designed to commemorate the look of the exhibition, had history in mind and has endured, but, ironically it had lost the reading that tied Steichen's work most closely to its audience. The bomb was not there" (Sandeen 1995, 74). Sandeen speculates, "It could be that [Steichen] avoided constricting a representation of fundamental annihilation to the rectangular confines of a book layout in which it could be compared to other images. In any case, the bomb was left out" (Sandeen 1995, 74).

7   The exhibit became a global phenomenon, touring in different versions for seven years under the auspices of the United States Information Agency and, attracting nine million viewers worldwide. The shelf life of the exhibit was extended even further by the publication of a book under the same title (Steichen 1955).

8   Palumbo-Liu's comment connecting a stereotype of Asia with modern forms is echoed in the research on the "modern girl" trope of global proportions in the 1920s and 1930s. As the members of the Modern Girl around the World Research Group contend, the "Asianization" of the Modern Girl in modernist art deco images included "caricatured, elongated, often slanted eyes" (2008, 32). Indeed, through the transformation of cosmetics and dress, white women could engage in a "racial masquerade" and put on a "yellow face," or at least acknowledge this version of the Asian woman as a desirable, exotic aesthetic and commodity (Weinbaum 2008, 121). As Alys Weinbaum argues, "In the United States, the modern consumer's objective was neither to become Asian through purchase of Asian things or an Asian aesthetic. . . . Rather, she sought to embrace a cosmopolitan aesthetic so as to distance herself from the racial 'otherness' that she had the power to purchase. In this sense representations of racial masquerade suggest . . . what might aptly be labeled 'racist cosmopolitanism'" (ibid., 128).

9   The perduring image of the geisha continued through the 1990s and beyond. The sensationalized publication of Arthur Golden's *Memoirs of a Geisha* in 1997 and the subsequent film in 2005 touched off a mini-industry in geisha fascination. The book became a phenomenon, with sales of over four million copies, translations into thirty-two languages, criticism by scholars (Allison 2001), and a memoir by the woman on whom the book was based (Iwasaki with Brown 2002).

10   The plot centers around the love story between a Japanese woman, Cio-Cio-san (Madame Butterfly), who waits in vain for the return of her American lover, Lieutenant B. F. Pinkerton; in the end she commits the ultimate act of self-sacrifice.

11   Nearly 100,000 Asian war brides also came to the United States from Korea as a result of the Korean War (1950–53) and the continued American military presence there. Ji-Yeon Yuh's excellent study of these women demonstrates that they must be seen through a complex prism that reflects not only the relationship between Korea and the United States but also Japanese colonialism, Korean patri-

archy and nationalism, and American race politics (2002). Like Japanese war brides shunned by the Japanese American community, Yuh found that Korean war brides were shunned by the Korean American community as double failures: "people who failed both to achieve the American Dream and to maintain their Koreanness" (2002, 185).

12 The list includes no fewer than ten films in ten years: *Japanese War Bride* (1952), *The Gentle Wolfhound* (1955), *Three Stripes in the Sun* (1955), *Teahouse of the August Moon* (1956), *Sayonara* (1957), *The Barbarian and the Geisha* (1958), *The Crimson Kimono* (1959), *Bridge to the Sun* (1961), *Cry for Happy* (1961), and *A Majority of One* (1961). Several of these films were adaptations from earlier novels and plays, such as *Teahouse of the August Moon*: originally a novel published in 1951 by Vern J. Sneider about the Okinawan occupation, it was adapted by John Patrick in 1953 into a play that won a Pulitzer Prize and a Tony Award; the film version, from 1956, was directed by Daniel Mann.

13 Ji-Yeon Yuh discusses how American men who married Korean women similarly "wanted the traditional, all-American housewife of a bygone era and believed that Korean women—whom they viewed as docile and subservient—would be able to fulfill that role" (2002, 136). Typically the men in these marriages were not interested in Korean culture so much as a Korean woman who would fulfill the role of an (old-fashioned) American wife.

   Asian women are not the only ones constructed as paragons of "old-fashioned" femininity. Denise Brennan's work on sex tourism in the Dominican Republic finds similar images of Caribbean women: "European men . . . compare Dominican women to European women. They imagine Dominican women as more sexual, more compliant, and having fewer financial demands than European women. European men also often expect Dominican women to adhere to very traditional—and regressive—understandings of gender roles. And race plays a central role in how the white European sex tourists imagine Afro-Dominican sex workers. Women's skin color was mentioned again and again in my interviews with sex tourists, as well as on the Internet" (2004, 194–95). Brennan's work focuses on sex workers; mine does not, but it is useful to note the overlap in the imaging of women of color by white men.

14 The persistence of the stereotype of Japanese and other Asian (not American) women fuels the market for overseas brides: "The distressing popularity of the Asian Bride catalog business attests both to the continuing perception of Asian women as 'cute (as in doll-like), quiet rather than militant, and unassuming rather than assertive' (except sexually), as well as more 'feminine, loyal, [and] loving'" (Lai 1992, 168; quoted in Yamamoto 1999, 66). Nicole Constable's work on Asian bridal websites uncovers more contemporary constructions along the same lines. An item on the China Bride website is entitled "Why Choose Women from Asia": "The Asian woman is 'upstanding and gentle.' . . . Women from Asia are feminine. They are normally petite and slender with delicate bone structure. . . . They typically have smooth, silky, hairless skin. . . .

Women from Asia value family. Family is all important. Husband, children, parents, relatives come first. Husband and children never take second place to her career" (quoted in Constable 2003, 96). And similarly, from the World Class Service website: "Had your fill of feminists, gold-diggers, air heads, unfaithful partners and party girls? Too busy to find the right woman? This is your best opportunity in the world to find a beautiful and well educated woman of traditional values who is dedicated to marriage as a lifelong commitment" (quoted in Constable 2003, 96). Not only does this construction create a nostalgic, family-oriented image of the Asian woman, it also highlights the counter-image of the Euroamerican woman: the feminist, gold-digging slut.

More recently, since the 1990s the market for Asian overseas brides has seen intra-Asian traffic, as Southeast Asian women have become sought after as brides by men in Taiwan and Japan. After the United States, Japan has become the second-largest destination for Filipina bride migration. Nobue Suzuki notes the complex refractions of global hierarchy and prestige in these kinds of matches: given the longstanding presence of the United States in the Philippines, the Filipinas are often better versed in the English language and Americanisms than their Japanese husbands. Thus, "'Americanness' allows Filipina wives to position themselves and their self-claimed 'mono-cultural,' monolingual Japanese husbands onto an East-West axis, where the women are powerful 'Westerners'" (2005, 161).

15 Japanese women later dominated the field of interpreting and translation in American-Japanese business transactions. In fulfilling this essential position they significantly acted primarily as mouthpieces for other people's—typically men's—ideas.

16 The image has pre-aviation antecedents in rail travel: "Harvey Girls," young, well-trained, uniformed waitresses who worked at train-stop "Harvey Houses" throughout the American West from the late 1880s to the mid-twentieth century. In the hands of Fred Harvey, founder of the restaurant chain, Harvey Girls became more than mere waitresses—they were emblematic of the "civilizing" of the "wild West." That civilizing process lay not only in the white tablecloths that Fred Harvey set down but in his use of young, white women from the eastern and Midwestern United States, trained according to company standards and transported to work in Harvey's rail-stop restaurants, where he kept close watch over them. They became the girls next door of train service. Many of the recruits were from the lower-middle classes—not wealthy, but "respectable" (http://www.oerm.org/pages/Harveygirls.html). They may have been selected for their manners, neatness, and articulateness, yet they received considerable training to regulate and educate them by "Harvey standards." They lived in company housing with a strict 10:00 p.m. curfew and a senior Harvey Girl supervisor. The "Harvey way" taught them middle-class practices of dress, comportment, and service. The tenure of their work was not meant to be long, around eighteen to twenty-four months; like the work of stewardesses, theirs was "temporary

employment," after which the women were expected to quit and marry. In fact Harvey Girls were the ultimate marriage candidates: girls next door who had learned the ways of middle-class dress and comportment through their training.

17 At about the same time that Pan Am's "Nisei" stewardess program was diversifying and thus coming to an end in the 1970s, another Asian airline was promoting the Asian woman as a company icon. Singapore Airlines developed its "Singapore Girl" as a key symbol of the company in 1972. The two developments are not unrelated: Pan Am helped to conduct training for Singapore Airlines. The brainchild behind the "Singapore Girl," the advertising agent Ian Batey, describes her as follows: "Physically, she has the attractive, natural looks of most young Asian women. . . . Character-wise, she mirrors her Asian heritage—natural femininity, natural grace and warmth, and a natural, gentle way with people" (quoted in Whitelegg 2007, 135). As the signature persona of the airline, the Singapore Girl in distinctive *sarong kebaya* uniform symbolized gracious hospitality and aestheticized charm. Like the "Nisei" stewardess, she was racialized as the ultimate "natural" hostess, as Asia's dreamgirl next door.

CHAPTER 2: "THE WORLD'S MOST EXPERIENCED AIRLINE"

1 Trippe's tenure lasted until 1968. He was succeeded as CEO by Harold Gray (1968–69), Najeeb Halaby (1969–71), William T. Seawell (1971–81), C. Edward Acker (1981–88), and Thomas G. Plaskett (1988–91). None of his successors garnered the kind of corporate identity and charismatic personal style as Trippe.

2 Roosevelt and all his successors later flew a noncommercial aircraft officially designated Air Force One (the air traffic control call sign of any U.S. Air Force aircraft carrying the president of the United States). These aircraft have had nicknames, such as *Guess Where Two* for Roosevelt's, *Independence* for Harry Truman's, and *Columbine* for Dwight Eisenhower's.

3 These guidebooks include *Complete Reference Guides* (one devoted to each European country), *New Horizons World Guide* (useful reference on thirty-six countries), *New Horizons U.S.A.* (covering ninety cities in fifty states, plus Puerto Rico and the Virgin Islands), *New Horizons Living Abroad* (information on eighty-eight countries for those relocating), *New Horizons in Education* (information on 177 universities in thirty-eight countries), *Ski New Horizons* (information on ski facilities in thirty countries), *Round the World with Famous Authors* (fiction set in different countries), and *Round the World Cookbook* (recipes from eighty-one foreign countries).

More tongue-in-cheek, libidinal guide books obliquely associated with Pan Am include those on international sexual matters. One example is *How to Date a Foreign Man* (1989), in which a former Pan Am stewardess, Fumiko Takahashi, gives tips to Japanese women (Kelsky 2001, 162).

4 Like other airlines, Pan Am made significant changes to its flight attendant uniforms over the years. The original Don Loper uniform (1952–59) was succeeded

by a second version (1952–59), a further modification that included a box-style jacket and pillbox hat (1965), an Evan Picone uniform with a shorter skirt and bowler hat (1969; the first uniform to give women a choice of colors, either "Galaxy gold" or the more familiar blue); and a navy-blue uniform by the Spanish designer Adolfo (1980s).

5   The skyscraper was built not by Trippe but by the New York real estate developer Erwin Wolfson. Through a lengthy series of clandestine meetings and memoranda, Trippe agreed to occupy nine floors and a sales office at street level for approximately thirty years, in what was then the largest commercial lease on a property in Manhattan (Bender and Altschul 1982, 487).

6   The "Pan Am building" built in 1969 in Honolulu is still known by that name and bears the words "PAN AM," even if there has been no connection with the airline for over twenty years. Ernie Albrecht, Pan Am's Honolulu district traffic and sales manager, recalls how the building in Honolulu was named: "They were building [what came to be known as] the Pan Am building, and someone came to me and asked if we had any need for more space, or would they like to take a look at the plan. So I looked at it and I spoke with the company. To make a long story short, I indicated to the owners of the building that if we take two floors, would you name that building after Pan American. And in those days, no one was permitted to have a sign on the building. . . . They came back and said they would name the building after Pan American. We signed a lease, and I had that sign made, and caused a little trouble with the Outdoor Circle [a private organization that lobbied for regulating the size of signs]. And even to this day, we're the only building I think with a sign on top [in Honolulu]. That's how that came about." Albrecht's negotiations to occupy a portion of an independently owned skyscraper, and in the process place a large Pan Am sign on the building, follow a pattern set by Juan Trippe's dealings in New York.

7   American Airlines, for example, had its *Air-Age Education News.*

8   Pan Am distributed these publications at schools and upon request throughout the United States and Canada, as well as through application in foreign countries.

9   The air trips promoted in 1951, primarily for teachers, included summer sessions in Europe at the Sorbonne, the University of Lille, the University of Toulouse, and the University of Barcelona; seven-week tours to Europe promoted by *Scholastic Magazine* (tour A to England, Denmark, Sweden, and Norway; tour B to England, the Netherlands, Germany, Switzerland, and France; tour C to Italy, Austria, Switzerland, and France); three-week tours to the Caribbean, also sponsored by *Scholastic Magazine* (Mexico, Guatemala, Panama, Colombia, Jamaica, Cuba); sessions of the Institute of Latin American Studies in Colombia; summer courses sponsored by International House in the Yucatan, Costa Rica, and Colombia; summer courses at San Marcos University; and the Central American and South American branches of the Institute of World Studies in Washington ("Educational Air Travel" 1951).

10 Other sponsors of the event were Catalina Swimsuits, Universal-International Studios, and the City of Long Beach.

11 In the following year, 1955, Japan Airlines donated the Queen's scepter, which became known as the "JAL scepter" (Yano 2006b, 66–67).

12 "Paparazzi" was a word born in the Jet Age: in Federico Fellini's film *La Dolce Vita* (1960) Paparazzo is a photographer who ruthlessly pursues celebrities.

13 James Bond films from the 1970s on often featured exotic, nonwhite women.

14 Several stewardesses whom I interviewed told me that they went to see this movie in particular because the stewardesses depicted in it were wearing the uniform from their era. The Miami chapter of World Wings International, a group of retired Pan Am flight attendants, invited Abagnale to speak to their group.

15 Close observers of the film have noted inaccuracies in the scene, including the presence of a Russian aircraft, the Antonov AN-2, that Pan American never flew and the fact that the decals and registration on the aircraft appear backwards (http://www.moviemistakes.com/film7362/page1).

16 The color, size, style, and decoration varied over the years.

17 Pan Am was not the only airline to receive requests for space flight reservations. In the excitement that surrounded the lunar landing of Apollo 11 in 1969, TWA received 3,000 requests, Air Canada 2,500, and Pan Am 15,000 (*Aviation Daily*, 25 July 1969, 127).

18 Vanessa Schwartz's study of the mutual influences of France and the United States amid the development of Cold War culture in the 1950s and 1960s is useful. Schwartz reminds us that the transatlantic conversation accompanying the emergence of cosmopolitanism encompassed not only the Americanization of France by way of popular culture, but also the popularity of "Frenchness" on screen in the United States (2007, 8–10; cf. Endy 2004).

CHAPTER 3: "NISEI" STEWARDESSES

1 Approximately twenty years later Pan Am did the same thing in Africa. I interviewed one woman from Ghana who was hired in 1973. According to her, at the time Pan Am was recruiting widely in Ghana, Liberia, and along the western coast with advertisements proclaiming that the airline wanted to add "a look of Pan-Africanism" and "needed a flair of the international" on board its aircraft. The woman flew for Pan Am until its end in 1991, at which time she joined Delta Airlines, with which she still flies. Her language was French, but she says this was not the critical factor in her hire.

2 See Okihiro 1991 for an excellent discussion of pre-war anti-Japanese sentiment in Hawai`i. See also Roland Kotani's discussion of the politics of "Speak English" campaigns and other language issues for Japanese Americans in Hawai`i (1985).

3 The men pictured were Yoshio Koike, principal of the McCully Japanese School, Hideyuki Serizawa of the Toyogakuen School, and Toraki Kimura of the Moi-

liili Japanese School. A further check into the names of the men confirms that all three appear to have been internees. Serizawa and Kimura were in the first group to leave Hawai`i in February 1942 for camps on the continental United States (Camp McCoy in Wisconsin, Camp Forrest in Tennessee, Camp Livingston in Louisiana; the group was then split up and dispersed to other locations); Koike was in the third group, leaving Hawai`i in May 1942 and eventually arriving in New Mexico. Thanks to Brian Niiya for helping to determine the men's wartime status by examining the records held at the Resource Center of the Japanese Cultural Center of Hawai`i.

4 "English standard schools" were public schools requiring a particular level of English fluency, as determined by a test or interview. As Evelyn Nakano Glenn writes, "Ostensibly, their purpose was to encourage Americanization, but their actual result was segregated schooling. Virtually all 'Caucasians' in the public schools were enrolled in the English Standard schools, while only a small number of Japanese [Americans and other students] were able to gain entrance into them" (2002, 227). The schools reinforced the power structure of the islands: the proportion of all public school students attending English Standard school ranged from a low of 2 percent in 1925 to a high of 9 percent in 1947, with a disproportionately high number of whites (Tamura 1994, 113). For more on the schools' history and social impact see Eileen Tamura's fine study *Americanization, Acculturation, and Ethnic Identity; The Nisei Generation in Hawaii* (1994).

5 By contrast, not speaking English—or speaking Japanese—linked one closer to Japan. Ien Ang, an Australian resident of Chinese ancestry, comments on her own lack of knowledge of Chinese language. Australians or even Chinese who look upon her racialize her and assume that she can speak Mandarin or some other Chinese dialect. Ang identifies the racial bias at work: a German Australian, for example, at a parallel remove from Germany as Ang is from China, would not necessarily be expected to speak German (2001, 33).

6 Some of the family circumstances engendering Japanese linguistic fluency include close contact with grandparents; having at least one parent who was *kibei-Nisei* (that is, was born in Hawai`i or elsewhere outside Japan, was raised in Japan, and then returned to the United States); and living or studying in Japan.

7 Once Pan Am began hiring Japanese nationals, the book included announcements written in Japanese characters, since native speakers found the romanized versions difficult to read.

8 Pan Am hired nonwhites in jobs other than stewarding. Albert Mills points out that Pan Am hired male and female African Americans, Hispanics, and other "locals" of color, especially for menial tasks and in locations outside the United States (2006, 246 n. 72).

9 One stewardess points out that typically it is the college-bound students who study foreign languages in high school.

10 Most "Nisei" hires were done in groups, but a few women were hired singly and thus trained as the only "Nisei" stewardess of their graduating class.

11   The previous history of Japanese flight attendants on foreign carriers begins in
     1951 with the hire of Japanese women by Thai Airways Company. Their employ
     only lasted one month because of a lack of Japanese customers. In 1952 North-
     west Orient Airlines hired Japanese stewardesses for its flights between Tokyo
     and Pusan, and continued their employ in the years to come. In 1955 three other
     foreign carriers hired Japanese stewardesses: Air India International, KLM Royal
     Dutch Airlines, and Air France (*Nippon Times*, 29 June 1955, 10; 20 September
     1955, 6). A photograph in the *Nippon Times* depicts seven "Japanese" women
     flying internationally as stewardesses on the following airlines: Pan Am, North-
     west Airlines, KLM, Japan Airlines, Air France, CAT, and Air-India International
     (*Nippon Times*, 20 September 1955, 6).

12   Retitled from the Japanese original ("Ue Wo Muite Arukou," I Will Walk Hold-
     ing My Head High"; music by Nakamura Hachidai, lyrics by Ei Rokusuke,
     United States release on Capitol Records), Sakamoto's song burst onto the
     American scene and garnered the number one spot on hit charts for four weeks
     running. Sakamoto's subsequent tour of the United States began with his arrival
     at Los Angeles International Airport aboard a Pan Am jet, met by thousands of
     screaming teenagers (Bourdaghs 2005, 249).

13   I thank one of the reviewers for Duke University Press for pointing out some
     of the parallels between the "Nisei" stewardesses leaving their hometowns and
     young men going into the military. Although the subject warrants a fuller dis-
     cussion than is possible here, see the rich literature on the military, includ-
     ing Elder 1986, Elder, Gimbel, and Ivie 1991, Gill 1997, and Woodward 2006.
     See also *Armed Forces and Society*, an interdisciplinary journal published by
     the Inter-University Seminar on Armed Forces and Society (founded in 1960,
     housed at Loyola University Chicago).

14   The other ethnic groups in Hawai`i at the time were as follows: 23.0 percent
     white (including Spanish and Portuguese), 17.3 percent Hawaiian and part-
     Hawaiian, 12.2 percent Filipino, 6.5 percent Chinese, 1.9 percent Puerto Rican,
     1.4 percent Korean, 0.8 percent others (U.S. Census of 1950, quoted in Lind
     1980, 34).

15   The teaching profession attracted Nisei men as well as women, especially in the
     1920s and 1930s when racial discrimination may have prevented them from
     entering other fields. See Tamura 1994, 233, figures 14 and 15, for ethnicity of
     teachers and nurses in Hawai`i, 1910–50.

16   Although some of my analysis may be applied in general to women who choose
     the flight attendant profession, my comments here pertain specifically to Japa-
     nese American stewardesses during 1955–72. The situation may be quite differ-
     ent for other groups of women who flew for Pan Am.

17   For further discussion of the socioeconomic life of Japanese Americans in the
     mid-1950s in Hawai`i see Yano 2006b, 41–51.

1   "Nisei" women's experiences inevitably overlap with those of other stewardesses of the period. However, by focusing on race and class, I demonstrate how Pan Am's "Nisei" stewardesses dealt with the stereotypes and made the airplane cabin their own.

2   By tradition, airlines have not accepted tips from passengers. This has important ramifications for the job. Removing tipping from the occupation elevates the way service on an airplane is perceived, because it is not reduced to cold, hard cash. Instead, it takes on the veneer of a personal relationship whose script emulates a master-servant relationship. By contrast, a waitress dependent on tips occupies a low position: "She is placed in the symbolically demeaning position of receiving the greater part of her income in the form of tips conferred as gifts by strangers" (Paules 1991, 9). Although the master-servant (or passenger-stewardess) relationship ultimately rests on an economic transaction, the absence of tipping obscures its financial basis. In contrast with service jobs that rely on tips, stewardessing takes on the appearance of work that is voluntary, performed "out of the goodness of one's empathetic heart," even if that heart is well practiced in the "deep acting" of thorough training.

3   Green notes that Bell telephone operators too acted as public representatives of the company: "As a part of the intense drive to create favorable public relations, Bell System managers advocated a personnel policy designed to transform each employee into an advertisement for the company. In order to divert these young women from unionism and to mold them into good, uncomplaining, and productive workers who would be good public relations examples and mouthpieces, managers devised several projects [to this end]" (Green 2001, 144).

4   The twenty-two "hospitality flights" covered the following cities: San Diego (California), Phoenix and Tucson (Arizona), Albuquerque (New Mexico), Las Vegas (Nevada), Fresno, San Jose, Stockton, and Sacramento (California), Boise (Idaho), Spokane (Washington), Great Falls (Montana), and Portland (Oregon). Each flight lasted approximately an hour and fifteen minutes, long enough to showcase Pan Am's international service and stewardesses.

5   Darrell Hamamoto notes that there are two sides to what he calls the "Connie Chung Syndrome": female Asian American newscasters are overrepresented even as their male counterparts are underrepresented (1994, 244–47). The explanation lies in an unspoken industry belief that "Asian women are exotic looking and thus more appealing to white audiences while Asian men are not" (1994, 245).

6   In fact Japanese women during this period were not buying kimono in large numbers. Formal kimono were expensive and the occasions for wearing them relatively few. To counteract the decline in kimono wearing, the industry introduced a line of inexpensive, easy-care polyester kimono, pre-matched with the necessary accessories (Wada 1996, 158). These kimono may be found in depart-

ment stores and in the tourist shops that Pan Am stewardesses frequented (e.g. Oriental Bazaar).

CHAPTER 5: BECOMING PAN AM

1   I acknowledge here the related and rich field from business psychology of organizational socialization, defined by Meryl Reis Louis as "a process by which an individual comes to appreciate the values, abilities, expected behaviors, and social knowledge essential for assuming an organization role and for participating as an organization member" (1980, 229–30). However, here my research goals, methods, and discussion differ. Undoubtedly a parallel study of Pan Am and its employees from an organizational socialization perspective would yield valuable insights.

2   I assume that this woman refers to the uniformity of the final outcome. Some "Nisei" stewardesses with straight hair may have required a permanent wave to emulate the requisite hairstyle.

3   Although Japanese American women were not depicted in this way, as few wore kimono or other clothing of ethnic distinction before entering Pan Am, the company often drew upon representations of them in uniform to imply their transformation.

4   The manual lists the following items as "things that detract": "dangling slips, peek-a-boo straps, loose threads, roaming hemlines, runaway shoulder straps, bulging purses, tobacco-y or dirty handkerchiefs, wavy stocking seams, and powder or make-up remnants" (ibid.).

5   A company manual from 1966 lists the following maximum height and weight standards for stewardesses:

5'2" (158 cm)	116 lb. (52.7 kg)
5'3" (160 cm)	120 lb. (54.5 kg)
5'4" (162 cm)	125 lb. (56.8 kg)
5'5" (165 cm)	129 lb. (58.6 kg)
5'6" (167 cm)	133 lb. (60.4 kg)
5'7" (170 cm)	136 lb. (61.8 kg)
5'8" (173 cm)	140 lb. (63.6 kg)

(*Horizons Unlimited* 1966, 79)

These proportions give a body mass index (BMI) of approximately 21.5, in the middle of the normal range for adults.

6   This is not so different from scrapbooks that one might purchase to record a child's milestones, such as first photo, first birthday, first words, and first day at school. The scrapbook was not specific to Pan Am but was more generally available for purchase. The stewardess does not recall where she purchased the book, and the manufacturer's information is not clearly retained in the present scrapbook. However, one may easily interpret such a scrapbook as promoting bonding between those in the profession. At the very least, the categories predefine

the milestones of one's profession and provide a sorority of those engaged in it. Note that all the illustrations depict female flight attendants.

7   This includes the date when she terminated employment with Pan Am and began flying for United Airlines in February 1986.

8   The supervisor rates appearance in the categories of uniform, shoes, hair, facial, and weight; however, the evaluator provides explanatory comments, which include an assessment of "endurance" (rated as "above"). The evaluative categories under passenger relations are poise, friendliness, anticipation, enthusiasm, and helpfulness. The comments that she received: "outstanding personality; excellent attitude." Crew relations warrant evaluation for cooperation, guidance, teamwork, follow-up, and initiative.

CHAPTER 6: FRONTIER DREAMS

1   Pan American's promotional culture always grabbed the headlines and spotlighted the company's place at the frontier of air travel. To this end the company created events and commemorations celebrating its own accomplishments and place in history. One such event was held on 26 October 1983, the twenty-fifth anniversary of the inaugural Boeing 707 flight from New York to Paris. At a time when airlines—including Pan Am—were fast losing their luster and economic robustness, the company mustered pomp and celebrity to stage its own spectacle, heralding its place in the Jet Age. In the 1980s this was already the stuff of nostalgia.

Pan Am invited eighty-four government officials, media representatives, and celebrities from entertainment, sports, and the arts, as well as eleven passengers on the original flight, to join the celebration. Beginning with a pre-flight red-carpet champagne reception in New York displaying the flags of all the countries to which the airline flew, and capped by a gala Napoleonic era ball at the Hotel Intercontinental in Paris, Pan Am aimed to achieve an impressive scale, as well as to recreate as many details as possible from the original flight. None of this was lost on the media, which covered the event as an example of lavish, stylish nostalgia for a bygone era. Undoubtedly the airline knew how to put on a good show. But what was also poignantly dramatized was the degree to which Pan Am was an airline whose glory had passed into the realm of nostalgia.

2   To this end the foundation boasts over two thousand members, publishes a quarterly newsletter, holds annual meetings, maintains a close relationship with the Pan Am archives at the Otto G. Richter Library of the University of Miami, and awards a yearly scholarship for researchers wishing to use the Miami collection. It also actively collects memorabilia and acts as an official center for Pan Am corporate memory—a status that has not come without contention as to who should control and profit from that memory.

3   The beginnings of the organization date to the 1950s, when Pan Am stewardesses formed separate groups on the West Coast in 1952 and on the East Coast

in 1957. In 1959 the two groups united as World Wings International, Inc. The Hawai'i chapter of World Wings International was established in 1969 under the name Na Eheu Lani (Soaring Wings in the Sky). With thirty members at the time, the group elected Joyce Yoshizu Mitsumori as its first president; other "Nisei" stewardesses continue to figure prominently among its officers.

4 Female and male flight attendants have joined the group, but the number of women far exceeds that of men, and all its officers in 2007 were women.

5 World Wings International pays more than lip service to community service. Officers include a vice-president of charity, whose duties are to act as a liaison to CARE and coordinate the charitable efforts of local chapters. Members of the organization have traveled worldwide in conjunction with CARE, in behalf of which a group travels to Washington every April to lobby. The women also organize fundraising events such as fashion show luncheons, sporting events, and an international charity drawing in conjunction with the annual convention. (Coincidentally, World Wings International focuses Pan Am's public ethos of "caring" on the international organization CARE.)

6 Among the more popular American cities for the conventions are Honolulu (1973, 1985, 2004), San Francisco (1970, 1976, 1995), Los Angeles (1980, 1997), Miami (1979, 1999), New York (1977, 2003), and Seattle (1971, 1991). Conventions have been held in Europe in London (1983), Oslo (1990), Berlin (1994), Brussels (1998), and Paris (2005). The cruise-ship conventions have been to Alaska (2002) and New England (2007).

7 The thirtieth-anniversary commemoration of the "Last Pan Am Flight Out of Vietnam," as it is known, was held from 22 to 24 April 2005 in Washington, with over three hundred former Pan Am employees, family members, and friends. Participants in the symposium and reunion included former war orphans, in an emotional meeting with the Pan Am employees who had carried them out of the country and onto Pan Am airplanes. A highlight of the event was a showing of the made-for-television film *Last Flight Out* (1990). As a result of the commemoration, the Pan Am Vietnam Wings of Freedom Planning Committee started a fundraising campaign to help the needy in Vietnam through three organizations: Help the Hungry (co-founded by the CNN anchor Betty Nguyen), Sister Teresa's Orphanage in Danang, and the Daughters of Charity of St. Vincent de Paul in Ho Chi Minh City. The Vietnam commemoration's website www.paavn.net was active during my period of research but was scheduled to close.

8 As of April 2007 the store did not have a website.

9 Articles of clothing included, for $15, a women's nightshirt in bright pink or blue with the Pan Am logo and the legend "I slept around the world . . ."

10 www.marchanddelegumes.com.

11 The map is geographically jumbled, juxtaposing London, Paris, Boston, Buenos Aires, and New Delhi. Although one may ascribe this confusion to an art director's prerogative, one may also take it as a cryptic view of Pan Am's deterritorial-

ized world, in which geography and national borders meant less than point-to-point destinations and in-flight hours.

12 Released in 1958 with music by Jimmy Van Heusen and lyrics by Sammy Cahn and arranged by Billy May, the song was also the title of an album put out by Sinatra on Capitol Records. The album was meant as a musical tour around the world, as demonstrated by the other songs included: "Around the World," "Isle of Capri," "On the Road to Mandalay," "April in Paris," "London by Night," "Brazil," "Blue Hawaii," "South of the Border," and "I Love Paris." Not coincidentally, the year of the album, 1958, was the same year that Pan Am ushered in the jet age with regular transatlantic jet service.

Abbas, Ackbar. 2000. "Cosmopolitan De-scriptions: Shanghai and Hong Kong." *Public Culture* 12, no. 3, 769–86.

Abelmann, Nancy. 2003. *The Melodrama of Mobility: Women, Talk, and Class in Contemporary South Korea.* Honolulu: University of Hawai'i Press.

Acocella, Joan. 2006. "The Girls Next Door: Life in the Centerfold." *New Yorker,* 20 March, 144–48.

Adinolfi, Francesco. 2008. *Mondo Exotica: Sounds, Visions, Obsessions of the Cocktail Generation.* Durham: Duke University Press.

"Airborne Dreams." 2006. *Honolulu Star-Bulletin,* 20 November, § D, 7.

"Alice Erasing Effects of Myths." 1971. *Clipper* 22, nos. 23–24 (20 December), 10.

Allison, Anne. 2001. "Memoirs of the Orient." *Journal of Japanese Studies* 27, no. 2, 381–98.

Ang, Ien. 2001. *On Not Speaking Chinese: Living between Asia and the West.* London: Routledge.

Anzaldúa, Gloria. 1987. *Borderland / La Frontera: The New Mestiza.* San Francisco: Aunt Lute.

Arey, James. 1983. Unpublished memorandum to G. J. Beck, 16 September.

Auge, Marc. 1995. *Non-places: Introduction to an Anthropology of Supermodernity.* London: Verso.

Aviation Daily. 1969. "TWA Files for Route to Moon." *Aviation Daily,* 25 July, 127.

Baker, Trudy, and Rachel Jones. 1967. *Coffee, Tea, or Me? The Uninhibited Memoirs of Two Airline Stewardesses.* New York: Bantam.

———. 1970. *Coffee Tea or Me Girls' Round-the-World Diary.* New York: Bantam.

———. 1972. *The Coffee, Tea or Me Girls Lay It on the Line.* New York: Bantam.

———. 1974. *The Coffee, Tea or Me Girls Get Away from It All.* New York: Bantam.

Ballantyne, Tony, and Antoinette Burton. 2009. "Introduction: The Politics of Intimacy in an Age of Empire." *Moving Subjects: Gender, Mobility, and Intimacy in an Age of Global Empire*, ed. Tony Ballantyne and Antoinette Burton, 1–28. Urbana: University of Illinois Press.

———, eds. 2009. *Moving Subjects: Gender, Mobility, and Intimacy in an Age of Global Empire*. Urbana: University of Illinois Press.

Banet-Weiser, Sarah. 1999. *The Most Beautiful Girl in the World: Beauty Pageants and National Identity*. Berkeley: University of California Press.

Banning, Gene. 2001. *Airlines of Pan American Since 1927*. McLean, Va.: Paladwr.

Barry, Kathleen. 2002. "Femininity in Flight: Flight Attendants, Glamour, and Pink-Collar Activism in the Twentieth-Century United States." Ph.D. diss., New York University.

———. 2007. *Femininity in Flight: A History of Flight Attendants*. Durham: Duke University Press.

Bell, Reginald. 1978. *Public School Education of Second-Generation Japanese in California*. New York: Arno.

Bender, Marylin, and Selig Altschul. 1982. *The Chosen Instrument: Juan Trippe, Pan Am*. New York: Simon and Schuster.

Bialystok, Ellen, and Kenji Hakuta. 1994. *In Other Words: The Science and Psychology of Second-Language Acquisition*. New York: Basic.

Bilstein, Roger E. 2001. *Flight in America*. Baltimore: Johns Hopkins University Press.

Borstelmann, Thomas. 2001. *The Cold War and the Color Line*. Cambridge: Harvard University Press.

Bourdaghs, Michael. 2005. "The Calm Beauty of Japan at Almost the Speed of Sound." *Minor Transnationalism*, ed. Françoise Lionnet and Shu-mei Shih, 237–58. Durham: Duke University Press.

Bourdieu, Pierre. 1977. *Outline of a Theory of Practice*. Cambridge: Cambridge University Press.

Brennan, Denise. 2004. *What's Love Got to Do with It? Transnational Desires and Sex Tourism in the Dominican Republic*. Durham: Duke University Press.

Bruner, Edward. 1999. "Return to Sumatra: 1957, 1997." *American Ethnologist* 26, no. 2, 461–77.

Burawoy, Michael. 1979. *Manufacturing Consent*. Chicago: University of Chicago Press.

Burdick, Eugene, and William Lederer. 1958. *The Ugly American*. New York: W. W. Norton.

Calhoun, Craig. 2002. "The Class Consciousness of Frequent Travellers: Towards a Critique of Actually Existing Cosmopolitanism." *Conceiving Cosmopolitanism: Theory, Context, and Practice*, ed. Steven Vertovec and Robin Cohen, 86–109. London: Oxford University Press.

"Cape Canaveral: Spaceport, U.S.A." 1963. *Classroom Clipper* 30, no. 3 (February–March 1963), 1.

Chin, Frank. 1976. "Backtalk." *Counterpoint: Perspectives on Asian America*, ed. Emma Gee, 556–57. Los Angeles: Asian American Studies Center, University of California.

Chinen, Karleen, and Arnold S. Hiura. 1997. *From Bento to Mixed Plate: Americans of Japanese Ancestry in Multicultural Hawai`i*. Los Angeles: Japanese American National Museum.

Ching, Leo T. S. 2001. *Becoming "Japanese": Colonial Taiwan and the Politics of Identity Formation*. Durham: Duke University Press.

Choy, Catherine Ceniza. 2003. *Empire of Care: Nursing and Migration in Filipino American History*. Durham: Duke University Press.

"Chronology: Pan Am's Assistance during Times of Crisis." 1980. Unpublished manuscript. Special Collections Division, University of Miami Libraries, collection 341, box 41, folder 11.

Clifford, James. 1992. "Traveling Cultures." *Cultural Studies*, ed. Lawrence Grossberg, Cary Nelson, and Paula Treichler, 96–112. New York: Routledge.

———. 1997. *Routes: Travel and Translation in the Late Twentieth Century*. Cambridge: Harvard University Press.

Cohen, Lizabeth. 2003. *A Consumers' Republic: The Politics of Mass Consumption in Postwar America*. New York: Vintage.

"College Rules/Regulations and Information." 1966. Unpublished classroom guide. Special Collections Division, University of Miami Libraries, collection 452, box 27, folder 267, World Wings.

"Company Aids Eight Universities." 1959. *Clipper*, February, 9.

"Company's Humanitarianism Saluted." 1959. *Clipper*, February, 8.

Conrad, Barnaby. 1999. *Pan Am: An Aviation Legend*. Emeryville, Calif.: Woodford.

Constable, Nicole. 2003. *Romance on a Global Stage: Pen Pals, Virtual Ethnography, and "Mail Order" Marriages*. Berkeley: University of California Press.

Cook, Alice. 1982. Introduction, *From Sky Girl to Flight Attendant: Women and the Making of a Union*, xiii–xxii. Ithaca, N.Y.: ILR Press.

Coontz, Stephanie. 2000. *The Way We Never Were: American Families and the Nostalgia Trap*. New York: Basic.

Corn, Joseph. 1983. *The Winged Gospel: America's Romance with Aviation, 1900–1950*. New York: Oxford University Press.

Courtwright, David T. 2005. *Sky as Frontier: Adventure, Aviation, and Empire*. College Station: Texas A&M University Press.

Cresswell, Tim. 2006. *On the Move: Mobility in the Modern Western World*. New York: Routledge.

Crockett, Lucy Herndon. 1949. *Popcorn on the Ginza: An Informal Portrait of Postwar Japan*. New York: William Sloan Associates.

Daley, Robert. 1980. *An American Saga: Juan Trippe and His Pan Am Empire*. New York: Random House.

Davies, R. E. G. 1987. *Pan Am: An Airline and Its Aircraft*. New York: Orion.

————. 1991. *Lufthansa*. New York: Orion.

Davila, Arlene. 2001. *Latinos Inc.: The Marketing and Making of a People*. Berkeley: University of California Press.

"Division to Hire Chinese-Speaking Stewardesses." 1959. *Clipper: Pacific-Alaska Division* 15, no. 9 (December), 15.

Dower, John. 1999. *Embracing Defeat: Japan in the Wake of World War II*. New York: W. W. Norton.

"Educational Air Travel." 1951. *Pan American World Airways Teacher* 7, no. 3, January–February, 1, 6.

Elder, Glen H., Jr. 1986. "Military Times and Turning Points in Men's Lives." *Developmental Psychology* 22, no. 2, 233–45.

Elder, Glen H., Jr., Cynthia Gimbel, and Rachel Ivie. 1991. "Turning Points in Life: The Case of Military Service and War." *Military Psychology* 3, 215–31.

Endy, Christopher. 2004. *Cold War Holidays: American Tourists in France*. Chapel Hill: University of North Carolina Press.

Faragher, John Mack. 1994. *Rereading Frederick Jackson Turner*. New York: Henry Holt.

Feldstein, Ruth. 1994. "'I Wanted the Whole World to See': Race, Gender, and Constructions of Motherhood in the Death of Emmett Till." *Not June Cleaver: Women and Gender in Postwar America, 1945–1960*, ed. Joanne Meyerowitz. Philadelphia: Temple University Press.

Ferguson, R. G. 1966. Unpublished memo to Juan T. Trippe, 21 February. Special Collections Division, University of Miami Libraries, collection 341, box 492, folder 21, SCLF box.

"First of New Japanese Stewardesses Graduate." 1966. *Clipper*, 1 November, 8.

"Flight Service Indoctrination." 1966. Unpublished classroom guide. Special Collections Division, University of Miami Libraries, collection 452, box 27, folder 267, World Wings.

Foreman, Kelly. 2005. "Bad Girls Confined: Okuni, Geisha, and the Negotiation of Female Performance Space." *Bad Girls of Japan*, ed. Laura Miller and Jan Bardsley, 33–47. New York: Palgrave Macmillan.

"For Finer Service: Flight Service Announces Plans to Put Japanese Speaking Stewardesse [*sic*] on All TYO-SFO-TYO Trips." 1955. *Clipper: Pacific-Alaska Division* 11, no. 4 (17 February), 5.

Foucault, Michel. 1977. *Discipline and Punish: The Birth of a Prison*. New York: Vintage.

Frank, Katherine. 2004. *G-Strings and Sympathy: Strip Club Regulars and Male Desire*. Durham: Duke University Press.

Fritzsche, Peter. 1992. *A Nation of Fliers: German Aviation and the Popular Imagination*. Cambridge: Harvard University Press.

Fujikane, Candace. 2000. "Asian Settler Colonialism in Hawai`i." *Amerasia Journal* 26, no. 2, xv–xxii [special issue: *Whose Vision? Asian Settler Colonialism in Hawai`i*, ed. Candace Fujikane and Jonathan Okamura].

Galbraith, John Kenneth. 1958. *The Affluent Society*. New York: New American Library.

Gandt, Robert. 1999. *Skygods: The Fall of Pan Am*. McLean, Va.: Paladwr.

Garon, Sheldon, and Patricia Maclachlan. 2006. Introduction, *The Ambivalent Consumer: Questioning Consumption in East Asia and the West*, ed. Sheldon Garon and Patricia Maclachlan, 1–15. Ithaca: Cornell University Press.

Gill, Lesley. 1997. "Creating Citizens, Making Men: The Military and Masculinity in Bolivia." *Cultural Anthropology* 12, no. 4, 527–50.

Glenn, Evelyn Nakano. 2002. *Unequal Freedom: How Race and Gender Shaped American Citizenship and Labor*. Cambridge: Harvard University Press.

Goffman, Erving. 1959. *The Presentation of Self in Everyday Life*. New York: Doubleday Anchor.

Golden, Arthur. 1997. *Memoirs of a Geisha*. New York: Alfred A. Knopf.

Gordon, Alastair. 2004. *Naked Airport: A Cultural History of the World's Most Revolutionary Structure*. New York: Henry Holt.

"Government Urges Measures to Improve Aviation Accounts." 1966. *Air News Japan* 6, no. 19 (11 July), 2–3. Special Collections Division, University of Miami Libraries, collection 341, box 492, folder 21, SCLF box.

Green, Venus. 2001. *Race on the Line: Gender, Labor, and Technology in the Bell System, 1880–1980*. Durham: Duke University Press.

Grooming Newsletter. 1960. 10 June, 1–3.

Grooming Program. 1959. Unpublished classroom lectures. Special Collections Division, University of Miami Libraries, collection 452, box 28, folder 278, World Wings.

Hall, Stuart. 1990. "Cultural Identity and Diaspora." *Identity: Community, Culture, Difference*, ed. Jonathan Rutherford, 222–37. London: Lawrence and Wishart.

———. 2002. "Political Belonging in a World of Multiple Identities." *Conceiving Cosmopolitanism: Theory, Context, and Practice*, ed. Steven Vertovec and Robin Cohen, 26–31. London: Oxford University Press.

Hamamoto, Darrell Y. 1994. *Monitored Peril: Asian Americans and the Politics of TV Representation*. Minneapolis: University of Minnesota Press.

Hannerz, Ulf. 1990. "Cosmopolitans and Locals in World Culture." *Global Culture: Nationalism, Globalization and Modernity*, ed. Mike Featherstone, 237–51. London: Sage.

Havighurst, Robert J., et al. 1951. *The American Veteran Back Home: A Study of Veteran Readjustment*. New York: Longmans, Green.

"Hawaii Girls Join First Nisei Stewardess Class." 1955. *Clipper: Pacific-Alaska Division* 11, no. 7 (31 March), 2.

Heller, Joseph. 1961. *Catch-22*. New York: Simon and Schuster.

Herman, Elizabeth. 1995. *The Romance of American Psychology: Political Culture in the Age of Experts*. Berkeley: University of California Press.

"Hints on Polite and Gracious Conversation." 1966. Unpublished classroom guide.

Special Collections Division, University of Miami Libraries, collection 452, box 27, folder 267, World Wings.

Hochschild, Arlie Russell. 1983. *The Managed Heart: Commercialization of Human Feeling*. Berkeley: University of California Press.

Homan, Lynn M., and Thomas Reilly. 2000. *Pan Am*. Charleston, S.C.: Arcadia.

Hopgood, James. 1998. "Another *Japanese Version*: An American Actor in Japanese Hands." *The Social Construction of Race and Ethnicity in the United States*, ed. Joan Ferrante and Prince Brown Jr., 470–77. New York: Longman.

Horizons Unlimited. 1959, 1966. New York: Pan American World Airways, Sales and Service Training System.

Houston, Velina Hasu. 1988. *Tea*. New York: Theatre Communications Group. Repr. Dramatist's Play Service, 2006.

Howe, Louise Kapp. 1977. *Pink Collar Workers: Inside the World of Women's Work*. New York: Avon.

Hume, Bill, and John Annarino. 1953. *Babysan: A Private Look at the Japanese Occupation*. Columbia, Mo.: American.

———. 1956. *Babysan's World: The Hume'n Slant on Japan*. Rutland, Vt.: Tuttle.

"International Tourism Booming." 1967. *Japan Times*, 2 October, 20.

Iwasaki, Mineko, with Rande Brown. 2002. *Geisha: A Life*. New York: Atria.

"Japanese Girls Join Ranks of Stewardesses for Pan Am." 1964. *Pan American Clipper: Latin American Division* 21, no. 2 (March), 3.

"Japanese Hostesses." 1955. *Nippon Times*, 29 June, 6 [pictorial caption].

"Jet Clippers Are Here." 1958. Promotional pamphlet. Author's possession.

Josephson, Matthew. 1972 [1943]. *Empire of the Air: Juan Trippe and the Struggle for World Airways*. New York: Arno.

Kakutani Osamu. 2005. *Joshi Kouseifuku Zukan 2005 Nendo-han* [High school girl uniforms picture book, 2005 edition]. Tokyo: Bunkasha.

Kane, Paula, with Christopher Chandler. 1974. *Sex Objects in the Sky: A Personal Account of the Stewardess Rebellion*. Chicago: Follett.

Kaplan, Amy. 1993. "Left Alone with America: The Absence of Empire in the Study of American Culture." *Cultures of United States Imperialism*, ed. Amy Kaplan and Donald E. Pease, 3–21. Durham: Duke University Press.

Kaplan, Caren. 1996. *Questions of Travel: Postmodern Discourses of Displacement*. Durham: Duke University Press.

Kawada, Jean. 2004. "¡Bienvenidos!" *Aloha Clipper* 11, no. 2 (February), 6–7.

Kawauchi Kazuko. 2004. "Aru Hi, Aru Toki" [One day, some time]. *Pan Am Kaisouroku [Pan Am memoirs]*. Tokyo: Pan Am Alumni Association, Japan.

Kelly, Frank, and Cornelius Ryan. 1947. *Star-Spangled Mikado*. New York: Robert M. McBride.

Kelsky, Karen. 2001. *Women on the Verge: Japanese Women, Western Dreams*. Durham: Duke University Press.

Kim, Elaine. 1982. *Asian American Literature: An Introduction to the Writings and Their Social Context*. Philadelphia: Temple University Press.

Kitayama, Glen. 2001. "Model Minority." *Encyclopedia of Japanese American History*. Los Angeles: Japanese American National Museum.

Klein, Christina. 2003. *Cold War Orientalism: Asia in the Middlebrow Imagination, 1945–1961*. Berkeley: University of California Press.

Kodama, Marie. 2007. "The Art of Japanese Gift Wrapping." *Hawaii Herald*, 5 January, § B, 6–8.

Kolm, Suzanne Lee. 1995. "Women's Labor Aloft: A Cultural History of Airline Flight Attendants in the United States, 1930–1978." Ph.D. diss., Brown University.

———. 2003. "Who Says It's A Man's World? Women's Work and Travel in the First Decades of Flight." *The Airplane in American Culture*, ed. Dominick A. Pisano, 147–64. Ann Arbor: University of Michigan Press.

Kotani, Roland. 1985. *The Japanese in Hawaii: A Century of Struggle*. Honolulu: Hawaii Hochi.

Kujawa, Anthony. 2006. "Citizen Diplomats Nurturing Japanese-U.S. Understanding, Peace." International Information Programs, USINFO.STATE.GOV, 7 August, Http://usinfo.state.gov. Accessed 5 June 2007.

Kurashige, Lon. 2002. *Japanese American Celebration and Conflict: A History of Ethnic Identity and Festival in Los Angeles, 1934–1990*. Berkeley: University of California Press.

Lacerda, John. 1946. *The Conqueror Comes to Tea: Japan under MacArthur*. New Brunswick: Rutgers University Press.

Lai, Tracy. 1992. "Asian American Women: Not for Sale." *Race, Class, and Gender*, ed. Margaret L. Andersen and Patricia Hill Collines, 163–71. Belmont, Calif.: Belmont.

Leibowitz, Neil. 1973. "Minority Recruiting Difficult at Pan Am; Enlisting Aid Shows Lack in Interest." *Inside Travel News*, March, 12–13.

Leidner, Robin. 1993. *Fast Food, Fast Talk: Service Work and the Routinization of Everyday Life*. Berkeley: University of California Press.

Leopold, Todd. 2005. "The 50-Year-Old Song That Started It All." CNN.com, http://www.cnn.com/2005/SHOWBIZ/Music/07/07/haley.rock. Accessed 15 January 2007.

Lessor, Roberta. 1982. "Unanticipated Longevity in Women's Work: The Career Development of Airline Flight Attendants." Ph.D. diss., University of California, San Francisco.

Lester, Valerie. 1995. *Fasten Your Seat Belts! History and Heroism in the Pan Am Cabin*. McLean, Va.: Paladwr.

Lewisohn, Mark. 2003. "Pam Ann's Mile High Club." http://www.bbc.co.uk/comedy/guide/articles/p/pamannsmilehighc_66602740.shtml. Accessed 27 May 2007.

Lim, Shirley Jennifer. 2006. *A Feeling of Belonging: Asian American Women's Public Culture, 1930–1960*. New York: New York University Press.

Limerick, P. N. 1994. "The Adventures of the Frontier in the Twentieth Century."

The Frontier in American Culture, ed. J. R. Grossman, 66–102. Berkeley: University of California Press.

Lind, Andrew. 1980. *Hawaii's People.* Honolulu: University of Hawai`i Press.

Loti, Pierre. 1888. *Madame Chrysanthème.* Paris: Calmann-Lévy.

Lotman, Yuri M. 1990. *Universe of the Mind: A Semiotic Theory of Culture.* Trans. Ann Shukman. London: I. B. Tauris.

Louis, Meryl Reis. 1980. "Surprise and Sense Making: What Newcomers Experience in Entering Unfamiliar Organizational Settings." *Administrative Science Quarterly* 25 (2 June), 226–51.

Lowe, Lisa. 1996. *Immigrant Acts: On Asian American Cultural Politics.* Durham: Duke University Press.

Lutz, Catherine A., and Jane L. Collins. 1993. *Reading National Geographic.* Chicago: University of Chicago Press.

Manderson, Lenore, and Margaret Jolly. 1997. Introduction, *Sites of Desire, Economies of Pleasure: Sexualities in Asia and the Pacific,* ed. Lenore Manderson and Margaret Jolly, 1–26. Chicago: University of Chicago Press.

Marchetti, Gina. 1993. *Romance and the "Yellow Peril": Race, Sex, and Discursive Strategies in Hollywood Fiction.* Berkeley: University of California Press.

Marling, Karal Ann. 1998. *As Seen on TV: The Visual Culture of Everyday Life in the 1950s.* Cambridge: Harvard University Press.

Mascia-Lees, Frances E., and Nancy Johnson Black. 2000. *Gender and Anthropology.* Prospect Heights, Ill.: Waveland.

Massey, Doreen. 1994. *Space, Place, and Gender.* Minneapolis: University of Minnesota Press.

May, Elaine Tyler. 1988. *Homeward Bound: American Families in the Cold War Era.* New York: Basic.

McHugh, Kathleen. 2005. "Giving 'Minor' Pasts a Future." *Minor Transnationalism,* ed. Françoise Lionnet and Shu-mei Shih, 155–77. Durham: Duke University Press.

McVeigh, Brian. 2000. *Wearing Ideology: State, Schooling and Self-Presentation in Japan.* Oxford: Berg.

Meyerowitz, Joanne. 1994. "Introduction: Women and Gender in Postwar America, 1945–1960." *Not June Cleaver: Women and Gender in Postwar America, 1945–1960,* ed. Joanne Meyerowitz, 1–16. Philadelphia: Temple University Press.

Michener, James. 1953. *Sayonara.* New York: Random House.

Miles, Agnes. 1991. *The Neurotic Woman: The Role of Gender in Psychiatric Illness.* New York: New York University Press.

Millard, D. Ralph, Jr. 1955. "Oriental Pereginations." *Plastic and Reconstructive Surgery* 16, 319–36.

Miller, Laura. 2006. *Beauty Up: Exploring Contemporary Japanese Body Aesthetics.* Berkeley: University of California Press.

Milley, H. F. 1955a. Unpublished memo, 31 January. Special Collections Division, University of Miami Libraries, collection 341, box 225, folder 11.

———. 1955b. Unpublished memo, 4 March. Special Collections Division, University of Miami Libraries, collection 341, box 225, folder 11.

———. 1955c. Unpublished memo, 11 July. Special Collections Division, University of Miami Libraries, collection 341, box 225, folder 11.

Mills, Albert. 2006. *Sex, Strategy, and the Stratosphere: Airlines and the Gendering of Organizational Culture.* Basingstoke: Palgrave Macmillan.

Mills, C. Wright. 1951. *White Collar.* New York: Oxford University Press.

"Miss Universe and Miss U.S.A. to Serve as Co-hostesses aboard Pan Am's 747SP Round the World Anniversary Flight." 1977. Unpublished news release, 28 October. Smithsonian National Air and Space Museum FIP-167000-70 PAA releases.

Modern Girl around the World Research Group. 2008. "The Modern Girl around the World; Cosmetics Advertising and the Politics of Race and Style." *The Modern Girl around the World: Consumption, Modernity, and Globalization,* 25–54. Durham: Duke University Press.

Montgomery, James. N.d. Unpublished letter, "Dear Moon First Flighter." Special Collections Division, University of Miami Libraries, collection 341, box 42, folder 5.

Moore, Brenda L. 2003. *Serving Our Country: Japanese American Women in the Military during World War II.* New Brunswick: Rutgers University Press.

Morris, Narrelle. 2002. "Innocence to Deviance: The Fetishisation of Japanese Women in Western Fiction, 1890s–1990s." *Intersections: Gender, History and Culture in the Asian Context* 7 (March), http://intersections.anu.edu.au/issue7/morris.html. Accessed 30 May 2008.

"Most Beautiful Girls in the World, The." 1952. *Clipper: Pacific-Alaska Division* 8, no. 15 (24 July), 7.

Murray, M. F. 1951. *Skygirl: A Career Handbook for the Airline Stewardess.* New York: Duell, Sloan and Pearce.

"Newest Stewardess Fad: A Japanese in Every Jet." 1967. *Life* (Asia edn), 1 May, 42–46.

New Horizons in Education: The Benefits of Study Abroad. 1961. New York: Pan American Airways.

Nielsen, Georgia Panter. 1982. *From Sky Girl to Flight Attendant: Women and the Making of a Union.* Ithaca, N.Y.: ILR Press.

Ni, Ching-Ching. 2007. "Fresh Faces in the Sky." *Los Angeles Times,* 20 November, http://www.latimes.com/news/la-fg-stew20nov20,0,3213263.story?page=2&coll=la-tot-topstories. Accessed 20 November 2007.

"Nihongo de Kiyasui Pan American no Nikkei Koukuujou" [One can relax comfortably with Japanese-speaking Pan American's Nikkei stewardesses]. 1955. *Hawaii Hochi,* 15 June, 2.

Niiya, Brian, ed. 2001. "Chronology of Japanese American History." *Encyclopedia of Japanese American History,* 27–100. Los Angeles: Japanese American National Museum.

"Nippon Hostesses Enjoy Big Demand." 1955. *Nippon Times,* 20 September, 6.

"Nisei Stewardess Anniversary." 1958. *Clipper: Pacific-Alaska Division* 14, no. 6 (June), 7.

Nordyke, Eleanor C. 1989. *The Peopling of Hawai`i*. Honolulu: University of Hawai`i Press.

Ogasawara, Yuko. 1998. *Office Ladies and Salaried Men*. Berkeley: University of California Press.

Okamura, Jonathan Y. 2001. "Race Relations in Hawaii during World War II." *The Japanese American Historical Experience in Hawaii*, ed. Jonathan Okamura, 67–89. Dubuque: Kendall/Hung.

———. 2008. *Ethnicity and Inequality in Hawai`i*. Philadelphia: Temple University Press.

Okihiro, Gary. 1991. *Cane Fires: The Anti-Japanese Movement in Hawaii, 1865–1945*. Philadelphia: Temple University Press.

———. 1994. *Margins and Mainstreams: Asians in American History and Culture*. Seattle: University of Washington Press.

Oldenziel, Ruth. 1999. *Making Technology Masculine: Men, Women and Modern Machines in America, 1870–1945*. Amsterdam: Amsterdam University Press.

Omelia, Johanna and Michael Waldock. 2003. *Come Fly with Us! A Global History of the Airline Hostess*. Portland: Collector's Press.

Ong, Aihwa. 1999. *Flexible Citizenship: The Cultural Logics of Transnationality*. Durham: Duke University Press.

———. 2007. *Neoliberalism as Exception: Mutations in Citizenship and Sovereignty*. Durham: Duke University Press.

Ong, Paul, and John M. Liu. 2000. "U.S. Immigration Policies and Asian Migration." *Contemporary Asian America: A Multidisciplinary Reader*, ed. Min Zhou and James V. Gatewood, 155–74. New York: New York University Press.

"Over 93,000 on Pan Am's First Moon Flight Waiting List." News release. Special Collections Division, University of Miami Libraries, collection 341, box 42, folder 3.

Packard, Vance. 1957. *The Hidden Persuaders*. New York: David McKay.

———. 1960. *The Waste Makers*. New York: David McKay.

Palumbo-Liu, David. 1999. *Asian/American: Historical Crossings of a Racial Frontier*. Stanford: Stanford University Press.

Pan Am Employees Advertising Fund. 1972. "We Don't Have to Work for Pan Am . . . We Want to." *Life*, 29 December.

———. 1974. "An Open Letter to the American People from the Employees of the World's Most Experienced Airline." *New York Times*, 23 September.

"Pan Amerikan Koukuugaisha [Pan American Airline Company], Which Means 'Compliments of Pan American World Airways: The World's Most Experienced Airline.'" 1953. *Clipper: Pacific-Alaska Division* 9, no. 11 (11 June), 8.

"Pan Am Flight Bag Honored by Orient Counterfeiters." 1958. *Clipper: Pacific-Alaska Division* 14, no. 9 (September), 4.

Pan Am Flight Service Interview Rating. 1972. Unpublished. Author's possession.

PanAmOne. 2006. Promotional brochure. Author's possession.

"Pan Am to Employ Six Isle Nisei Stewardesses." 1955. *Honolulu Advertiser*, 11 February, § A, 14.

Park, Robert E. 1950. *Race and Culture: Essays in the Sociology of Contemporary Man.* New York: Free Press.

Parker, Bradley J., and Lars Rodseth, eds. 2005. *Untaming the Frontier in Anthropology, Archaeology, and History.* Tucson: University of Arizona Press.

Patterson, Peggy. 1961. "Stewardess Finds Constant Flying Very Educating." *Honolulu Star-Bulletin*, 25 August, 17.

Petersen, William. 1966. "Success Story, Japanese American Style." *New York Times Magazine*, 9 January, 20–21, 33, 36, 38, 40–41.

Poling-Kempes, Lesley. 1989. *The Harvey Girls: Women Who Opened the West.* New York: Paragon House.

Pollock, Sheldon, Homi K. Bhabha, Carol A. Breckenridge, and Dipesh Chakrabarty. 2000. "Cosmopolitanisms." *Public Culture* 32, no. 4, 577–89.

Pratt, Mary Louise. 1992. *Imperial Eyes: Travel Writing and Transculturation.* London: Routledge.

Reida, Ellis. 1983. "Service, Care . . . and History: Pan Am Story: A Conversation with James Frank." *Ninnescah: International Service* 1, no. 5 (September), 2–7. Special Collections Division, University of Miami Libraries, collection 341, box 41, folder 11.

Richter, Amy. 2005. *Home on the Rails: Women, the Railroad, and the Rise of Public Domesticity.* Chapel Hill: University of North Carolina Press.

Rodseth, Lars, and Bradley J. Parker. 2005. "Introduction: Theoretical Considerations in the Study of Frontiers." *Untaming the Frontier in Anthropology, Archaeology, and History*, ed. Bradley Parker and Lars Rodseth, 3–21. Tucson: University of Arizona Press.

Ross, Kristin. 1995. *Fast Cars, Clean Bodies: Decolonization and the Reordering of French Culture.* Cambridge: MIT Press.

Ross, Walter. 1976. *The Last Hero: Charles A. Lindbergh.* New York: Harper and Row.

Saldizar, Jose. 1997. *Border Matters: Remapping American Cultural Studies.* Berkeley: University of California Press.

Sampson, Anthony. 1984. *Empires of the Sky: The Politics, Contests and Cartels of World Airlines.* New York: Random House.

Sandeen, Eric J. 1995. *Picturing an Exhibition: The Family of Man and 1950s America.* Albuquerque: University of New Mexico Press.

Schivelbusch, Wolfgang. 1979. *The Railway Journey: Trains and Travel in the 19th Century.* New York: Urizen.

Schwartz, Vanessa R. 2007. *It's So French! Hollywood, Paris, and the Making of Cosmopolitan Film Culture.* Chicago: University of Chicago Press.

"Second Nisei Class Wins Wings." 1955. *Clipper: Pacific-Alaska Division* 11, no. 13 (7 July), 3.

"Sekai no Sora o Iku Nisei Musume" [The Nisei girls who fly the skies of the world]. 1956. *Hawaii Hochi*, 1 January, 1–2.

Sennett, Richard, and Jonathan Cobb. 1973. *Hidden Injuries of Class*. New York: Vintage.

Serling, Robert. 1985. *Eagle: The Story of American Airlines*. New York: St. Martin's / Marek.

Sherman, Dallas. 1951. "Note to Vice President Bixby." Unpublished memo, 15 November. Special Collections Division, University of Miami Libraries; collection 341, box 225, folder 12.

Sherman, Rachel. 2007. *Class Acts: Service and Inequality in Luxury Hotels*. Berkeley: University of California Press.

Sharpley, Richard. 2002. "Tourism: A Vehicle for Development?" *Tourism and Development: Concepts and Issues*, ed. Richard Sharpley and David J. Telfer, 11–34. Bristol, England: Channel View.

Shibusawa, Naoko. 2006. *America's Geisha Ally: Reimagining the Japanese Enemy*. Cambridge: Harvard University Press.

Simpson, Caroline Chung. 2001. *An Absent Presence: Japanese Americans in Postwar American Culture, 1945–1960*. Durham: Duke University Press.

"Six Beauties from Malaysia Flying Pacific for Pan Am." 1965. *Pan American Clipper: Overseas Division* 24, no. 6 (15 August), 4.

Smith, Robert. 1983. "Selling the Moon: The U.S. Manned Space Program and the Triumph of Commodity Scientism." *The Culture of Consumption: Critical Essays in American History 1880–1980*, ed. Richard Wightman Fox and T. J. Jackson Lears, 176–209. New York: Pantheon.

Solberg, Carl. 1979. *Conquest of the Skies: A History of Commercial Aviation in America*. Boston: Little, Brown.

Steichen, Edward. 1955. *The Family of Man*. New York: Museum of Modern Art. Repr. in large format, 2003.

Stoler, Ann Laura. 2001. "Tense and Tender Ties: The Politics of Comparison in North American History and (Post)Colonial Studies." *Journal of American History* 88, no. 3, 829–65.

———. 2006. "Intimidations of Empire: Predicaments of the Tactile and Unseen." *Haunted by Empire: Geographies of Intimacy in North American History*, ed. Ann Stoler, 1–22. Durham: Duke University Press.

———, ed. 2006. *Haunted by Empire: Geographies of Intimacy in North American History*. Durham: Duke University Press.

"Students from Abroad Explore American Life, Find Many Surprises in Families, Schools." 1962. *Classroom Clipper* 18, no. 5 (June), 1–2.

Sturken, Marita. 1993. "Absent Images of Memory: Remembering and Reenacting the Japanese Internment." *positions* 5, no. 3, 693.

Suzuki, Bob. 1977. "Education and Socialization of Asian Americans: A Revisionist Analysis of the 'Model Minority' Thesis." *Amerasia Journal* 4, no. 2, 23–52.

Suzuki, Nobue. 2005. "Filipina Modern: 'Bad' Filipino Women in Japan." *Bad Girls* of Japan, ed. Laura Miller and Jan Bardsley, 159–74. New York: Palgrave Macmillan.

Tajima, Renee. 1989. "Lotus Blossoms Don't Bleed: Images of Asian Women." *Making Waves: An Anthology of Writings by and about Asian American Women*, ed. Asian Women United of California, 308–18. Boston: Beacon.

Takita, Kazuo. 1956. "Int'l Airlines Spearhead Tourist Drive." *Nippon Times*, 14 February, 15.

Tamura, Eileen H. 1994. *Americanization, Acculturation, and Ethnic Identity: The Nisei Generation in Hawaii*. Urbana: University of Illinois Press.

Telotte, J. P. 1999. "Lindbergh, Film, and Machine Age Dreams." *South Atlantic Review* 64, no. 4, 68–83.

Tobin, Joseph J., ed. 1992. *Re-made in Japan: Everyday Life and Consumer Taste in a Changing Society*. New Haven: Yale University Press.

Trask, Haunani-Kay. 2000. "Settlers of Color and 'Immigrant' Hegemony: 'Locals' in Hawai`i." *Amerasia Journal* 26, no. 2, 1–24 [special issue: *Whose Vision? Asian Settler Colonialism in Hawai`i*, ed. Candace Fujikane and Jonathan Okamura].

Trippe, Juan Terry. 1939. "America Unlimited." Speech, with later interview by NBC, 29 September, on the theme of "Business Frontiers." National Air and Space Museum, Juan Terry Trippe Collection, box 1, folder A(II).

———. 1944. "America in the Air Age." Address delivered at the Charter Week Ceremonies of the University of California at Los Angeles and Berkeley, 23 March, 1–10. National Air and Space Museum, Juan Terry Trippe Collection, box 10, speeches, vol. 2, 1940–49.

———. 1958. Address at the christening of Jet Clipper America. Quotations from Speeches and Public Statements of Juan T. Trippe, National Air and Space Museum, Juan Terry Trippe Collection, box 4, JTT 1968.

———. 1960. Address delivered by Juan T. Trippe upon receiving the Chicago Association of Commerce and Industry's International Achievement Award for World Peace, 23 June 1960. National Air and Space Museum, Juan Terry Trippe Collection, box 4, Awards and Honors.

———. 1963. Pan Am Building's Grand Opening. *Pan American Clipper: Overseas Division* 22, no. 2 (March–April), centerfold.

Tuan, Mia. 2003. *Forever Foreigners or Honorary Whites? The Asian Ethnic Experience Today*. New Brunswick: Rutgers University Press.

Turner, Frederick Jackson. 1992 [1920]. *The Frontier in American History*. Tucson: University of Arizona Press.

Umemoto, Karen. 2000. "'On Strike!' San Francisco State College Strike, 1968–1969: The Role of Asian American Students." *Contemporary Asian America: A Multidisciplinary Reader*, ed. Min Zhou and James V. Gatewood, 49–79. New York: New York University Press.

Urry, John. 2007. *Mobilities*. Cambridge: Polity.

Vogel, Ezra. 1963. *Japan's New Middle Class*. Berkeley: University of California Press.

Von Moltke, Johannes. 2005. *No Place like Home: Locations of Heimat in German Cinema.* Berkeley: University of California Press.

Wada, Yoshiko. 1996. "The History of the Kimono: Japan's National Dress." *The Kimono Inspiration: Art and Art-to-Wear in America,* ed. Rebecca Stevens and Yoshiko Wada, 131–62. Washington: Textile Museum.

Warn, Sue. 1999. *Recreation and Tourism: A Changing Industry.* London: Nelson Thornes.

Waters, Mark. 1963. "Isle Girls Who Speak Japanese or Chinese Scarce, P.A.A. Finds." *Honolulu Star-Bulletin,* 26 February, 7.

Weinbaum, Alys Eve. 2008. "Racial Masquerade; Consumption and Contestation of American Modernity." *The Modern Girl around the World: Consumption, Modernity, and Globalization,* ed. Modern Girl around the World Research Group, 122–46. Durham: Duke University Press.

Weitekamp, Margaret A. 2004. *Right Stuff: Wrong Sex: America's First Women in Space Program.* Baltimore: Johns Hopkins University Press.

Whitelegg, Drew. 2007. *Working the Skies: The Fast-Paced, Disorienting World of the Flight Attendant.* New York: New York University Press.

Whitfield, Stephen J. 1996. *The Culture of the Cold War.* Baltimore: Johns Hopkins University Press.

Wilson, Richard Guy, Dianne H. Pilgrim, and Dickran Tashjian. 1986. *The Machine Age in America, 1918–1941.* New York: Harry N. Abrams.

"Wings to Japan." 1955. *Honolulu Advertiser,* 5 June, "Hawaii Weekly," 4.

Woodward, Rachel. 2006. "Warrior Heroes and Little Green Men: Soldiers, Military Training, and the Construction of Rural Masculinities." *Country Boys: Masculinity and Rural Life,* ed. Hugh Campbell, Michael M. Bell, Margaret Finney, 235–50. University Park: Pennsylvania State University Press.

"World of Neighbors, A." 1946. Promotional brochure, Pan American World Airways. National Air and Space Museum FIP-167000-04, PAA documents.

World Wings International 2002 Calendar. 2001. Miami: World Wings International.

World Wings International 2004 Calendar. 2003. Miami: World Wings International.

World Wings International 2006 Calendar. 2005. Miami: World Wings International.

World Wings International 2007 Calendar. 2006. Miami: World Wings International.

Yamamoto, Traise. 1999. *Masking Selves, Making Subjects: Japanese American Women, Identity, and the Body.* Berkeley: University of California Press.

Yano, Christine R. 2006a. "Airborne Dreams." Videorecording, co-produced by Chris Conybeare. Honolulu: Japanese Cultural Center of Hawai`i.

———. 2006b. *Crowning the Nice Girl: Gender, Ethnicity, and Culture in Hawai`i's Cherry Blossom Festival.* Honolulu: University of Hawai`i Press.

Yoshimi Shun'ya. 2006. "Consuming America, Producing Japan." *The Ambivalent*

Consumer: Questioning Consumption in East Asia and the West, ed. Sheldon Garon and Patricia Maclachlan, 63–84. Ithaca: Cornell University Press.

Yuh, Ji-Yeon. 2002. *Beyond the Shadow of Camptown: Korean Military Brides in America.* New York: New York University Press.

WEB SITES

Air Scouts: http://www.geocities.com/Yosemite/Falls/8826/airscouts.html, accessed February 2007.

Armed Forces and Society: http://www.iusafs.org, accessed 9 June 2008.

Flight 001: http://www.flight001.com, accessed 6 June 2007.

Harvey Girl Historical Society: http://www.oerm.org/pages/Harveygirls.html, accessed 30 January 2007.

Japan Airlines: http://www.jal.com/en/history/history, accessed 12 April 2007; http://www.jal.com/en/history/uniform, accessed 4 June 2008.

Modelminority: http://www.modelminority.com, accessed 29 May 2008.

Moviemistakes: http://www.moviemistakes.com/film7362/page1, accessed 7 June 2008.

Pan Am Clipper Connection: http://www.flypanam.com, accessed 7 June 2007.

Pan Am Historical Foundation: http://www.panam.org, accessed 28 February 2007.

Pan Am Railways: http://www.guilfordrail.com, accessed 7 June 2007.

Pan Am Vietnam Wings of Freedom, http://www.paavn.net, accessed 17 April 2007.

Pam Ann: http://www.pamann.com, accessed 27 May 2007.

Retro to Go: http://www.retrotogo.com, accessed 7 June 2007.

World Wings International: http://www.worldwingsinternational.org, accessed 7 April 2007.

Mitchell, Ernie, 167

Miyamasu, Jean, 70

Mizuno, Ruby, 65, *66*

Mobility: double-sided, 14; as pendulum, 181; as symbol of modern, 29–30

Model minorities, 7, 9–10, 17, 20, 22, 24, 54, 73, 93

Modernity, 4, 11, 14, 27, 29, 31, 47, 179

Monroe, Marilyn, 49

Montgomery, James, 51–52

Moore, Brenda, 25–26

Moriwaki, Frances, 70

Multicultural marketing, 20

Murakami, Tule, 70

Museum of Modern Art, 21

Na Eheu Lani (Soaring Wings in the Sky), 201–2 n. 3

Nakamoto, Seiko, *71*

National Airlines, 173

NATO (North Atlantic Treaty Organization), 11

New Horizons, 136

Newton, Wayne, 125–26

Nichols, Bob, 82, 110

Nisei flight attendants: airborne dreams of, 3–4, 15–16, 24, 81–83, 85–86, 161, 179; branding and, 43, 178–79; as career women, 127–28; Chinese, 122; class background of, 86–91; company loyalty and, 103, 110, 139, 152–53, 165; consent concept and, 152; conservatism of, 88, 103–4, 117, 145; corporate control of, 138–42, 145, 148; cosmopolitanism of, 4, 7, 13, 15, 35, 166, 170, 180–81; described, 1; differences among, 57–58; discrimination toward, 59, 112–16; emotional depletion of, 111; empathetic service of, 105–6; end of, 167–69; frontiers and, 161, 162–64, 172; girl-next-door image of, 27–28, 41, 78–81; group

character of, 93, 113; hair policies and, 133–34; home countries of, 165–66; interviews with, 2; Japanese, 72–73; Japanese-American, 58–64, 162–64; June Cleaver ideal and, 18–19; language skills of, 13, 20–21, 58–64, 75, 95–97; loneliness of, 63, 111, 112; Malaysian, 70; media and, 65–69, 72–73, 108; memories of, 155; mobility and, 14; as model minority, 7, 24, 54, 93, 97; multicultural image and, 43, 47–48, 54–55, 171; multitasking by, 143; on-the-job demands of, 111–12; Pan Am legacy and, 155–60; Pan Am program beginnings and, 58–60; parents' reactions toward, 88–90; passengers' friendship with, 122–24; passengers' gifts for, 102–3; as pioneers, 10–11; prejudice against, 59; prestige and, 119, 162; promotional work by, 107, 109–10, 134–35; purser promotions of, 167; racialized, 3, 20, 25, 57, 63, 75–76, 100–101, 112, 163–64, 181; recruitment of, 58–60, 77–81, 95–97; reputation of, 97–110; resistance techniques of, 150–52; sexual harassment of, 116–18; skills learned by, 119–22; subjectivity of, 13–14, 25, 130, 152; subservience of, 104–6, 119; training of, 130–37, 156; transculturation and, 124–25; transformations of, 158–60, 166; translational identities of, 168; whites' interaction with, 100, 114; work ethic of, 97, 98, 102, 104; work-play mix and, 145, 147, 148; wow factor and, 83, 85, 88, 91, 93

Nisei women. *See* Asian and Asian American women

Nishi, Minnie, 167

North Atlantic Treaty Organization (NATO), 11

CHRISTINE R. YANO is a professor of anthropology
at the University of Hawai`i, Manoa.

Library of Congress Cataloging-in-Publication Data

Yano, Christine Reiko.
Airborne dreams : "Nisei" stewardesses and Pan American World Airways /
Christine Yano.
p. cm.
Includes bibliographical references and index.
ISBN 978-0-8223-4836-8 (cloth : alk. paper)
ISBN 978-0-8223-4850-4 (pbk. : alk. paper)
1. Pan American World Airways, Inc.
2. Japanese American women—Employment.
3. Flight attendants—United States.
I. Title.
HE9803.P36Y36 2011
3877'42089956073—dc22
2010035869